ato)

ٹ

LOCH CLASS
FRIGATES

HMS. Loch Lomond. F437
3rd. Frigate Squadron,
Far East Fleet.
Commission — 1962/64.
Jamieat in Hong Kong left.
Dec 1964 on. B I S N Co "NAVASA"
arrived at Southampton Dec 19th 1964.
Last Seagoing Ship then to
H M S SULTAN (Engineering Base)
      Demobed. (Some have all
the luck — Could have done
another 12 years)(Far East Station)."
Rank on leaving POM(E).

LOCH CLASS
FRIGATES

by

Patrick Boniface

Previous Page: HMS Loch Lomond   (*Ken Kelly Collection*)

CONTENTS

APPENDICES

INTRODUCTION

During the dark early years of World War Two, Great Britain stood alone against the Axis powers and at times it appeared that Britain too would, like its European neighbours, fall to the Nazis.

In 1940 and 1941 the War in the Atlantic seemed to be being won by the German U-boats. These submarines sank merchant shipping quicker than it could be replaced and in so doing almost starved Great Britain of precious resources and food.

Through sheer determination, the introduction of new technologies and strategies and in no small part through luck the tide of the war started to change in mid 1941. The use of sonar, convoys and depth charges started to even the score between the U-boats and the escorts defending the precious convoys across the North Atlantic. After years of struggle, sacrifice and loss eventually the odds were in the Allies favour with new American warships joining the fight plus long range anti submarine aircraft able to detect submarines and prosecute them with rockets, bombs, depth charges and cannons.

The existing escorts were, on the whole, not ideal as they had, for the most part, been built or designed before the war. Their sterling service had highlighted where improvements could be made and accordingly plans were drawn up for a new frigate construction programme to utilise pre-fabrication techniques to both speed construction and to reduce the risk from enemy attack by using multiple dispersed construction sites.

The resulting ships all shared a common hull, engines and equipment and as the programme progressed construction times were rapidly reduced.

The ships were to be numerous so the Admiralty decided to name them after Scottish lochs, of which there were many to choose from. The Loch class was to prove to be amongst the best frigates produced by Great Britain during the war, although most of the class only entered service from 1944 onwards. One hundred and ten ships of the Loch class were projected, but with the end of the war only 28 were completed as such, with another 18 being finished as Bay class frigates. A further eight vessels were completed for use as survey ships, despatch vessels and depot ships.

Although designed primarily for anti submarine warfare the frigates proved themselves more than capable of long distance patrols in isolated and remote regions of the world. Many Loch's went onto serve long deployments in the Persian Gulf and Indian Oceans as a result. The ships would prove to be popular with Commonwealth nations with three examples serving with the South African Navy and six in the New Zealand Navy.

The class was steadily withdrawn from service throughout the 1950's and 1960's as newer, more capable vessels became available but the Loch class was popular with their ships companies and served the nation with distinction.

Flower Class.

Frank Ripley **DESIGN** Oppo Nottingham

HMS. Leeds Castle. (Castle Class)

North Atlantic Convoys USA - Russia

During World War Two the Royal Navy relied on corvettes like Clematis *for anti-submarine warfare. Their design was used as the basis for the follow classes such as the Loch class frigates.* *(Syd Goodman Collection)*

In designing the Loch class, the Admiralty decided early on that they should have good sea keeping qualities and to be able to keep pace with the latest German U-boat designs. The existing Flower and River classes were chosen as a starting point for the design that was enlarged to improve upon the sea keeping of the earlier designs. Indeed the Flower class corvettes had been massed produced in small shipyards and had made a vast contribution to the war effort despite their relatively small size and poor levels of weaponry. Throughout the Second World War, new innovations and technologies were steadily introduced onto each successive class of ships such as new engines, radar, sonars, more capable anti aircraft guns and crucially the development of new ever more lethal methods of detecting and destroying enemy submarines. With the introduction of the Black Swan class frigates of around 1,300 tons displacement, the basic standard for the Loch class was established. Each ship was armed with six 4-inch high angle guns plus steam turbines giving the ships enough speed to catch and attack enemy submarines. Yet despite an impressive war record of 28 known U-boats destroyed, they were expensive to produce as they had been designed to full military standards and only a handful of shipyards had the skills necessary to construct Black Swan class vessels. Added to this was the limited space onboard that prevented them from carrying the latest Squid and Hedgehog anti submarine weapons.

This problem was rectified to some degree in the subsequent River class frigate that had started out in

Another class of warship that led to the development of the Loch class was the Black Swans. The layout of Woodcock *is noticeably similar to the Loch class, except with a heavier gun armament.*

(Crown Copyright/MoD)

1940 as a 'twin screw corvette'. Displacing 1,400 tons this class was larger than the Flower and Black Swan classes and allowed the installation of two single 4-inch guns, backed up with a layer of light anti-aircraft guns. The most significant improvement was the positioning ahead of the forward gun of a Hedgehog anti submarine weapon in addition to the normal complement of depth charge throwers on the quarterdeck. Being larger ships the River's also provided their ships companies with better, although still relatively basic, accommodation standards. Crucially though, having been designed to commercial standards construction times on the class were significantly quicker than the Black Swans and a total of 57 warships were built in the United Kingdom, with more being built in Canada and a derivative of the design being constructed by the US Navy.

After the River class, came the Castle class. At 50 feet longer than the Flower class corvettes, the Castle's saw into service as standard equipment the Squid anti submarine mortar. The Squid consisted of a three barrelled mortar which fired depth charges out to a distance of 275 yards from the parent ship. The mortars could be arranged to fire a set pattern of depth charges each weighing 390 lbs (177kg). The system was ordered by the Directorate of Miscellaneous Weapons Development in 1942 and first went to sea on trials in *HMS Ambuscade* in May 1943. *HMS Hadleigh Castle* received the first production unit and Squid mortars were later fitted to over 70 frigates and corvettes. *Loch Killin* made the first successful anti submarine attack on 31 July 1944 when *U-333* was sunk. By the end of the Second World War Squid had accounted for 17 submarines. Such was the success of Squid that the last operational example was only retired in April 1977 onboard the Type 61 frigate *HMS Salisbury*.

The knowledge and wartime experience gained from operating Flower, Black Swan, River and Castle class corvettes and frigates was used when defining the requirements of the Loch class. Each of the new frigates was to be armed with a variety of weapons to combat the submarine threat and also to be able to attack surface targets and to offer some degree of self

protection capabilities.

The limited capacity of British shipyards was a critical consideration in the design and the opportunity to innovate in their construction became increasingly important. Each ship was to be made up of a number of separate units, which could be built in dispersed areas, sometimes many miles from the shipyard. These sections would not be any larger than 29 feet long, 8 foot 6 inches wide and 8 foot 6 inches tall and a maximum weight of 2.5 tons. This size was chosen for a number of reasons, principal amongst them being the available size of cranes at shipyards and the size of the British road and rail network upon which these building blocks were set to travel. Up to eighty percent of the ships were prefabricated and brought to the designated shipyard either by rail or road or where practicable by sea. Once the sections were delivered the frigates were constructed in the usual manner on the slipways. The final twenty percent of the construction work being carried out by the contracted

shipyard. Critical to the success of the process was a minute control of standards – any slip in measuring a component part could have a disastrous result later in the build programme.

Another important factor in the success of the programme was the elimination, wherever possible, of curved structures. Producing curves in metal was time consuming and could result in unforeseen errors, which could delay construction considerably.

Throughout the design process sometimes heated discussions were had between the Director of Naval Construction and the Admiralty over the layout and composition of the weapons fit. It would prove to be a delicate balancing act focussed between heavy anti submarine and heavy anti aicrcraft. The emergence of the threat posed by fast modern aircraft to ships at sea had at the start of the war been somewhat overlooked and it was essentially to provide the new class with suitable high angle guns capable of deterring, defending against and destroying enemy aircraft. This

The River class frigate Ness *seen during World War Two.*   *(Syd Goodman Collection)*

The Loch class owed much to the Castle class corvettes. This is Dumbarton Castle. *(Syd Goodman Collection)*

requirement was set against the limited deck space available and the principal role of the frigate, that of anti submarine warfare in the North Atlantic.

The final design was approved in May 1943 and gave the frigates a length overall of 307 feet 4 inches, a beam of 38 feet 6 inches and a mean draught of 12 feet 3.5 inches.. Displacement was set at 2,260 tons. Speed was estimated at 18.5 knots and endurance at an economical speed of 15 knots over a range of 7,000 nautical miles.

Each Loch class ship was fitted with two sets of triple expansion reciprocating engines each developing 5,500 ihp, these being fitted to twin screws. The use of these merchantile engines was twofold, on the one hand they were relatively simple to manufacture, rugged, reliable and straightforward to maintain,

whilst secondly they were familiar to the mainly reservist crews, drawn from the merchant marine who manned the new frigates. The frigates were each given two 3 drum watertube Admiralty boilers. Two ships of the class *Loch Tralaig* and *Loch Arkaig* were fitted instead with Double Reduction turbine machinery, which produced 6,000 shp. The fitting of this equipment resulted in these two ships having slightly different internal arrangements than the rest of the class and each also had a three bladed propeller of 9 ft 9 inch diameter.

For armament the Loch's were initially fitted with a single Mk V 4-inch gun, a quadruple 2-pdr Pom Pom and several 20mm guns. To attack submarines each ship was equipped with two 3-barrelled Squid Anti Submarine mortars mounted ahead of the bridge and a

depth charge thrower on the quarterdeck. These weapons were tied in with the Type 144 sonar set for the Squid and the Type 147B for the depth charge throwers.

For the detection of approaching enemy aircraft out to a range of around 40 miles the Loch's were fitted with the Type 277 search radar atop a lattice foremast. The same set could detect enemy shipping out to around 20 miles distant. IFF and HF/DF aerials were also fitted to each ship.

The design of the Loch class received varying degrees of approval but, in early 1945 investigations were initiated into the habitability of the class. In a report dated 3 March 1945 the Director of Naval Construction stated that the *Natal*, under South African control, would be a test bed for enhanced accommodation. The report stated: "*Investigations have been proceeding with methods of making living spaces more attractive and comfortable. As a result*

HMSAS Natal, has been decorated with various colour schemes, furnishings and improved internal lighting for trial, with a view to their adoption in new construction if found to be serviceable and popular. Natal will visit Scapa for two days on passage to Tobermory about 13 March to give the Home Fleet the opportunity of inspecting and remarking on the schemes."

When the Loch class started entering service from late 1944 some vessels experienced worrying levels of hull warping and distortion. Later analysis proved that the design of the bows and forward structures of the ships were insufficient to cope with the hammering the warships received from the brutal North Atlantic wind and waves. Early in their careers the ships were all strengthened with the addition of extra stiffening bars that cured the problem of hull strength.

Postwar the class and the very similar Bay class frigates constituted a large percentage of the Royal

The similarities with the Flower, Black Swan and Castle classes are evident in this view of Loch Fyne.

(Crown Copyright/MoD)

Navy's surface fleet until 1946 when most of the class, except six ships (*Loch Glendhu, Loch Quoich, Loch Arkaig, Loch Fada, Loch Tralaig* and *Loch Veyatie*) entered lengthy periods in the reserve fleet. The need for surface units following the outbreak of the Korean War saw the reactivation of nine members of the class, which were formed into two frigate squadrons. One squadron comprising *Loch Craggie, Loch Dunvegan, Loch Lomond, Loch More* and *Loch Scavaig* was allocated to the Mediterranean where they replaced C class destroyers. The other four Loch class frigates, (*Loch Alvie, Loch Fyne, Loch Insh* and *Loch Killisport*) were destined to serve in the Home Fleet until 1952.

The Loch class modernisation programme of the early 1950's would see the single 4-inch gun replaced with a twin 4-inch Mk XVI gun together with a direc-

tor on the bridge. The mix of various calibre smaller guns were standardised to six Mk V 40mm guns with the units positioned two in the bridge wings and abaft the funnel. Seven ships received Loch class Modernisation Programme refits, being *Loch Alvie, Loch Fada, Loch Insh, Loch Killisport, Loch Lomond* and *Loch Ruthven*. Their un-modernised sister ships were soon deleted from service.

Of particular note in the design of the Loch class is *Loch Insh*, she was the prototype vessel of the Modernisation Programme, but would be further enhanced once sold to the Royal Malayan Navy and renamed *Hang Tuah*. After an extensive refit at Portsmouth Dockyard, *Hang Tuah* emerged with a flight deck and hangar facilities and an enclosed bridge structure.

HMS LOCH ACHANALT
(HMNZS PUKAKI FROM 1948)

HMS Loch Achanalt *seen during World War Two on escort convoy duties. The Loch class were ideally suited to the demands of anti-submarine warfare in the North Atlantic.* *(Crown Copyright/MoD)*

Henry Robb shipyard, known colloquially as Robbs, received an order on 24 July 1942 for the construction of *Naver*, a River class frigate. This order was subsequently changed to that of the Loch class frigate with construction finally starting with the first steel being laid on the slipway on 14 September 1942. After just over a year's work the ship was prepared for launching. The ceremony saw the ship, having been christened as *Loch Achanalt*, being launched into the waters of the Firth of Tay on 23 September by Mrs A.V Alexander, wife of the First Lord of the Admiralty. In February 1944 the need for escorts with the Royal Canadian Navy saw the frigate being transferred to the Canadian Navy. The frigate was completed swiftly with the build finished by 11 August 1944. After initial sea trials the warship was accepted for service on 31 July

1944 as part of the 6th Canadian Escort Group.

After more sea trials in the Forth areas and storing at Tobermory *Loch Achanalt* commenced wartime operations on 7 September when she operated in the North West Approaches area with the 6th Escort Group.

On 16 October the ship detected a submarine on the surface near to the Faroe Islands. The U-boat was later found to be *U-1006* a Type VIIC/41 U-boat under the command of Oberleutnant zur see Horst Voight. The boat had been brought to the surface by action with the Canadian warship HMCS *Annan*, which had dropped depth charges on her. *U-1006* fired a torpedo towards the Canadian vessel, which detonated prematurely.

The submarine would not surrender and when confronted with *Annan* started firing back at the

approaching warships with its deck gun. This action claimed the lives of eight of the warships crew. *Loch Achanalt* joined in the fight and together the two escorts sank the *U-1006*. Forty four Germans were taken into custody as prisoners of war including her commanding officer Horst Voight.

At the beginning of November *Loch Achanalt* escorted the damaged frigate *Whittaker*, under tow into Belfast. The *Whittaker* had experienced a misfiring of her Hedgehog anti-submarine mortars and these subsequently led to a serious structural weakness in the ship.

Loch Achanalt herself was suffering with a similar problem, a lack of hull stiffness and on 11 November she crossed the Irish Sea and made for the Welsh port of Holyhead where extra bracing was added to the ship, in common with the rest of the Loch class ships. The work took until 29 December to complete with Christmas being spent ashore or on leave.

When the ships company were back up to strength the frigate sailed from Holyhead to resume her war patrols on the North West approaches. A duty she would continue only until January 1945 when she transferred south to the Portsmouth and Channel areas. *Loch Achanalt* remained in the region until redeployed to Belfast at the beginning of April.

On 18 April 1945 *Loch Achanalt* sailed from Londonderry to the Canadian Navy's base at Halifax in Nova Scotia. With the end of the European War in sight the frigates last operational duties involved convoy defence along the Canadian coastline until 23 May when the 6th Canadian Escort Group was formally disbanded.

Five days later, she sailed for Great Britain where it was planned for her to be reduced to reserve status. On 5 June she arrived at Sheerness Dockyard to pay off into reserve. After de-storing she was formally accepted into the reserve fleet on 20 June and officially handed back to the Royal Navy by the Canadians the following month. The frigate remained at Sheerness until offered for sale to the Government of New Zealand in February 1948.

After the sale had been completed it was also arranged for a refit to be carried out at Sheerness Dockyard. The frigate was taken in hand on 19 May

for mostly restorative work on the engines and machinery to be undertaken with the work being completed by the end of July. Following sea trials minor modifications were made to the ship but on 6 August the frigate made the short voyage to Chatham Dockyard up the River Medway where she was to be formally handed over to the New Zealand Government. The ceremony took place on 13 September where she was renamed HMNZS *Pukaki* by Mrs H V P McClintock wife of the Captain Superintendent, Sheerness Dockyard. (The name chosen had been originally Manpouri but had been changed at a late stage). The ship was under the command of Lieutenant Commander Laurence 'Larry' Edward Herrick DSC RN. He carried out his training onboard the cadet cruiser *Frobisher* before serving as a midshipman for two years in China onboard the modern cruiser *Suffolk*. Following promotion to Lieutenant he was appointed on 15 February 1940 to the submarine *Tigris* and later in 1941 to submarine *P34*. His first command as a full lieutenant was of *P31*, which in February 1943 was renamed *Ullswater* only to renamed for a third time two months later as *Uproar*. He completed eight combat patrols in the Mediterranean and sank a number of vessels for which he was awarded the DSC.

After the war he stayed in the Navy and saw service in the aircraft carrier *Indefatigable* and the cruiser *Mauritius* before taking command of the *Pukaki*.

On 15 October the ship sailed from Portland for work up in and around Malta, which continued until the end of the year. In January 1949 she finally arrived at her new home port of Auckland and was absorbed as part of the 11th Frigate Flotilla.

The first role for the new frigate was to visit a number of islands and colonies in the South Seas with visits paid to Suva and Samoa before returning to the naval base at Auckland in April. Summer 1949 found *Pukaki* taking part in a major joint Australian and Kiwi exercise that culminated in a very successful visit to the Australian city of Hobart with the other ships taking part in the exercise. The rest of the year was spent in home waters.

After spending Christmas at home *Pukaki* carried out a small exercise in January 1950 in the Bay of

The Royal New Zealand Navy frigates Pukaki *and* Tutira *were ordered at very short notice to proceed to Hong Kong for service in the Far East, in accordance with the resolution of the United Nations Security Council. The photo shows* Pukaki *leaving Auckland for Hong Kong on 3 July 1950.* (Ken Kelly Collection)

Islands before carrying out a cruise that took in visits to Suva, Tabiteuea, Fanafuti and Ocean Island. The worsening conditions in Korea, however, saw a change in fortunes for the frigate when on 25 June she was placed at the disposal of the United Nations.

The Korean War developed out of unresolved issues from the Second World War. Korea had been occupied by Japan as far back as 1904 and an agreement had been reached between the Soviet Union and the United States on power sharing the country after the removal of Japanese forces. The Russians would occupy the north of the country as far south as the 38 parallel with American forces occupying the south.

These two forces did not understand the Korean's demands for independence and unification of their entire country.

The Americans later supported a Korean nationalist called Syngman Rhee, who had been exiled in 1907 from Korea and through the United Nations pressed for elections to be held across all of Korea. Communists in the South boycotted the elections and disallowed it in the North. Subsequently in October 1948 Rhee became President of the independent South Korea. Meanwhile North of the 38th parallel the Soviets installed Kim el Song as leader of North Korea.

When the American military forces left South Korea they left behind a small force equipped with mostly light weapons, whilst the North was heavily supplied with tanks and armoured vehicles from the Soviet Union. The US policy in the region was one of containment of Communism but primarily through non military means with economic and military aid being handed out to non communist governments across Asia.

With the last American soldier withdrawn from South Korea the North saw their chance to finally unify the country by force and in June 1950 Kim el Song launched the first wave of the Korean War with backing from China and the Soviet Union.

The United Nations immediately responded by gathering together a coalition of forces from across the globe to combat the threat posed to independent South Korea from the North and one of the countries that committed men and equipment was New Zealand.

On 3 July *Pukaki* and sister ship *Tutira* sailed from Auckland to Hong Kong and then onto Sasebo in Japan where she would be based during her deployment to Korea. The frigate arrived at Sasebo in August and the ships complement soon settled into a pattern of operations and leave at Sasebo. Her first deployment saw her becoming part of Task Group 96.5 in August but the following month when escorts were required to cover the American Marines landings at Inchon, she was temporarily transferred to Task Group 90.7.

In October having resumed her original tasking with TG 96.5 *Pukaki* worked her way along Korea's east coastline supporting the work of the United Nations minesweepers as they prepared the area around Wonsan for the planned amphibious assault.

On 26 October *Pukaki*'s crew were given leave at the Japanese port city of Kure, where in November they were relieved by Rotoiti. *Pukaki* then sailed to Hong Kong for a short visit before heading home to Auckland in time for Christmas.

Commonwealth warships dressed overall when anchored in Singapore Roads on Her Majesty the Queen's Birthday in June 1955. In the foreground is the New Zealand cruiser Black Prince. *Also in the picture are HMNZS* Pukaki, HMS Modeste *and* HMS Opossum.
(Ken Kelly Collection)

In December 1950 the ship was declared suitable for a reduction to reserve status and on 3 December she arrived at Auckland. She received a refit that lasted until August when she was placed in reserve. She remained in this state until December 1952 when she re-commissioned for further service with the 11th Frigate Flotilla.

After the pressures of the Korean War *Pukaki*'s operational record in 1953 was far from dull with the ship patrolling the vast ocean expanses between New Zealand, Singapore and Hong Kong. The frigate also undertook frequent naval exercises with Australian navy units throughout the year.

In January 1954 with tensions still strained in Korea *Pukaki* was sent to the North China Sea as a fall back if the Korean situation were to flare up once more and also to protect merchantmen sailing in the region from pirate attack. After a brief maintenance period in March, *Pukaki* returned to the Formosa Strait region where on the 29 April in company with the British destroyer *Concord* she helped obtain a resolution in a most delicate diplomatic situation. A Chinese Nationalist warship had seized the British ship SS *Inchuvla* in the Formosa Straits after China claimed it had crossed into its territorial waters. After many hours of diplomacy the ship was released and allowed to proceed after the intervention of the British and New Zealand warships.

The summer was dominated by the worsening situation in Malaya where on a number of occasions *Pukaki* operated with other Royal Navy units in bombarding enemy positions on the west coast.

The Malayan Emergency was a guerrilla confrontation fougtht between the Malayan National Liberation Army (MNLA) and Commonwealth forces. The Malayan economy and infrastructure were devastated by the Second World War, but postwar the British were trying to quickly re-establish the pre war situation, of British controlled industries. Protestors were dealt with harshly and militancy steadily grew. As a consequence the British authorities brought in draconian laws that restricted movement and outlawed communist and left wing political parties. The police were even given the powers to arrest communists and imprison them without trial. As a consequence the

MNLA started a campaign against the British colonial rule in Malaya using weapons left over from the Second World War.

After being relieved by *Kaniere*, *Pukaki* returned home arriving at Auckland on 28 September. *Pukaki* remained in home waters for the rest of the year operating with the 11th Frigate Squadron. In 1955 she would spend a great deal of time operating with US, Australian and British warships in the Pacific taking part in numerous exercises throughout the spring months ending up in Singapore in May.

The ever present threat from a rejuvenated North Korea would mean that the frigate returned there in October after a visit to Hong Kong the previous month. *Pukaki* along with the rest of the 4th Frigate Squadron patrolled the coastline on the lookout for pirates and illicit smuggling operations into South Korea. The patrols were broken up with visits to Japanese ports and a number of interesting and complex naval challenges presented by American Admirals during joint training opportunities with the US Navy.

1956 saw *Pukaki* operate in both hot and cold conditions with early visits to Bangkok, Sasebo and Singapore before, in late May, an official port of call to Port Moresby in Papua New Guinea.

After a two month refit at Auckland from October the frigate was detailed to be escort for a Royal visit to Chatham Island in December. The frigate, together with sister ship, *Hawea* escorted the Royal Yacht *Britannia* with HRH Prince Phillip, Duke of Edinburgh onboard during his visit to the island. Upon completion of this duty she continued escorting, but this time HMNZS *Endeavour*, a ship specially designed for operations in Antarctica. The pair sailed south to McMurdo Sound where scientific measurements were made and also to support fellow Kiwi Sir Edmund Hilary on his transpolar crossing. Christmas Day was celebrated in the snow and ice and two days later the frigate crossed the Antarctic Circle. The pressure of the ice pack in the region, however, meant a return to base as it had started to pose a threat to the safety of the frigate. *Pukaki* sailed to Dunedin and then back to her home port.

1957 started with *Pukaki* at Auckland before exer-

cising in the Hauraki Gulf the following month. 1957 was also the year that Great Britain was in the South Pacific testing their new nuclear weapons (the name given to the operation was Operation Grapple). Grapple was the largest tri-service operation staged since World War Two and would result in the detonation of nine hydrogen bombs at Malden Island and Christmas Island between 1956 and 1958. The Royal Navy had assembled a large fleet of ships and also requested help from the Commonwealth including New Zealand. *Pukaki* was detailed to the operation and used as a weather reporting ship at Christmas Island throughout the spring and summer months.

After witnessing some of the biggest explosions in human history and studying the weather both before and after the blasts, *Pukaki* sailed home to Auckland in August 1957. After a short period of leave for the crew, she sailed in September for joint exercises with Australian and Kiwi units off the coast of Australia. The exercises finished with a wash up at Sydney.

The British nuclear tests, however, resumed in October and the frigate was once again required to study the weather for the tests at Christmas Island. This time *Pukaki* was on station for around a month before once again sailing for New Zealand and some leave.

Just prior to Christmas the frigate was once again at sea off Australia before spending Christmas and New Year in Australia.

1958 started in a similar pattern to the previous year with the frigate stationed at Auckland in January where she was soon in dockyard hands for a much needed maintenance period until late February. After some joint Australian/Kiwi exercises *Pukaki* was once again in demand for her weather reporting skills by the British at Christmas Island for the continuing Operation Grapple nuclear tests. The New Zealand frigate shared this task with sister ship *Rotoiti* until May, when *Pukaki* returned home. En route she had visited the small islands of Manihiki and Danger Island before entering Auckland Harbour on 19 May.

The commitment to Operation Grapple resumed after a short summer leave period for the ships company with further operations off Christmas Island throughout the summer months. Only in September did *Pukaki* return home with the remainder of 1958 being spent in home waters.

In January 1959 *Pukaki* remained in home waters only venturing further afield in March when she sailed to Australia, entering Sydney Harbour at the start of a joint Australian/Kiwi exercise part of which saw her visiting the city of Townsville.

The summer months were extremely busy ones for the New Zealand frigate with participation, in August, in the annual SEATO Exercise JET59 that also saw the presence of HMS *Cardigan Bay* and the Indian cruiser *Mysore*. Indeed it was this cruiser that collided with the Battle class destroyer *Hogue* crushing the destroyers bow and killing a British sailor. *Pukaki* escorted the heavily damaged British ship back to Singapore.

The frigate remained in the Singapore area throughout October before visiting Hong Kong prior to a major naval exercise at the end of the year in Australian waters.

1960 started with a passage to Singapore, en route the frigate called at Sourabaya for an unofficial visit just ahead of the SEATO naval exercise JET60. Upon completion *Pukaki* made for Hong Kong and then onto Kobe and other Japanese ports during a short cruise round to Japan. Before returning to New Zealand *Pukaki* made another visit to Port Moresby and Suva before rejoining the other ships of the 11th Frigate Squadron at Auckland in June.

In July the ship operated around Auckland before being paid off prior to a lengthy refit that lasted until January 1961. The frigate then undertook a series of harbour and sea trials before finally re-commissioning in April at Auckland. The trials were interrupted when she was called upon to assist the government of Tawara in the Gilbert and Ellice Islands to restore order following civil unrest.

Having successfully assisted in the restoration of law and order, the warship returned home to New Zealand. In June she sailed for Australia where she participated in a number of local exercises before sailing on to Singapore where she arrived in July. Throughout the summer months she operated with

HMNZS Pukaki *amongst the ice of the Southern Ocean, having deployed in 1964 as part of Operation Deep Freeze.*
(Steve Bush Collection)

Royal Navy units in the region and with them visited Hong Kong, Penang and Langkawi.

The summer gave way to autumn and in October *Pukaki* spent most of the month at Singapore before a return visit to Hong Kong in November for fleet exercises that lasted until the end of the year.

1962 started with a journey to Japan with ports of call paid to Beppu, Yokohama and Kobe. The return journey to Singapore was routed via Hong Kong where a fantastic time was had by all the sailors onboard who discovered the many nooks and crannies and special places that sailors always discover on port visits to Hong Kong. After a short spell in dock at Singapore for necessary repairs the ship took part in the naval exercise JET62 that also saw the participation of HM ships *Woodbridge Haven* and the despatch vessel *Alert*. April saw the frigate operating in and around Hong Kong before once again returning to Singapore. The early summer was spent taking part in numerous naval exercises that culminated in a port

visit to the Philippine Capital of Manila plus Darwin and Brisbane in Australia. Finally after a long deployment the men of *Pukaki* were relieved to arrive home at Auckland after a short stop at Taranaki.

The remainder of the summer months were spent in New Zealand waters before carrying out a South Seas cruise in November and early December.

Upon her return home to Auckland in December she patrolled locally for a while before being taken in hand for a refit that lasted until early February 1963. After post refit trials and work up the frigate embarked a cadre of new recruits and sailed on a training cruise in May in the South Seas. The cruise took in visits to Raoul, Apia Fakaofa and Suva before returning to Auckland in June.

After a brief respite alongside, the frigate resumed her training role the following month taking another batch of trainees to sea with visits to Gisbum, Wellington and Wanganui. *Pukaki* also took part in an exercise with other Royal New Zealand Navy units at

 Loch Class Frigates

Wellington.

Upon completion she sailed in August for another training cruise taking the younger sailors to such exotic locations as Chatham Island, Lyttleton, Picton and Wellington before joining Australian warships for a joint Australian New Zealand exercise off the coast of Australia. As a reward the ships company of *Pukaki* were granted leave at Sydney and later at Jervis Bay during ports of call at the two towns. The return journey to New Zealand saw a brief stopover at Launceston before arriving home in October.

The final months of the year were spent either in dock at Auckland for routine work to be carried out or operating in the waters off Auckland.

1964 started with an interesting deployment for the frigate as part of the US Operation Deep Freeze. The American bases on Antarctica were in constant need of resupply by air and a large number of American and Allied warships were deployed along the flight path to act as air sea rescue should an aircraft develop difficulties in the treacherous conditions.

Pukaki was, in early, January deployed in the Southern Ocean at 60 degrees South before breaking from Deep Freeze duties in February at Dunedin.

Later in the month she returned to the Southern Ocean and resumed her weather reporting and air sea rescue duties into March. Upon release she sailed north to Auckland and also took time out to pay a courtesy call on the community of Tamanga before sailing for joint Australian and Kiwi exercises in May off Sydney. *Pukaki* made a brief farewell tour of Australian ports including Newcastle and Brisbane before returning home to Auckland in July.

The summer months passed with the frigate operating out of Auckland, but in September *Pukaki* was once again called upon to assist in Operation Deep Freeze for the Americans. For most of October the ship battled heavy seas in the Southern Ocean again at 60 degrees south before taking rest and recreation leave at Lyttleton. In November she resumed her duties through into the new year of 1965. Periodically the warship would return for R&R at either Dunedin or Auckland, but in March the future of *Pukaki* came under discussion. The decision was taken to refit the frigate prior to putting her into reserve in May. The following October she was placed on the disposal list and towed away in January 1966 to be broken up in Hong Kong.

14

Battle Honours

ENGLISH CHANNEL 1945

Chronology

24.07.1942	Ordered from Henry Robb
14.09.1942	Laid down
23.09.1943	Launched
02.1944	Transferred to the Royal Canadian Navy
31.07.1944	Joined 6th Canadian Escort Group
07.09.1944	Commenced wartime operations
16.10.1944	Attacked *U-1006*
11.1944	Extra hull stiffening added at Holyhead
01.1945	To Portsmouth and Channel areas
04.1945	To Belfast
18.04.1945	Sailed to Nova Scotia
28.04.1945	Returned to United Kingdom
28.05.1945	Arrived at Sheerness to pay off into reserve
20.06.1945	Formally returned to Royal Navy control
02.1948	Sold to New Zealand Government
19.05.1948	Start of refit at Chatham Dockyard
13.09.1948	Renamed *Pukaki*
01.1949	Sailed to New Zealand
03.07.1950	Joined United Nations forces in Korea
03.12.1950	Reduced to reserve at Auckland
12.1952	Recommissioned with 11th Frigate Flotilla
01.1954	North China Sea area
29.04.1954	SS *Inchuvia* incident in Formosa Strait
10.1955	Off South Korea
08.1956	Antarctic mission with HMNZS *Endeavour*
1957	Weather reporting ship for Operation Grapple at Christmas Island as part of British nuclear tests.
1958	Operation Grapple in continuation
Summer 1959	Exercise JET59. Escorted damaged RN destroyer *Hogue* into Singapore
07.1960	Paid off into refit
04.1961	Recommissioned into service
1962	Japan: Visited Beppu, Yokohama and Kobe
1962	JET62
02.1963	Became training ship

01.1964	American Operation Deep Freeze in Antarctica
05.01.1965	Paid off into reserve
10.1965	Disposal list
01.1966	Towed from Auckland to Hong Kong for breaking up

HMS LOCH ACHRAY
(HMNZS KANIERE from 1948)

HMS Loch Achray *seen on 29 January 1945, shortly after completion.*   (*Crown Copyright/MoD*)

Loch Achray was ordered from Smiths Dock in Middlesborough on 25 January 1943. Construction started with the first steel plates on the slipway on 13 December the same year and she was subsequently launched on 7 July 1944. The shipbuilders took the ship out on her initial sea trials during January 1945 and handed her over to the Royal Navy on 1 February. Lieutenant Commander L H Stammers RNVR receiving the ship on behalf of the Navy.

Loch Achray like many of the early Loch class frigates was found to suffer from a lack of stiffness and arrangements were made for her to enter a commercial shipyard on the Clyde for extra stiffeners to be fitted. Before she arrived she stored at Tobermory finally arriving on the Clyde on 9 February. She remained in Glasgow until 7 March after which she

entered the 8th Escort Group in the Western Approaches together with *Aire, Natal, Loch More* and *Loch Glendhu.*

The five ships operated in the Irish Sea throughout April. April also saw a change of command with Lieutenant Commander Stammers being replaced in command by Commander John Henry Eaden DSC RN as Senior Officer 8th Escort Group. Eaden was born in the Dominica British West Indies on 23 February 1910 as the son of a lime plantation owner. He was sent to preparatory school in the United Kingdom and developed a love of the sea whilst there. On the 1 May 1927 he joined the Royal Navy as a cadet at Dartmouth and spent his first years at sea as a midshipman on the battleships *Royal Sovereign* and *Royal Oak* in the Mediterranean.

After attending promotion courses in the United

Kingdom he was posted to the cruiser *Canterbury* in 1931. Eaden had always had an interest in submarines and his wish to become part of the silent service was granted when he joined the depot ship *Medway* before joining the submarine *Orpheus* on the China Station. He would later serve on *Swordfish, Clyde, Titania* and *Cyclops* before being given his own command on 17 December 1938 with the submarine *Spearfish*. He was her commanding officer as the Royal Navy faced up to the threat of the Second World War.

Later in the war he would command the submarine *Upmost* and the destroyers *Venetia, Walpole, Inconstant, Mackay* and the frigate *Chelmer* before being given command of *Loch Achray*.

After a brief visit to Belfast the frigate conducted anti-submarine patrols in the Irish Sea where together with *Loch Glendhu* she forced the German submarine *U-1024* to the surface with gunfire. *U-1024* was a Type VIIC/41 boat built by Blohm and Voss at Hamburg and commissioned into service on 28 June 1944. Kapitanleutnant Hans Joachim Gutteck was given command. After training with 31 Flotille *U-1024* was transferred to the front line 11 Flotille and made just the one patrol starting on 1 February 1945. At 1723 on 7 April the submarine attacked the American SS *James W Nesmith* part of convoy HX-246 with the result that the cargo vessel had to be beached near Holyhead. Five days later the submarine attacked the American SS *Will Rogers* part of convoy BB-80 again near Holyhead. This ship faired better than the previous vessel and was later repaired. The submarine was boarded and taken in tow by *Loch More*. Onboard were a large cache of documents and equipment. It also transpired that Kapitanleutnant Gutteck had been injured during the initial attack and had subsequently shot himself dead. Thirty seven members of his crew survived and became prisoners of war. Sadly the U-boat started taking on water during heavy weather whilst on tow and sank some distance off Anglesey the following day.

Loch Achray was, on 28 April, allocated to the defence of convoy OS129/KMS99 to bolster its forces en route to Gibraltar. The ship meanwhile had celebrated VE Day whilst on the Clyde. Her war was far from over, however, after it had been decided that the

frigate should be sent to the Indian Ocean to boost forces in the region.

After refuelling at Belfast on 19 May *Loch Achray* became involved with escorting the numerous surrendered and surrendering German U-boats. This was a more pressing concern and accordingly *Loch Achray* became involved in Operation Deadlight, the escorting of U-boats into British ports most notably Londonderry in Northern Ireland and Loch Ryan in Scotland. On 21 May she was at the Loch Ryan Assembly Point to control the submarines as they arrived. Operation Deadlight was orchestrated immediately after the end of the conflict to ensure that all Axis submarines were surrendered en masse to Royal Navy control. When the German U-boat commanders received their orders to surrender they were told to fly black flags and to remain on the surface at all times. Failure to comply these rules would have resulted in the U-boats being attacked as they were thought to still be active warships. Once detected the submarines were escorted by Royal Navy to ports such as Loch Ryan where they were impounded.

Loch Achray was then under refit on the Clyde that would last until August. On 27 June Lieutenant Commander C J Aldridge RNR was appointed to command the frigate upon her return to service. In September with the refit completed the ship conducted her first post refit sea trials in and around the Clyde. No major problems were discovered and on 26 September she set sail for Colombo routed through the Mediterranean and the Suez Canal.

Two days later Lieutenant Commander H G Chesterman was appointed to command the frigate upon her arrival at Colombo. The frigate duly arrived safely at Colombo on 7 November and joined the East Indies Escort Force that comprised *Loch Craggie, Loch Eck, Loch Katrine, Loch Scavaig* and *Loch Tarbert*.

The repatriation of service personnel scattered around the South East Asia region was the most pressing requirement and *Loch Achray* and her sister ships were in constant demand undertaking this important task in areas such as Java, Sumatra and Batavia.

In January 1946 the frigate returned to Singapore but was soon active in air sea rescue duties off

Gwadar, in what is now Pakistan, for the air transportation to and from the United Kingdom of service personnel. She assumed the role from *Loch Gorm* and spent most of February in this role until relieved herself by sister ship *Loch Katrine*.

The frigate's time in the Far East was fast coming to a close and in March she received notification that she was being recalled to the United Kingdom to enter the reserve fleet at Portsmouth. There was still plenty of work to do before heading home with the ship visiting Port Blair and Trincomalee under the command of Lieutenant Commander C C Anderson RN who had joined ship in May.

Further visits were paid to Rangoon and Penang, but in June 1946 *Loch Achray* finally headed for home. On 10 June the frigate collided with sister ship Loch Scavaig in the Malacca Strait, the damage only being slight on both ships. First stop on the journey was Trincomalee before calling at Malta and Gibraltar. When she finally arrived at Portsmouth she was paid

off into reserve until sold to the Government of New Zealand in 1948.

January 1948 started with the frigate being laid up in Portsmouth, but, after having been sold to New Zealand for £232,750, she was taken in hand for a refit that would suit the conditions to be found in the Southern Oceans. The refit started in June and continued until 27 September when she commissioned as *Kaniere*, the naming ceremony being carried out by Lady Willis, wife of the CinC Portsmouth. The frigate had provisionally been given the name *Haipo* but this was changed just before the commissioning took place.

Kaniere's new commanding officer was Lieutenant Commander B E Turner and he carried out sea trials with the ship until October. Upon completion of an exhaustive list of sea trials the warship sailed to Malta to join the rest of the Mediterranean fleet for a period of work up in and around the island. These evolutions continued for a month at the end of which the frigate

HMNZS Kaniere *departing Auckland bound for operations off Korea.* *(Steve Bush Collection)*

was allowed to sail for New Zealand via the Suez Canal. En route she called at Aden and Singapore before finally arriving at Auckland early in January 1949 to join the 11th Frigate Flotilla.

The following months saw *Kaniere* operating in coastal waters before sailing for a Pacific Ocean patrol that would last until July and involve numerous visits to outlying islands such as Fiji, Somoa and Suva. In many respects the patrols in New Zealand waters were something of a come down from the deep ocean patrols but they occupied the ship and crew during August and September. Another change of command took place in September when the frigate's new commanding officer, Commander C C Stevens took command.

Towards the end of the month she sailed for Sydney where in October she took part in exercises with the Australian fleet in the Jervis Bay area after which she made port calls to the cities of Melbourne and Hobart. After a hugely successful deployment *Kaniere* returned home to Auckland in time for Christmas leave to be granted.

In January 1950 the frigate made a series of visits to ports around the region and also took part in a number of exercises particularly with the Australian Navy before being taken in hand in August for a refit. Whilst under refit the ship had a change of commanding officer with Lieutenant D B Holdsworth RN assuming command. In November she put to sea for sea trials and when these proved satisfactory she was re-commissioned into the New Zealand Navy.

The new year of 1951 saw the frigate undertake her usual mixture of port visits and exercises during a Pacific patrol that lasted until August. Lieutenant

HMNZS Kaniere *had an active wartime role during the Korean War and was often called upon to provide shore bombardments for the Allied land forces ashore.*
(Steve Bush Collection)

20

Commander J O'C Ross relieved Lieutenant D B Holdsworth in September and he took the frigate further into the Pacific with visits to Apia, Ellice Islands, Suva and Tonga before returning home to Auckland in October.

The Korean War developed out of unresolved issues from the Second World War. Korea had been occupied by Japan for as far back as 1904 and an agreement had been reached between the Soviet Union and the United States on power sharing the country after the removal of Japanese forces. The Russians would occupy the north of the country as far south as the 38 parallel with American forces occupying the south. These two forces did not understand the Korean's demands for independence and unification of their entire country.

The American's later supported a Korean nationalist called Syngman Rhee, who had been exiled in 1907 from Korea and through the United Nations pressed for elections to be held across all of Korea. Communists in the South boycotted the elections and disallowed it in the North. Subsequently in October 1948 Rhee became President of the independent South Korea. Meanwhile north of the 38th parallel the Soviets installed Kim el Song as leader of North Korea.

When the American military forces left South Korea they left behind a small force equipped with mostly light weapons, whilst the North was heavily supplied with tanks and armoured vehicles from the Soviet Union. The US policy in the region was one of containment of Communism but primarily through non military means with economic and military aid being handed out to non communist governments across Asia.

With the last American soldier withdrawn from South Korea the North saw their chance to finally unify the country by force and in June 1950 Kim el Song launched the first wave of the Korean War with backing from China and the Soviet Union.

The United Nations immediately responded by gathering together a coalition of forces from across the globe to combat the threat posed to independent South Korea from the North and one of the countries that committed men and equipment was New Zealand.

In November 1951 the frigate was paid off into reserve at Auckland where she remained until recommissioned into service in November 1952 with the 11th Frigate Squadron. The following month she worked up around Auckland before starting 1953 attached to the United Nations Naval Task Group based at Sasebo in Japan under the command of Lieutenant L G Carr RNZN. She left New Zealand for Sasebo on 2 January visiting Sydney, Singapore and Hong Kong en route, finally arriving at Sasebo on 23 April. The very next day the frigate made her first patrol of the west coast of Korea. Throughout the next month *Kaniere* was used for gunfire support of Army and Marine forces ashore and was exceptionally useful for the extraction of wounded personnel from Chodo Island during an operation there.

The frigate was withdrawn from the frontline in early June and the ships company were given leave at Hong Kong but by the 15th June she was back on the frontline. With the declaration of the ceasefire on 28 July the warship remained in the area under United Nations control until January 1954 when she was ordered to Hong Kong and onward passage to New Zealand. The route chosen involved a brief stop at Suva before finally arriving home at the end of March. There she rejoined the 11th Frigate Squadron and operated in local waters.

In July the frigate was prepared for a period of detached service with the 3rd Frigate Squadron, Far East Fleet, in Japan under the control of the United Nations. First, however, she visited Australia and made ports of call to Brisbane, Sydney and Cairns before joining the squadron in September based out of Sasebo. The following month the New Zealand warship joined units from the US Navy in a major international exercise.

In January 1955 *Kaniere* was at Hong Kong for a period of maintenance. Upon completion she resumed her United Nations support role based at Sasebo. This role kept the frigate busy throughout the first five months of the year with occasional port visits to Singapore or Hong Kong.

With the end of her detachment to the United Nations *Kaniere* was released for more routine operations allowing her to visit Celebes and Cairns in July.

HMNZS Kaniere would go on to serve the Royal New Zealand Navy well beyond most of her sisters in the Royal Navy. She was finally broken up in 1967. *(Ken Kelly Collection)*

The following month saw another period in dockyard hands as they cleaned the frigates bottom and gave her a fresh coat of paint.

In September the ship undertook fleet exercises and visits were made to a number of seaside communities including Wellington, Bluff and Suva. Upon completion the ship was taken in hand for a refit that would last until January 1956 when she commenced her post refit trials.

The New Zealand Government signed onto the Commonwealth Strategic Reserve, the idea being to maintain a force of warships in a central location for tasking should the need arise and *Kaniere* was one of the vessels declared to the force based in Singapore. The frigate made her passage in February and rejoined the 3rd Frigate Squadron upon her arrival. Until August the Kiwi frigate took part in fleet exercises and port visits across the region.

The next item on the agenda for the ship and her crew was the unhealthy situation growing in Borneo. The island of Borneo was, in 1961, divided into four separate states, Kalimantan, the Sultanate of Brunei, Sarawak and British North Borneo. The conflict grew out of a British desire to withdraw from its colonies in South East Asia after the Second World War and the British Government proposed combining its three colonies with the new Federation of Malaya.

Many local's protested against the proposal and eventually took up arms against it. The North Kalimantan National Army (TNKU) sparked the conflict on 8 December 1962 when they staged an abortive insurrection to seize oil fields and capture the Sultan of Brunei. The insurrection failed faced with a superior British force comprising, amongst others, Gurkha troops. Operations to capture the remains of the TNKU took until May 1963 to complete.

On 20 January 1963, the Indonesian Government, which had previously supported the planned joining of

the colonies dramatically reversed its decision and announced a policy of Kronfrontasi with Malaysia. On 27 July 1963 President Sukarno of Indonesia went as far as to state that he was going 'to crush Malaysia'.

Kaniere was one of the armada of vessels assembled to patrol the coastline and try and prevent arms and ammunition from reaching the rebels ashore. She continued in this role until leaving in December to spend Christmas at Hong Kong.

1957 started for the frigate with duties off the coastline of Borneo and in February she took part in a major naval exercise before spending a period of time at Hong Kong. In April *Kaniere* undertook another major exercise called Astra held in the waters off Singapore, the rest of her squadron also taking part all designed to test interoperability and communications as well as anti submarine warfare. At the end of the exercises the frigate made for Auckland where she was soon in dockyard hands being prepared for a brief refit.

The work was completed by the end of September and during that time the decision was taken to convert the ship to a training role with the addition of extra classrooms at the expense of some weapons. In future *Kaniere* would be home to cadets and midshipmen on initial sea training courses. Her first deployment in this capacity started in October and one of the more interesting places the trainees visited was Christmas Island. The frigate returned home to Auckland at the end of November whilst the following month saw exercises undertaken with the Royal Australian Navy.

At the beginning of 1958 the frigate visited Melbourne and Hobart in Australia, whilst in March and back in home waters she undertook the training of more young officers and midshipmen in local waters. As part of this process the frigate sailed to Suva on one of a number of training cruises that year. On her return to Auckland the ship was taken in hand for a two month refit and maintenance period before resuming her training role at Auckland until the end of the year.

1959 started as the last had ended with the frigate conducting a series of training deployments that also included periods of anti submarine training. In March 1959 the frigate took part in Exercise Star Globe, which was an anti submarine exercise staged in the Tasman Sea. It was the first exercise of its kind for nearly two years and was one of the most ambitious

HMNZS Kaniere *departing Auckland bound for operations off Korea.*   *(Syd Goodman Collection)*

undertaken. The exercises were centred on the flagship HMAS *Melbourne*, attended by the escorts *Voyager* and *Quiberon* plus two New Zealand frigates *Rotoiti* and *Kaniere*. For the targets the Royal Navy provided two submarines - *Andrew* and *Anchorite*.

In April she was taken in hand for a refit at Auckland. The work onboard continued until June when she started her post refit sea trials programme. In November 1959 *Kaniere* took part in Exercise Enzex under the control of Flag Officer Commanding the Australian Fleet. The force assembled was again centred on the aircraft carrier HMAS *Melbourne* and her escorting warships *Voyager, Vampire* and the New Zealand cruiser *Royalist* and frigate *Kaniere*. A wide field of activity was covered during the exercises that also saw the Royal New Zealand Air Force provide aircraft for the anti aircraft gunnery practice and fighter defence exercises. Upon completion *Kaniere* resumed her training role within the fleet that also saw visits paid to Sydney in January 1960. November, however, saw *Kaniere* collide with the British submarine Anchorite whilst both vessels took part in a series of naval exercises. The damage to both vessels was later repaired.

Perhaps the damaged sustained was sufficient to call into question the frigates long term future. In December *Kaniere* was based at Auckland and in early 1961 became a harbour training ship until she paid off for disposal four years later. In 1966 *Kaniere* was declared surplus to requirements and a scrapyard in Hong Kong took the hulk back to the colony where she was scrapped in 1966.

Battle Honours

ATLANTIC 1945   KOREA 1953

Motto

Kia Maia : 'Be firm'

Chronology

25.01.1943	Ordered from Smiths Dock Middlesborough
13.12.1943	Laid down
07.07.1944	Launched
01.02.1945	Handed over to Royal Navy
Early 1945	Extra stiffening added
07.03.1945	Joined 8th Escort Group
03.1945	With *Loch Glendhu* forced *U-1024* to surface
28.04.1945	Escorted convoys OS129/KMS99
05.1945	Operation Deadlight at Loch Ryan
06.06.1945	Under refit on the Clyde
26.09.1945	Took passage to the Far East
07.11.1945	Colombo and joined the East Indies Escort Force
Late 1945	Java, Sumatra and Batavia
Early 1946	Gwandar, Port Blair and Trincomalee
10.06.1946	Collided with *Loch Scavaig* in Malacca Strait
07.1946	Arrived Portsmouth to pay off into reserve
1948	Sold to New Zealand
06.1948	Refitted at Portsmouth and renamed *Kaniere*
10.1948	Sea trials
11.1948	Mediterranean with British fleet at Malta
01.1949	Auckland and joined 11th Frigate Flotilla
08.1949	Refit at Auckland
11.1949	Paid off into reserve at Auckland
11.1952	Recommissioned into 11th Frigate Flotilla
1953	UN Naval Task Group at Sasebo for Korean conflict
23.04.1953	Sailed from Sasebo for first Korean War patrol
28.07.1953	Korean ceasefire announced – remained on station under UN Control
01.1954	Ordered to Hong Kong

03.1954	In New Zealand waters with 11th Frigate Squadron
01.1955	Hong Kong for maintenance during UN support role
1956	Commonwealth Strategic Reserve at Singapore
Autumn 1956	Borneo Patrol
04.1957	Exercise Astra off Singapore
05.1957	Refitted as training ship at Auckland
01.1957	Collided with submarine *Anchorite*
Early 1961	Harbour training ship at Auckland
1966	Declared surplus to requirements
1966	Scrapped in Hong Kong

HMS LOCH ALVIE

A well presented Loch Alvie *leaving harbour.* (Syd Goodman Collection)

Loch Alvie was ordered from the Scottish ship-yard of Barclay Curle in Dundee on 2 February 1943. Workmen laid the first steel on 31 August the same year and quickly assembled the frigate to launching stage which occurred on 14 April 1944. Final fitting out of the hull took place at Dulmuir and it was from there that the sea trials by the shipbuilders took place in late August. On 21 August the build was officially complete and the warship joined the 9th Escort Group. She was manned by the Royal Canadian Navy including the frigates Commanding Officer Lieutenant Commander E G Old RCNVR.

After storing at Tobermory she started her first operational patrol on 29 August that took her to Londonderry and later in September to Gibraltar. At Gibraltar the frigate received some repairs before returning to Londonderry at the beginning of November to rejoin the Home Fleet.

Loch Alvie sailed on the 29 November as part of the escort for convoy JW62 comprising fifty four ships including no fewer than 34 escorts to the Kola Inlet. Other ships escorting the merchantmen included *Cygnet, Lapwing, Lark* and the Canadian ships *Monnow, Nene, Fort Colborne, St Johns* and *Stormont*. The convoy arrived safely at its destination and upon unloading *Loch Alvie* resumed escort of the return convoy RA62 comprising 30 ships plus 33 escorts.

RA62 arrived in British waters on 17 December and together with other Canadian warships *Loch Alvie* left the convoy just prior to arrival at Loch Ewe and instead made for Liverpool. One of the reasons behind this was to enter into a shipyard to have repairs made to parts of the ship that had suffered damage in the

fearsome Arctic waters around the Kola Inlet.

The repairs continued until February 1945 after which the frigate sailed under the command of Commander A F C Layard RN appointed as Senior Officer 9th Escort Group. The patrols, looking for enemy submarines, continued into the early Spring with little activity but on the 6th April the merchant vessel *Cuba*, part of Convoy VPW-16, was attacked and sunk by *U-1195*. The submarine was a Type VIIC and was fitted with the famed Schnorkel underwater breathing apparatus. On the day of the attack she was under the command of Ernst Cordes, a highly decorated German Reichsmarine officer. Cordes had joined the Navy in 1934 and had undergone training on the destroyer *Theodor Riedel* as well as the *Gorch Fock* and the old battleship *Schleswig-Holstein*. In May 1940 he joined the submarine service and served onboard both *U-123* and *U-103*. By August 1941 he had completed U-boat commander training with the 24th Flotilla and took command of *U-560* a training submarine. His first active U-boat command was as commander of *U-763* which operated from Danzig initially before transferring to the French port of La Rochelle. By this time Cordes had been decorated four times with an Iron Cross 2nd Class, a U-boat War badge 1939, Iron Cross 1st Class and on 19 July 1944 the German Cross in Gold.

In November 1944 he took command of *U-1195* at Kiel in Germany before sailing to Bergen in Norway. His final mission started on 1 January 1945 sailing into the English Channel. There on the 21 March he sighted and attacked the 7,194 ton American merchantman *John R Parks* and sank her. On the 6 April he sighted his second victim, the large French troopship *Cuba* of 11,420 tons. 264 people were rescued by the frigate *Nene*.

The response from the Allied warships escorting the convoy was swift and decisive with the German U-boat being sunk by *Watchman* using depth charges. Only 18 German survivors were rescued, the submarine sinking in a position south east of the Isle of Wight.

For the remainder of the war in Europe *Loch Alvie* continued anti-submarine operations in the Irish Sea and South West Approaches. With the end of the war against Germany the frigate made for the Clyde area and escorted the final Russian convoy, JW-67, which sailed on 12 May and comprised 26 merchantmen and eight escorts. Part way to Russia *Loch Alvie* was ordered away to escort fourteen surrendered German U-boats from Norway to the United Kingdom as part of Operation Deadlight. This was the name given to the internment of all German U-boats after the end of the war in Europe. German submarines were ordered to surface and wear black flags prominently before following Allied ships into the nearest port. Large numbers of U-boats were taken to Scottish lochs but most ended their war service in Londonderry.

On 20 May *Loch Alvie* arrived at Loch Erribol with *U-668* under the command of Kapitänleutnant Fritz Henning which had surrendered at Narvik. The following month the Royal Canadian Navy formally handed the frigate back to the Royal Navy, who paid her off into reserve alongside many other warships. She was later stored at Sheerness Dockyard in Kent where she would remain in reserve until brought forward for further service in 1950.

Commander Peter Hankey took command of the ship on 11 April 1950. Commander Hankey was born in the Dorset town of Blandford on 2 October 1912 and in 1930 joined the Royal Navy as a cadet. Nine months later he passed out as a midshipman and was posted to the cruiser *Hawkins* in the Atlantic Fleet and later on the battlecruiser *Hood* in the Home Fleet. Peter Hankey would spend the next few years of his naval career in the Mediterranean onboard the destroyers *Codrington* and *Ardent*.

He was serving onboard the battleship *Warspite* when war broke out after which he was posted to HMS *St Angelo* in Malta in 1940 during the German bombing of the island. The following year he was onboard the destroyer *Cossack* during the epic battle with the German battleship *Bismarck* and later the night action in Svaerholt Fjord in 1941.

He later served on the aircraft carriers *Formidable* and *Implacable* before gaining his own command as captain of *Loch Alvie* on 11 April 1950.

Whilst at Sheerness Dockyard *Loch Alvie* was, on Thursday 18 May, struck by fire. The fire broke out at 1105 on a catamaran moored on the starboard side of

the frigate abreast the bridge. The catamaran had caught fire due to dockyard welding. Ten minutes later the heat from the fire transferred through the frigates hull and caused a small fire in the galley to ignite. It took another thirty minutes to extinguish all the fires within Sheerness Dockyard.

Apart from a run over the degaussing range in the Thames Estuary *Loch Alvie* remained at Sheerness until the final day of May when she sailed for Portsmouth. After a night in the Solent the frigate entered Portsmouth Dockyard on Friday 2 June and secured on *Cawsand Bay* on the North West Wall. Later at 1115 *Burghead Bay* secured on *Loch Alvie*.

Within twenty four hours the frigate was back at sea heading for her work up at Portland but en route went to the aid of a yacht in distress. Upon her arrival at Portland *Loch Alvie* entered the harbour and saw a vast assortment of Royal Navy vessels including the cruiser *Cleopatra*, the destroyers *Aisne, Agincourt* and *Jutland* and the frigate *Hedingham Castle*.

Loch Alvie remained at Portland until 13 June when she sailed together with the destroyer *Scorpion* for Swanage for three days of exercises before heading north to Invergordon having been joined by the cruiser *Swiftsure* and another weapon class destroyer *Battleaxe*. The ships exercised in the Dornoch Firth, Invergordon and Scapa Flow areas until 7 July when *Loch Alvie* dropped anchor in D1 berth in the wide natural harbour at Scapa.

After two days at anchor the frigate set sail early on Sunday 9 July bound for Egesund in Norway together with the destroyer *St Kitts*; both ships eventually berthing on the town quay where both were opened to the public throughout their stay. From Egesund the frigate and destroyer sailed south to Amsterdam where they secured on Saturday 15 July on the Javagarde jetty. Again many hundreds of local residents took the opportunity of being welcomed onboard and given a tour of these modern warships.

After five days *Loch Alvie* returned to sea and crossed the English Channel to visit the Kent port of Folkestone. On the third day of the visit the weather started to deteriorate and accordingly *Loch Alvie* sailed the short distance round the coast to anchor off Margate to weather the force 7 to 8 gale and twelve

foot swells; once the storm had blown through *Loch Alvie* returned to Folkestone to complete the visit to the town, remaining there until Tuesday 25 July. From Folkestone it was only a short journey to Sheerness, which was reached at 1700 the same day. After disembarking her ammunition at Sheerness *Loch Alvie* sailed up the River Medway on 27 July 1950 and entered Chatham Dockyard securing on the cruiser *Cleopatra* in No 3 Basin.

The following weekend saw the ships company meet and greet many thousands of people who toured the ship from stem to stern as part of the annual Chatham Navy Days. The frigate looked spick and span everyday as the ships company spent most of the three days cleaning the ship thoroughly as well as being dressed overall with flags and bunting from every possible location onboard.

After the general public had left on Wednesday 9 August *Loch Alvie* was moved by tug into No 2 Basin and was secured alongside the destroyer *Crossbow*. It was whilst she was there that news was received onboard that Princess Elizabeth had given birth to a son, who was given the name Charles.

Three days later on Monday 18 September 1950 *Loch Alvie* left Chatham Dockyard and sailed the short distance to Sheerness Dockyard where she embarked ammunition and stores. The next day she sailed for Spithead and then onto Londonderry for more exercises and training with the submarines *Tireless, Alliance* and *Amphion* and the destroyer *Crispin* and sister ship *Loch Arkaig*.

On Tuesday 3 October *Loch Alvie* left Londonderry for Harwich arriving at the port after three days steaming and secured to No 1 buoy in the harbour. The frigate only stayed at Harwich for a couple of days before returning to Margate to anchor overnight before once again returning to Harwich for a further four days of exercises in the North Sea. Upon completion she sailed around the south coast before arriving to secure to D13 buoy in Portland harbour. In harbour were the aircraft carrier *Indefatigable*, destroyers *Scorpion, Battleaxe, Crossbow, Zephyr* and *Myngs* and the frigates *Oakham Castle* and *Tintagel Castle*.

The force exercised in local waters until Saturday 21 October when *Loch Alvie* sailed for Londonderry

for a period of anti-submarine warfare training around Molville with Loch Insh. The two frigates then stayed together for the journey to Gibraltar, which started on Saturday 11November with both ships arriving at The Rock a week later. Highlight of the week for the ships company was undoubtedly the arrival on Wednesday 22 November of the Duke of Edinburgh, who was congratulated on the recent arrival of his first son Charles.

The end of November was spent exercising in local waters around Gibraltar before visiting the French port of Bayonne where *Loch Alvie* secured alongside the Quai de la Place d'Ares Bayonne. During the visit the frigate was again open to the public and hundreds of local residents toured the ship and asked many questions of the British crew.

On Monday 4 December the frigate slipped to sea bound for Sheerness and some well earned Christmas leave, which was granted once the ship had been secured in the floating dock AFD12 at Sheerness Dockyard on 12 December.

On New Year's Day 1951 the dock was flooded and *Loch Alvie* was towed out and secured alongside *Loch Killisport* on the West Wall of the Great Basin at Sheerness, where she would remain for the next ten days. On Friday 12 January she was loaded with ammunition whilst at Buoy 25 and finally on Saturday 20 January she sailed south to Gibraltar.

After five days steaming the frigate arrived at the British colony and immediately was tasked with a number of exercises that lasted until Thursday 8 January when she sailed for Arachi Bay where she anchored five days later. Her stay there was overnight as *Loch Alvie* together with sister ships *Loch Insh* and *Loch Scavaig*, the dispatch vessel *Surprise* and the frigate *Peacock* sailed for Savona.

After a pleasant visit the British ships sailed on to the crown jewel of the Mediterranean, Monaco, where the frigates provided a suitable escort for the battle-ship *Vanguard*, which was anchored in the harbour. The frigates, meanwhile, could secure alongside the Quai de Planance with five shackles keeping her safely alongside. From this location the ships company could see straight into the town and enjoy the nightlife in this most cosmopolitan resort without having to use a liberty boat.

The frigates were open to the public throughout the visit and many thousands had a sneak peak at the British warships. After five most enjoyable days *Loch Alvie* together with *Loch Insh* returned to Gibraltar, where she secured on the destroyer *Gabbard* at 27 berth on Monday 5 March.

Another four days were spent at the colony before the frigate, together with *Loch Insh* and *St Austell Bay*, sailed at 1820 bound for the United Kingdom. *Loch Alvie* arrived at Sheerness on Thursday 15 March and was soon taken in hand for a refit that lasted until 8 May. Post refit trials were carried out in the Thames Estuary before the ship sailed up the River Medway on 15 May to Chatham Dockyard where she was quickly taken into Dry Dock 7 for some repairs to be undertaken.

After two days at Chatham the frigate sailed at 1300 back to Sheerness for the conclusion of her sea trials programme. Upon completion *Loch Alvie* sailed to Invergordon for further training and exercises that included periods spent at Red Bay. These continued until the end of the month when the warship made for Portsmouth, securing on the destroyer *Zambezi* on Saturday 2 June. Two days later she was moved by tug onto *Ulster*, which was herself secured onto *Cavalier* on the North West Wall of the Dockyard.

The next day came the shocking news of the loss of the submarine *Affray*. The submarine had sailed on her last journey on 16 April 1951 at 1615 on a simulated war patrol that had been codenamed as Training Spring. Onboard the submarine was seventy five men under the command of Lieutenant J Blackman DSC. His orders were to conduct a series of simulated attacks on enemy shipping, land Commandos on an enemy shores and return to port at Falmouth three days later.

When *Affray* failed to make radio contact at 0900 on 17 April, in accordance with orders a rescue mission codenamed Subsmash was initiated. Every available warship that could be deployed in the search for the submarine was sent to sea including *Loch Alvie, Loch Insh, Loch Fyne* and *Loch Killisport*. On Thursday 7 June *Loch Alvie* searched for signs of the lost boat in Freshwater Bay before returning to Portsmouth the

HMS Loch Alvie *was one of six Loch class frigates that were modernised in the late 1950's and early 1960's. After their refits the ships served mostly on distant stations such as the Far East, Persian Gulf and South Atlantic.*   *(Crown Copyright/MoD)*

next day. On 11 June the frigate once again searched an area of the English Channel for *Affray* finally anchoring over the site of the wreck off Hurd Deep on Friday 15 June. Representatives from the media came onboard the frigate from the MV *Burhou* and recorded television programs and took photographs of the sea above where the men of *Affray* lost their lives.

On Monday 18 June, with the harrowing task completed *Loch Alvie* returned to Portland and from there back to Portsmouth on 20 June. After three days at the Hampshire naval base she once again sailed to Portland for a week of exercises.

July started with a much more pleasant task, a visit to the town of Berwick. *Loch Alvie* arrived there after two days steaming and anchored some distance off the town in 7 fathoms of water on Tuesday 3 July. The next day the Mayor of Berwick came onboard having arrived via the MV *Lady Forth* together with a number of local schoolchildren who had a personal tour of the ship by the ships company. The next four days were spent making contacts with the local community and also welcoming hundreds of people onboard, all of whom had taken the short ferry ride out to visit the ship.

Together with *Loch Killisport*, *Loch Alvie* left Berwick early on 9 July and sailed the short distance to Whitby where again the two ships were opened to the public throughout their stay which ended on Tuesday 17 when *Loch Alvie* sailed south to visit the Kent seaside resort town of Deal.

Although Deal is an ancient Cinque Port town it had no harbour or port and therefore, upon her arrival *Loch Alvie* anchored offshore and welcomed visitors and VIP's from the town via ferries. The six day visit ended on Wednesday 25 July when the frigate weighed anchor and made the short journey to Sheerness and onwards to Chatham Dockyard when for the second year running the frigate was to be one of the star attractions at Chatham Navy Days.

Before that, however, the crew were assembled on the forecastle on Friday 27 July for a ships company photograph to be taken. A copy of the photograph was presented to the departing Commander Hankey when the ship was transferred to the command of Commander C F Parker on the last day of July.

After Chatham Navy Days long summer leave was granted and *Loch Alvie* next set sail on 3 September 1951 when the frigate left Chatham Dockyard at 1345 bound for a few days of exercises off Portland. From there the frigate sailed on Saturday 8 September for the Norwegian port of Kristiansand together with the Bay class frigate *St Austell Bay* for anti submarine exercises. Upon their arrival the British ships anchored in the West Harbour and witnessed three Danish ships, *Huitfeadt*, *Krabbe* and *Kridel* enter the anchorage later followed by the Norwegian destroyer *Bergen*.

By Friday 14 September the force had been further bolstered by the addition of the Norwegian Trondheim and the Danish Springeren. Unfortunately much of the planned exercises had to be postponed due to bad weather, with the ships confined to sheltered bays to ride out the worst of the storms for twenty four hours.

After three days of intense exercises *Loch Alvie* visited the port of Horten before going onto the Norwegian Capital city of Oslo with *St Austell Bay* where the ships were opened up to the public. The ships enjoyed an almost unrivalled level of hospitality from the locals who made them all feel very welcome. Sadly, the British ships departed for Invergordon on Monday 24 September and another period of training in Scottish waters with the cruiser *Swiftsure*, the submarine *Alliance* and other Loch class frigates. The bulk of this force continued their training en route to Londonderry in early October.

Loch Alvie sailed south on 11 October for Gibraltar and four days later was joined by *Loch Arkaig*, *St Austell Bay* and *Veryan Bay*. The force finally arrived at Gibraltar after anti-submarine exercises on Friday 19 October. *Loch Alvie* operated around Gibraltar until visiting Tangiers on Saturday 17 November with the remainder of November given over to further training and exercises off the naval base at Gibraltar. On Thursday 29 November in company with *Loch Arkaig*, *St Austell Bay* and the Portuguese warship *Duaro*, *Loch Alvie* sailed for an official visit to Lisbon arriving the next day. The warships secured at Alfordega Wharf West in preparation for celebrating Portuguese Independence Day on 1 December. After the celebrations the British frigates set sail the next day for home.

After disembarking her ammunition at Sheerness into dockyard lighters *Loch Alvie* arrived home at Chatham on 6 December. Five days later she was moved by tugs into No 6 Dry Dock where she remained until New Years Day when the dock was flooded and the frigate moved next to *Opossum*.

On 16 January 1952 the frigate left Chatham Dockyard for Portland for exercises and training that included another visit to Gibraltar. *Loch Alvie*'s ships company were told on Wednesday 6 February of the death of King George VI. After the King had laid in state on the occasion of his funeral on Friday 15 February *Loch Alvie* fired a salute of 56 minute guns which were answered with 56 fired by Gibraltar Fortress.

The frigate sailed for home on 28 February and after disembarking stores and ammunition at Sheerness again returned to Chatham Dockyard at 0930 on 5 March. Commander C F Parker RN addressed the ships company on 24 March on the occasion of his leaving the ship.

Loch Alvie remained at Chatham Dockyard until 3 November 1952 and then continued to operate in homes waters.

On 8 March *Loch Alvie*'s new commanding officer was welcomed onboard the frigate, Commander Ian Graham Harrt Garnett had joined the Royal Navy as a cadet on New Year's Day 1932 and after training his first appointment had been to the battleship *Valiant* as a midshipman and a later appointment to the cruiser *Despatch*. In 1936 following a promotion course Ian Garnett served as a sub lieutenant on the battlecruiser *Hood* and later the cruiser *Capetown* and destroyer *Delight* both on the China Station.

Throughout the war Ian Garnett had served as a gunnery officer mostly on board destroyers such as *Vesper* and *Bedouin* but also on the aircraft maintenance ship *Unicorn*. His final wartime posting followed his promotion to Lieutenant Commander to assume the role of gunnery officer on the destroyer depot ship *Tyne*.

On 30 June 1949 he was promoted to Commander and on 8 March 1954 he stepped onboard *Loch Alvie* as her commanding officer. Garnett was promoted to Captain in June 1957 and took command of HMS *Cambridge*, the Royal Navy's Gunnery school near

Plymouth. Captain Ian Garnett died in July 1996 at his home in Dorset.

On 15 February 1954 *Loch Alvie* returned to Chatham to pay off and was taken in hand for a refit at Portsmouth. On 8 March at 1430 the ships company arrived from Barracks and the dedication ceremony took place. The following morning saw her shifted from No 2 Basin to the South Wall in the Tidal Basin and started a lengthy series of trials that lasted until Tuesday 30 March when *Loch Alvie* sailed for the start of her work up at Portland. At Portland she was put through her paces with a large variety of tasks with ships that included the aircraft carriers *Indefatigable*, *Implacable* as well as *Maidstone* and *Tyrian*.

On Saturday 3 April the frigate returned to Chatham where she stayed for the next four days before once again resuming her work up at Portland where she initially exercised with the Royal Yacht *Britannia*. After a short leave period for the ships company *Loch Alvie* was selected to escort the *Britannia* from Portsmouth to Malta in the Mediterranean the ships leaving on Friday 16 April.

On Tuesday 22 April the *Britannia* and her escort arrived at Malta with the frigate securing on No 7 buoy in Silema Creek. The following day the order was given to dress ship overall for the Queen's visit to the island and also to fire a 21 gun salute. Two days later *Loch Alvie* was back at sea at the start of a CASEX exercise with the wreck of the submarine Stubborn being used for the exercise. Later during her stay she would also get to exercise with the cruiser *Gambia* before taking passage to Port Said on Monday 24 May.

After passing through the Suez Canal, *Loch Alvie* visited Aden briefly and cheered ship as sister ship *Loch Quoich* passed by flying her paying off pennant. Throughout the next few months on the Persian Gulf station the frigate made a number of visits to the Seychelles and Aldabra Islands, Lamu Malindi, Mombasa, Mauritius, Trincomalee and Colombo.

In August the ship took part in a combined exercise with units of the Indian, Pakistani and Ceylon navies after which the frigate had the honour of visiting the Maldives. The closing months of the year were spent patrolling the Persian Gulf and also visiting Khor

Kuarai, Rasal Khaimaii and on Saturday 4 December arriving at Bombay where she secured alongside the breakwater pier. After a most successful four day visit *Loch Alvie* returned to sea bound for Colombo where the ships company enjoyed a traditional British Christmas whilst the ship was shifted into the Workers Dry Dock for dive days of work to be undertaken before sailing from Colombo on 7 January 1955 for Socotra on the East African Coast. The crossing was good and the weather was kind to the British ship and upon arrival *Loch Alvie* welcomed onboard the local Sultan who spent a week onboard on a mini cruise en route to Mukalla.

After a brief visit to El Ghaida the frigate continued onto Aden where she remained for two days before proceeding to transit into the Mediterranean via the Suez Canal. After further stops at Malta and Gibraltar on Monday 14 February she was back at Sheerness Dockyard. After disembarking her ammunition into lighters *Loch Alvie* proceeded into Chatham Dockyard the next day and was duly decommissioned. On Tuesday 26 April 1955 Commander Ian Garnett was succeeded in command by Captain E T Graham RN and the frigate was re-commissioned.

On Wednesday 6 June *Loch Alvie* was cold moved into No 7 dry dock within the dockyard and work commenced on her refit which would last until Tuesday 19 July at the start of her sea trials off Sheerness. By 25 July the work had been completed and when the frigate sailed she made for Portsmouth and Portland.

Loch Alvie sailed south on 1 August for Gibraltar en route to the Persian Gulf again. Off Malta she operated with the submarine *Truncheon* for a few days before proceeding to Messina for gunnery practice with aircraft from 1832 Squadron and a splash target towed by the cruiser *Birmingham*. Upon her arrival at the Italian Naval Base at Messina, Captain Graham left the ship to visit the Commanding Officer ashore as well as the Sub Prefect of Messina and the Mayor of the town.

The two day visit was a huge success with many friendships formed and sporting challenges undertaken between the British and Italian crews. On leaving Italy, *Loch Alvie* returned briefly to Malta before continuing onto the Suez Canal and Aden.

Port visits were made to Berbera in Somalia and the volcanic island of Perim in the Strait of Mandeb, before arriving at Aden on 28 September. The next day the frigate put to sea bound for Mukalla the capital of the Haudemaut coastal region of Arabia and experienced a mechanical breakdown when an oil pump failed. This resulted in an all stop of the engines for twenty minutes until engineers solved the problem.

October would see a number of high profile visits including those to Mukualla, Al Ghaida, Khor Dibai and Basra where the ship secured to the RAF Jetty on Wednesday 2 November. After a period on dhow patrol where the Royal Navy was tasked with intercepting pirates who attacked ships and stole cargoes as well as operated in various illegal trades such as smuggling and gun running. *Loch Alvie* sailed for Cochin and Colombo late in November.

On Friday 9 December whilst at Male in the Maldives the Sultan of Male came onboard the frigate and received a 21 gun salute. After the Sultan's tour of the ship was over it was time for local residents to be ferried out to the ship in the harbour and given a tour of the ship. After five days at anchor the frigate slipped out to sea bound for Addu Atoll and then Port de Galle and finally on Thursday 22 December arrived at Trincomalee for Christmas.

1956 started on Monday 2 January for the ship with exercises with the cruiser *Gambia* as both ships sailed to Colombo. The next morning the ships arrived and *Loch Alvie* secured between two buoys in the harbour at 1907. The frigate was in need of a brief maintenance period and after swinging at the buoy for six days was taken into the dry dock at Colombo, where she remained until Monday 16 January. The work on the ship continued until Wednesday 1 February when *Loch Alvie* slipped to sea for the return passage to Trincomalee.

February proved to be a busy month for the frigate with visits arranged to Quilan, Calicut and Mangalore where the ships cricket and football teams gave a good account of themselves against local teams. On Monday 27 February the frigate sailed to Ratnagiri in India where the gangway was opened to local visitors

to look over the warship during the ships two day port visit.

After a very brief visit to Bombay, *Loch Alvie* sailed back to the Persian Gulf at Dibba on Tuesday 6 March. Upon arrival the ships motorboat was lowered to collect the Sheik who had requested a personal tour of the British frigate. *Loch Alvie* remained anchored offshore for two days before continuing her planned programme returning to Bahrain for the rest of the month.

Loch Alvie started another dhow patrol on 5 April which also included visits to Das, Umh Said, Khor Dhuwein in Saudi Arabia and Khor Odaid in Qatar before once again returning to the familiar surroundings of Bahrain on 16 April. Only two days were spent alongside before she started the next phase of her patrol cycle with ports of call made on Khor al Bazm in Abu Dhabi, Dibau, Halal and Jazirat Halul in Qatar. On 30 April *Loch Alvie* was at Basra to honour the birthday of King Faisal of Iraq, on her arrival the ship fired a 21 gun salute in his honour and on 3 May the ships guard was paraded ashore and another 11 gun salute was fired to honour the commandant of the Garrison at Basra.

On Monday 7 May the frigate sailed back to Bahrain and remained alongside for nearly a fortnight as the ships company carried out routine maintenance onboard. Finally, on Tuesday 22, she resumed her patrols with calls made at Umh Said, Yas, Umm Al Qawain and Ras al Khaimah on Saturday 2 June. The intention had been to stay alongside for the next twelve days preparing the ship for the passage back to the United Kingdom, but at 1600 on Sunday 3 June the ship was ordered to raise steam with despatch and go to Jazirat Halul. The political agent at Qatar had received reports that five dhows containing some three hundred people were weather bound at that island and running short of food and water. *Loch Alvie* returned to Bahrain at the end of her humanitarian mission on Wednesday 13 June.

The passage back home started on Sunday 17 June, three days later than originally planned and saw the frigate routed through Aden, Suez and Gibraltar before finally arriving at the mouth of the River Medway at Sheerness on Wednesday 18 July.

After disembarking her ammunition she proceeded into Chatham Dockyard and was once again one of the star attractions at that year's Navy Days held over the August Bank Holiday weekend. Seasonal leave was granted to the ships company as the ship herself was on Wednesday 5 September moved by tugs into Chatham Dockyards No 7 dry dock where she remained for the rest of the month.

On 2 November 1956 at 1220 the frigate was re-commissioned for further service in the Persian Gulf. During her trials program in late November the ship was visited by Her Royal Highness the Duchess of Kent. Finally on Monday 26 November *Loch Alvie* put to sea through the dockyard's South Lock and into the River Medway and made for Portland where she exercised with Mounts Bay, Tumult, Keppel and the American submarine USS Cutlass.

After spending the weekend of 8 December at Portsmouth, *Loch Alvie* returned to Chatham the following Tuesday where seasonal leave was granted to the ships company as the frigate secured on the Type 14 frigate Hardy.

The frigate next put to sea on Tuesday 15 January 1958 and sailed for Sheerness, stayed for two hours at No 2 buoy and then returned to St Helens Roads in The Solent where she anchored overnight. Just after 1400 *Loch Alvie* slipped out to sea and took passage to Portland for further exercises that included the Dutch submarine Walrus as well as British ships and submarines Dundas, Murray, Pellew, Sleuth, Selene, Venus and Vigilant. After seven days of training the frigate returned to Portsmouth and secured alongside Fountain Lake Jetty on Friday 25 January.

Final preparations and storing the ship took four days before she left the Hampshire Navy Base and headed south to Freetown taking the long way round to the Persian Gulf. At Freetown she fuelled and proceeded upon completion. En route from Freetown *Loch Alvie* was escorted by a very large school of dolphins that rode and played in the ship's bow wave. King Neptune made his presence felt on Wednesday 13 February when he oversaw the Crossing the Line Ceremony held on the frigate's quarterdeck.

Finally on 23 February the frigate arrived at the Simonstown Naval Base in South Africa and secured

alongside the South African frigate Good Hope. During the next three days lots of sporting challenges were set by the host ship and honours were reasonably equally shared.

The following Tuesday at 1130 *Loch Alvie* left Simonstown and resumed her voyage to the Middle East via Mombasa, where upon arrival the frigate loaded 344 tons of fuel before proceeding to sea and onto Khor Kuwai in Oman.

Upon arrival the frigate spent four days alongside before commencing her first patrol that included visits to Basra in Iraq, Umm Qais in Jordan on the site of the ruined Hellenistic Roman city of Gadara, Nabiyu Tunb in Iran, Lingeh and the ruins at Hormuz in Iran, Bu Masa, Das and on Tuesday 16 April a return to Bahrain.

The following month started with the ship and her sisters in the Gulf taking part in the flotilla regatta with a wide variety of competitions and challenges presented to the three ships companies. After the regatta it was back to business as usual with the frigate patrolling the Persian Gulf but with the respite of a banyan at Ras al Khaimah.

On Monday 3 June the ship put to sea from Bahrain for Umm Said, where she arrived later the same day. Upon arrival at Midday she fired a 21 gun Royal salute for the Coronation. Later during the four day visit men from the ship arranged a children's party onboard and also a cricket match against a local team. At the end of the visit *Loch Alvie* sailed back to Sitra before spending some time operating with Loch Killisport en route to Abadan. The middle of June also saw visits paid to Kharramshahr for exercises with the Iranian Navy.

Amongst the many ports visited in July by *Loch Alvie* were Khor Kuwai, Quariyat, Sur, Tunh, Bu Masa and Muscat. At the later the Captain went ashore on Friday 19 July and the medical officer was despatched to assist a medical case onboard the oil tanker Galtex Canberra anchored in the harbour. The following night *Loch Alvie* sailed for Sawadi after an overnight passage; this visit was followed by Khor Kuwai, Dubai and Ras al Khaimah along with Loch Fada and the tanker RFA Gold Ranger.

August started with a dhow patrol where the frigate intercepted and inspected numerous dhows in the Persian Gulf looking for illicit cargoes. Usually nothing of interest was found but occasionally arms and ammunition were discovered and the vessel and crew arrested. Her first dhow patrol ended on Sunday 18 August upon the frigates return to Bahrain.

After three days alongside *Loch Alvie* put to sea in company with Loch Fada at the start of the Batina Coast Patrol that took in visits to Sohar, Khor Kuwai, Alkahdra and Muscat. By the middle of September the warship was in need of maintenance and arrangements were made for a docking in Karachi which was reached on Tuesday 17 September. Two days later she entered the graving dock and remained there until 4 October. *Loch Alvie* remained at Karachi for the final refit work to be completed until Sunday 5 October when she sailed for Trincomalee.

The wide harbour of Trincomalee was reached five days later as *Loch Alvie* secured on the oiling jetty. On Tuesday 15 October the Prime Minister of Ceylon, John Lionel Kotalawela, arrived onboard at 1135, along with other VIP's from his Government. He spoke with the Captain and addressed some members of the ships company before departing after some twenty five minutes.

The next morning, *Loch Alvie* put to sea and variously acted independently and also in company with the cruiser *Ceylon* before she returned to Trincomalee Harbour and secured alongside Saigan Berth. Leave was granted to the ships company and the frigate remained alongside until 2 November.

Having fuelled, *Loch Alvie* left the welcoming surroundings of Trincomalee for Cochin arriving after three days. At Cochin the frigate secured on the Naval Jetty No 2 and No 3 and witnessed the arrival of a number of Indian Navy warships including INS *Konkan*, INS *Godavari*, INS *Gomati* and INS *Ganga*. The next six days were spent at the Naval Base with many varied inter service activities laid on. Sports consisted mostly of cricket where the local teams invariably won the matches.

After six enjoyable days *Loch Alvie* sailed on Monday 11 November and briefly exercised with the Indian warship INS *Konkan* before proceeding to Bombay. At Bombay the ship was visited by numerous VIPs throughout her five day stay ahead of the

frigates participation in the large naval exercise Exercise Crescent.

The exercise involved a number of warships from Pakistan, India and Iran as well as *Loch Alvie* and *Loch Fada* and concluded with wash up's being undertaken at Karachi on 1 December. Upon completion the frigate made her way back to Bahrain by way of Sur, Muscat and Diamanyat Islands. On Friday 13 December she secured at Bahrain where five days later the colours were set at half mast for the funeral of AB Sullivan who had died a few days earlier. Christmas was spent alongside but Boxing Day saw the ship put to sea bound for Aden at the start of her return home to the United Kingdom.

The warship routed via Suez, Malta and Gibraltar finally arriving at Chatham Dockyard on 28 January 1958. Once inside the dockyard *Loch Alvie* was taken in hand for a five month refit. The work was complete by the beginning of May with the ship having been re-commissioned earlier on Tuesday 29 April for further service in the Middle East under the command of Captain C L F Webb DSC RN. During the Second World War he had been awarded the Distinguished Service Medal when flying for the Fleet Air Arm and carried out mine laying operations off Norway in 1944 and also provided an anti submarine escort role during Arctic convoys to Norway in March 1945.

The frigate first put to sea for initial sea trials on Wednesday 7 May and returned after a week. She next sailed to start her work up on 19 May and proceeded to Portland where she was met by a large assortment of escorts including *Brocklesby, Hardy, Dundas, Pellew, Grenville* and the submarine *Scout* and the Indian Navy's new Type 41 frigate INS *Brahmaputra*. Throughout the work up *Loch Alvie* exercised extensively with the Indian warship before visiting the French port of Cherbourg independently on the morning of Friday 13 June. During the visit the Captain called on Sous pre fet and the Mayor of Cherbourg, both of whom attended a cocktail party thrown in their honour onboard the frigate on the last day of her visit.

Upon completion it was back to Portland to complete her work up that ended with the frigate's arrival back at her home port of Chatham on Friday 27 June. After spending most of July alongside, the frigate ventured to sea on Monday 21 July bound for Gibraltar via Portland.

Upon arrival at Gibraltar *Loch Alvie* was visited by Rear Admiral R S Foster Brown, Flag Officer Gibraltar before proceeding onto Malta, Port Said and Aden after transiting the Suez Canal. Aden, as ever, was a barren and desolate location and after three days resupplying the ship with stores left on Tuesday 26 August and took passage to Bahrain. Throughout the summer and autumn months the frigate and her sister ships maintained patrols in the Persian Gulf and visited a wide variety of ports throughout the region including Muscat, Ras al Hadd and Das Island as well as conducting exercises with local navies, particularly that of Iran.

Loch Alvie returned to Aden on Tuesday 23 December and spent Christmas there secured alongside the West Wall of the Boom Defence Pier before sailing six days later for Mukalla.

On New Year's Day 1959 *Loch Alvie* sailed from Mukalla for Salala the capital and seat of the Governor of the Omani province of Dhofar and then onto Kuria Muria Islands a group of five islands in the Arabian Sea around forty miles off the southeast coast of Oman, The Sultanate of Masira, Muscat and then finally back to Bahrain in company with *Loch Insh*.

After a short period alongside the frigate returned to sea on Tuesday 20 January bound for Dubai. En route the flotilla comprising *Loch Insh* and *Loch Fada* conducted exercises in which the latter acted as an enemy destroyer. The ships arrived at Dubai after nine days at sea but only spent twenty four hours alongside before proceeding back to Bahrain for a Batina Coast Patrol.

On Thursday 12 February *Loch Alvie* was at Karachi where she was taken in hand for repairs in the drydock at the base. The work continued until Monday 9 March when she sailed for Bombay. In March visits were made to Cochin and Muscat before a further stint on the Batina Coast Patrol which took the warship well into April. On Monday 13 April, having returned to Bahrain, three days earlier, she put to sea for anti-submarine exercises and a sea inspection undertaken in company with *Loch Ruthven* and *Loch Fada*. Upon completion all the ships took part in a flotilla regatta before returning to Bahrain.

On Wednesday 22 April *Loch Alvie* sailed for Mena al Ahmadi in Kuwait, after which she made her way to Kharg Island in Iran for an extensive series of naval exercises with Iranian warships. The exercises started on Monday 4 May and involved *Loch Ruthven* and the Iranian *IINS Babr* and *IINS Palang*. Upon completion the ship sailed for Halul, Bahrain and Muscat. From there she headed south to Mombasa arriving in Kilindini Harbour on Tuesday 2 June and securing at No 2 Berth. The ship was properly dressed overall on the occasion of Queen Elizabeth II's Coronation Day and duly fired a 21-gun salute in her honour. At 1600 Commodore commanding Arabian Sea embarked and just under two hours later the ship sailed with *Bassingham* in line astern.

The next morning the ships arrived at Zanzibar where *Loch Alvie* was opened to the public with one hundred and thirty five people taking up the opportunity to look over a modern Royal Navy warship. The visit to Zanzibar was concluded on Friday 5 June when the frigate sailed arriving at Dar-es-Salaam later the same day. The ship was cleaned ahead of the arrival onboard of the Governor of Tanganyika and numerous other VIPs. After two days the port of call was complete and *Loch Alvie* sailed once again bound for Aden, with visits to Tanga and Mombasa before crossing the line at 2000 on Thursday 18 June. King Neptune and his court joined the ship and punished any and all defaulters.

On Wednesday 24 June 1959 *Loch Alvie* sailed from Aden to return to the United Kingdom, via the Suez Canal, Malta and Gibraltar. At the latter she picked up five Army officers for transit to Plymouth, which was reached on Sunday 19 July at just before midnight. The frigate anchored in Plymouth Sound overnight before proceeding into Devonport Dockyard the following morning once wives and families had boarded the warship from a launch. As the ship passed by at 0800 a 17-gun salute was fired to honour Commander in Chief Plymouth Admiral Sir Richard Onslow KCB, DSO who took the salute.

A few weeks later *Loch Alvie* was one of the attractions at Plymouth Navy Days held at the beginning of August. The frigate saw 2325 visitors on the Saturday and 3423 on the Sunday. Three days later *Loch Alvie*

was moved to the North Wall of Number 3 Basin as preparations were made for her withdrawal from service. By 28 August she had been turned over to civilian ship keepers.

The frigate remained in refit until Tuesday 4 October when, at 1130, colours were raised and the ship re-commissioned for yet more service in the Persian Gulf. The remainder of the month saw her undertake a variety of trials in local waters before working up at Torbay and Weymouth Bay with, amongst others, RFA *Black Ranger*, *Teazer* and the submarine *Tudor*. On 15 December *Loch Alvie* entered Chatham Dockyard and remained there for the Christmas leave period.

On Friday 6 January 1961 *Loch Alvie* was moved by tugs into Chatham Dockyards No 7 dry dock for maintenance work to be carried out. Upon completion she was undocked on Friday 13 and readied for sea. The frigate made a swift passage to Rosyth where she started a fishery protection patrol off Iceland during the Cod War. During her mission in the cold North Atlantic the frigate intercepted numerous British trawlers many of whom transferred supplies of fresh fish to the Royal Navy ships there to protect them. By Thursday 9 February *Loch Alvie*'s time on station was at and end and having been relieved by the Type 14 frigate *Palliser* she headed home to Chatham, where upon her arrival on Monday 13 February leave was granted to the ships company.

On Tuesday 28 February she sailed from Chatham bound south to Gibraltar and then onto the Middle East via Malta and Port Said. The ship berthed alongside No 11 Oiling Berth at Aden on Thursday 23 March and two days later sailed in company with the LST *Striker* for Bahrain.

After arriving at Bahrain the ships company took some time adjusting to the conditions before commencing a series of exercises with *Loch Fyne* and *Loch Ruthven*. At the end of the month the flotilla were at Kharg Island in Iran for the start of the regular Khargex IV naval exercise. The British ships operated with a number of Iranian warships including *Tiran, Mahan, Hanran* and *Keywan*. Throughout the summer months the frigate visited a number of local ports on both official and unofficial calls including

Lingeh in Iran, Charbahar in Pakistan, Dibba and Muscat at the start of another Dhow Patrol.

The patrol was cut short by the Kuwaiti crisis on Thursday 29 June when *Loch Alvie* was recalled to Bahrain to load 18 tons of ammunition for the reserve companies of 45 Commando. The leaders of Iraq had threatened to invade neighbouring Kuwait and because Britain had a treaty with Kuwait forces in the region were quickly assembled to defend the Gulf State from attack. The following day she was ordered to rendezvous with *Meon* and *Striker* for operations off Kuwait as required as part of Operation Vantage despite not having embarked 45 Commando onboard. The transport that the Royal Marines had been using to transport them from Aden had broken down en route.

On Saturday 1 July *Loch Alvie* detected what was probably a submarine off Kuwait ahead of anchoring at 1110 in six fathoms. With the immediate threat of invasion lessening slightly *Loch Alvie* was used over the next few weeks to patrol local waters and to operate with other Royal Navy units including the aircraft carrier *Victorious* and *Loch Fyne*, *Cassandra*, RFA *Tidereach* and RFA *Reliant*.

On Sunday 23 July *Loch Alvie* headed to Shuwaik and Ishuwaik both in Kuwait where the modern frigate berthed alongside. *Loch Alvie*'s commanding officer Commander J H Nethersole left the ship to visit the British troops ashore. The frigate remained there for five days before setting sail to join TF317 centred on the aircraft carrier *Centaur* together with *Camperdown*, RFA *Olna*, RFA *Reliant* and RFA *Retainer* en route to Bahrain.

The force arrived at Bahrain on Sunday 6 August and leave was granted. The Commanding Officer left the ship to take his leave in the United Kingdom, returning to the ship after a fortnight.

The day after his arrival *Loch Alvie* returned to sea and resumed her patrols in the waters off Kuwait until Tuesday 12 September when she returned to Bahrain. Having seen quite strenuous service over the previous months *Loch Alvie* was in need of repair and arrangements were made for her to enter dry dock in Karachi. On Tuesday 26 September the ship entered dry dock and remained there until Tuesday 10 October. Final

work on the ship continued until the following Tuesday which allowed the ships company the opportunity to arrange a party onboard for local children. *Loch Alvie* returned to Bahrain upon completion and following a successful Harbour Inspection by Rear Admiral Fitzroy Talbot prepared for the annual Midlink Exercises with a return to Karachi, securing alongside the replenishment tanker RFA *Wave Sovereign* on Friday 10 November. The exercises started the following Thursday and included *Loch Insh* as well as the USS *Haynsworth* and Pakistani PNS *Shah Jahan* (ex HMS *Charity*) and PNS *Babr* (ex HMS *Gabbard*). The exercises continued until Monday 27 November when the frigate sailed for Mombasa, Kenya. Upon arrival a week later the crew witnessed the arrival of the cruiser *Belfast*. The ships were to represent the British Government at the state opening of Parliament at Dar-es-Salaam with HRH The Duke of Edinburgh embarked in the cruiser.

In mid December the frigate visited Tanga in Tanzania before returning to Mombasa in company with *Centaur, Plymouth, Striker, Retainer, Reliant* and *Tidesurge*. After ten days at anchor, during which time the ships company were granted shore leave, the ship sailed for Aden at the start of the voyage home to the United Kingdom.

New Year's Day 1962 was celebrated onboard with the departure from Mombasa. The ship set a course for Aden. Sadly at 0900 Mr Danapala, head laundryman onboard the frigate died. Three hours later his body was placed in the forward gun shelter and the shelter was locked up. Two days later upon arrival at Aden Mr Danapala's body was removed for a post mortem to be conducted. His would not be the only death onboard the frigate that January. On Friday 5 January John A Smith died of Malaria whilst being treated ashore at the RAF Hospital. Colours were lowered in his honour and his funeral took place the next day at the Aden Cemetery.

Leaving Aden *Loch Alvie* sailed on Monday 8 January to Massawa where she joined the USS Soley in attending that year's Ethiopian Navy Days. The Captain left the ship the next day to pay an official visit on the Emperor at the Airport ahead of him attending the Naval Review. After a hectic few days at Massawa,

Loch Alvie spent the rest of early January visiting remote communities including the Perim Islands where the locals were treated to a film show onboard the frigate. After returning to Aden the frigate sailed for the Suez Canal on Monday 29 January.

On Thursday 1 February 1962 *Loch Alvie* was at sea heading from Aden to Suez and carried out some practice firings of her Squid anti submarine weapons. The following day she spoke to a number of British merchantmen including London Resolution, Clyde Gunner, Hereford Beacon and Mallua as well as the German tanker Esso Stuttgart and the Russian Tibilus. By Saturday she had arrived in Suez Bay. There she waited until she could join a North bound convoy through the Suez Canal.

A week later on 8 February the frigate secured alongside Parlatorio Wharf in Malta only remaining there long enough to refuel and restore the ship before proceeding onto Gibraltar on Saturday 10 February. En route *Loch Alvie* was over flown by a French Navy Neptune reconnaissance aircraft before arriving at Gibraltar at 1945 on Wednesday 14 February. She remained overnight before sailing early the next day for the four day voyage to Spithead.

She anchored at No 8 berth at Spithead late on Monday 19th and after customs had cleared the ship to proceed into Portsmouth she secured alongside the South Railway Jetty at 1046. De-ammunitioning of the ship commenced almost immediately. After six days the ship was ready to proceed to Chatham where, on Tuesday 27 February, she secured alongside sister ship *Loch Fada* at Chatham Dockyard Number 3 Basin.

On Wednesday 18 April 1962 Commander J de Beaufort Suchlick RN assumed command and the following Tuesday the new ships company joined from barracks at HMS *Pembroke* in Chatham. The men quickly got to work preparing the ship for service with the assistance of the dockyard workforce. On Friday 18th May the frigate was finally undocked and moved to No 2 Basin.

On 4 July the ship finally left Chatham at 1300 and sailed down the River Medway as far as Sheerness where she secured to No 8 buoy in the river. For the next few days she carried out her initial sea trials in the Thames Estuary areas before returning to Chatham Dockyard on 9 July.

On Wednesday 11 July the Commissioning Warrant was read onboard the frigate and the colours hoisted in the presence of Rear Admiral I W T Beloe DSC and final preparations made for the ship to leave port the following day. She made an overnight passage to Portsmouth arriving at 0930 on Friday 13 July to load ammunition.

After spending the weekend at Portsmouth the frigate returned to Chatham on Wednesday 18 July. Another two days were spent in Kent before once again returning to Portsmouth where she secured on the frigate *Virago* at Pitch House Jetty before sailing two days later for her work up at Portland.

At Portland the frigate carried out a number of training exercises with a variety of warships including *Undaunted, Agincourt, Carron, Aisne* and the submarine *Alcide*. The ships log for Monday 23 July also has an interesting reference to the Cross Channel ferry *Sarnia Cross*, which apparently embarrassed the Royal Navy frigate by refusing to give way.

On Wednesday 1 August *Loch Alvie* was at Portland operating with *Loch Fada, Barossa* and the submarine *Acheron* before arriving at Portsmouth nine days later for seasonal leave to commence. Once the ships company were back onboard the frigate left Pitch House Jetty on Monday 27 August to resume the work up programme at Portland where for twenty four hours she operated with the frigate *Blackwood* before returning to Portsmouth and entering No 15 Dock until Wednesday 5 September.

More work up exercises followed at Portland including bombardment practice with *Loch Fada* and *Dundas* and anti-submarine training with the submarine *Tireless* ahead of a Flag Officer Sea Training Inspection by Rear Admiral Law OBE, DSC. The inspection was passed successfully but *Loch Alvie* still carried out a CASEX exercise with the cruiser *Belfast* and *Loch Fada* for the next week before arriving at Portsmouth on Wednesday 19 September. Ammunition was taken onboard the frigate from the lighters *Howitzer* and *Cannon* over the next few days.

On Friday 21 September *Loch Alvie* sailed for Gibraltar at the start of her next deployment to the

Middle East. The transit of the Mediterranean took place in company with the minesweeper *Kemerton*. After brief stops at Port Said and Aden *Loch Alvie* arrived at Bahrain on Sunday 21 October having closed with the aircraft carrier *Bulwark* for the transfer of the carriers medical officer to treat a sick Somali seaman, who was later transferred to the carrier by helicopter for extra treatment.

A day after *Loch Alvie*'s arrival at Bahrain the frigate welcomed onboard the Kuwaiti Ambassador and the Minister of Defence, Sheik Mohammad al Amhed and Brigadier Mubarak. After almost two weeks in port *Loch Alvie* started her first patrol in the Gulf on Tuesday 6 November with a visit to Kharg Island in Iran. Onboard for the passage was Air Marshall Sir Charles Elsworthy Commander in Chief Middle East Station. The passage was dominated by bad weather with a severe squall and wind speeds of 77 knots. Such was the severity of the weather that the boat rope and lazy painter parted and the canopy to the Captain's motorboat was lost overboard.

After an enjoyable visit to Kharg Island, *Loch Alvie* went on to visit Jaz as Zarqua, Sohar, Jazirat Halal and Doha. December 1962 started with exercises with *Loch Fyne* and the submarine *Andrew* before visits to Dhunna and Bahrain where Christmas was spent. On Thursday 27 December *Loch Alvie* sailed to the ancient city of Muscat where a national salute was fired from Fort Maxim upon her arrival. The British frigate stayed at Muscat to see in the New Year 1963.

Having sailed from Muscat *Loch Alvie* went onto visit Bandar Khairan and Guadar before arriving at Karachi where she secured to the Pakistani warship PNS *Shah Jahan*. By 0900 an ammunition-lighter was secured alongside so that the frigates weapons could be safely unloaded and stored. Upon completion *Loch Alvie* was moved into the floating dock for a maintenance period. The ship was afloat again on Thursday 14 February and four days later was on her way back to Yas Island and Bahrain.

On 1 March *Loch Alvie* arrived at Bandar Mashur where the following day the welcome mat was laid out for local people to visit and tour the ship and ask questions. Hundreds of people eventually did and enjoyed some fine displays from the ships company. The visit

ended on Monday 4 March when, in company with *Parapet*, *Loch Alvie* took passage to Bahrain. After a week spent there the frigate was once again at sea this time bound for Abu Dhabi where the ruler of the country, Sheik Shabbut bin Sultan him Said called on the captain and took a brief tour of the British warship.

Upon completion of the official visit to Abu Dhabi, *Loch Alvie* resumed her role of patrolling the Persian Gulf making visits to numerous ports including Jaz Sir Abu Nu'Ar before returning to Bahrain to prepare for the FOMEX exercise in company with the modern Tribal class frigate *Ashanti*. The exercises lasted into April with the ship making a number of port visits including Halal, Jazirat Yas and the island of Dalma off Abu Dhabi before finally arriving back at Bahrain on Tuesday 2 April.

Loch Alvie remained at Bahrain until 15 April when she sailed for Dubai at the start of a Dhow Patrol. At Muscat on Sunday 28 April the frigate rendezvoused with the minesweepers *Chilcompton* and *Kemerton* before heading back to Bahrain for a period of rest and relaxation. Upon completion the frigate carried out a two week Trucial Coast Patrol from Thursday 2 May. When she returned the ships company were tasked with preparing the ship for her annual inspection, carried out off Bahrain, in company with submarines, the frigate *Nubian* and the LCT *Bastion*. Having successfully passed her inspection *Loch Alvie* was ordered to proceed to Aden, where she arrived on Friday 31 May.

On 1 June a patrol was landed at Aden and nine days later the ship sailed from Aden to the warmer climes of Mombasa where after a further seven days at sea she anchored in the harbour at just after ten in the morning. The next evening she sailed for an overnight passage to Pemba also known as Al Jazeera Al Khadra or Green Island, one of the islands that make up the Zanzibar archipelago where she arrived mid-afternoon of Wednesday 19 June; her arrival having been delayed by bad weather on approaching Port George Harbour. The two day visit was a complete success with many new friendships having been forged, but *Loch Alvie*'s itinerary was tight and she was required to visit Zanzibar in company with *Meon*. On arrival the frigate fired a 21-gun National Salute. Once safely anchored, *Loch Alvie*'s captain left the ship to call

on the Sultan to confirm the arrangements for the planned celebrations. The two Royal Navy warships were in attendance to participate in the celebration of Zanzibar's internal self governance from Great Britain.

The frigate was anchored in the harbour and welcomed onboard many local people but it was on Monday 24 June that the celebrations took place with another 21-gun salute fired from *Loch Alvie*.

From Zanzibar *Loch Alvie* sailed in company with *Meon* back to Mombasa where she was visited by the Vice President and Mayor. Whilst at Mombasa news reached the ship that the Sultan of Zanzibar, who the Captain had seen only days before, had died on Tuesday 2 July and accordingly the colours were lowered to half mast.

Loch Alvie sailed from Mombasa on Tuesday 9 July and took passage to the Seychelles where she refuelled and was also open to the public moored in the harbour at Mahe. On the fifth day of her stay the frigate was visited by Lord Oxford, Governor of the Seychelles and his wife Lady Oxford. The following morning *Loch Alvie* sailed again for the heat of the Persian Gulf.

The passage across the Indian Ocean was sometimes choppy with the ship experiencing a 15 degree roll, particularly at night. On Wednesday 24 July the ship rendezvoused with *Striker* for the transfer of mail before finally arriving at Bahrain on 27 July. The frigate remained at Bahrain until Friday 9 August when she took passage to the Indian port of Cochin and again experienced some poor weather conditions en route. After a four day stop over *Loch Alvie* sailed for Singapore, which was reached on Monday 26 August. The following Wednesday the ships company started moving out of their ship and into the accommodation at HMS *Terror* at the start of a much needed refit.

A new ships company had been flown out from Britain by Eagle Airways on 31 August from Stansted Airport with stops at Istanbul and Bombay.

On Monday 2 September at 0800 the main body of the ships company arrived onboard the frigate, which the following day was shifted into the floating dock AFD10. After an overnight stay in the dry dock *Loch Alvie* was, on Wednesday afternoon, back alongside Berth 9 at Singapore Dockyard. Final preparations and cleaning of the ship throughout occupied the ships company until Friday 6 September when *Loch Alvie* was re-commissioned.

Her first assignment was to proceed to sea in the Malayan Practice Areas for three days, from the following Monday, to test the ships systems and equipment before returning to Singapore. After further trials with the frigate *Lincoln* and submarine *Amphion* the frigate proceeded to Pulau Tioman where she carried out a series of exercises with *Loch Fada* and the submarine *Andrew*.

By 4 October *Loch Alvie* was once again back in Singapore where she remained for the next ten days. On Tuesday 15 October the frigate was in the Jahore Straits operating with the destroyer *Diana*, frigate *Quiberon* and *Alert*. On Thursday 17 October problems with her engines emerged when, during an exercise with RAF Shackleton aircraft, the starboard main engine failed and could not be restarted. Once back at Singapore the following Friday the ships company was saddened to hear of the assassination of the American President John F Kennedy in Dallas. The colours were half-masted as a mark of respect for the dead President.

Of more immediate concern for the crew was the frigate's future, with faulty main engines it was decided that the ship would be decommissioned and *Loch Lomond* would take her place with the former ship's company moving into *Loch Lomond*.

On Wednesday 27 November *Loch Alvie*'s ship company started the work of de-storing the ship whilst at 3 Berth South in Singapore. Some comics onboard quickly came up with a new name for the ship *Loch Almond*, a combination of both ships names.

The end for the frigate came quickly having been declared surplus to requirements and stripped of any useful equipment in 1964 the Royal Navy sought a buyer in the Far East for the frigate and found one in Hong Huat Hardware in Singapore. Demolition of the former *Loch Alvie* commenced on 20 September 1965.

Battle Honours

ARCTIC 1944-45 - ENGLISH CHANNEL 1945

Chronology

02.02.1943	Ordered from Barclay Curle, Dundee
31.08.1943	Laid down
14.04.1944	Launched with final fitting out completed at Dalmuir
21.08.1944	Completed and joined the 9th Escort Group with a Canadian Ship's Company
09.1944	Gibraltar
11.1944	Londonderry
29.11.1944	Escort for convoy JW62 to Kola Inlet. Return convoy RA62
12.1944	Repairs at Liverpool
02.1944	Returned to service
Spring 1945	Irish Sea and South West Approaches
Spring 1945	Operation Deadlight from Norway to United Kingdom
20.05.1945	Loch Eribol with *U-668*
06.1945	Ship returned to RN control and reserve at Sheerness
31.05.1950	Left Sheerness for Portsmouth
09.07.1950	Eggsund, Norway with destroyer *St Kitts*
15.07.1950	Amsterdam
20.07.1950	Folkestone
Autumn 1950	Home waters
Late 1950	Mediterranean
12.12.1950	At Sheerness in floating dock *AFD12*
01.1951	Mediterranean visiting Arachi Bay and Minorca
15.03.1951	Sheerness
07.06.1951	Searched for sunk submarine *Affray* in the English Channel
07.1951	Visited Berwick and Deal
08.08.1951	Kristiansand, Norway with *St Austell Bay*
17.09.1951	Oslo
24.09.1951	Invergordon with *Swiftsure* and submarine *Alliance*
17.10.1951	Tangiers
19.10.1951	Gibraltar
01.12.1951	Lisbon on Portuguese Independence Day
February 1954	Refit at Portsmouth
16.04.1954	Sailed for Mediterranean with *Britannia*
1954	Indian Ocean and Persian Gulf Service
January 1955	Colombo and Socotra
14.02.1955	Sheerness

06.06.1955	Chatham Dockyard No 9 dock for refit
19.07.1955	Start of post refit sea trials
01.08.1955	Sailed for Gibraltar
08.1955	Messina
09.1955	Indian Ocean and Persian Gulf Service
09.01.1956	Colombo for refit
02.1956	Visited Quilan, Calicut and Mangalore
07.05.1956	Bahrain
18.07.1956	Sheerness
02.11.1956	Duke of Kent onboard
29.01.1957	Sailed for service in Persian Gulf via Cape of Good Hope
19.07.1957	Medical emergency on tanker *Gallex Canberra*
15.10.1957	Prime Minister John Lionel Kotalaurela of Ceylon onboard whilst at Trincomalee
11.11.1957	Exercise Crescent with Indian Navy
28.01.1958	Chatham Dockyard for refit
29.04.1958	Recommissioned
13.06.1958	Cherbourg
21.07.1958	Sailed for Gibraltar
Autumn 1958	Persian Gulf Service
24.06.1959	Sailed for United Kingdom from Aden
19.07.1959	Plymouth for refit
04.10.1959	Recommissioned
13.01.1961	Fishery patrol off Iceland
28.02.1961	Sailed from Chatham for Middle East
03.1961	Exercise Khargex IV with Iranian Navy
29.06.1961	Kuwaiti Crisis – Operation Vantage
27.11.1961	State Opening of Kenyan Parliament with cruiser *Belfast*
14.02.1962	Gibraltar
20.02.1962	Portsmouth
27.02.1962	Chatham for refit
11.07.1962	Recommissioned
21.09.1962	Sailed for Middle East with minesweeper *Kemerton*
Summer 1962	Visited Aden, Pemba, Mombasa and Seychelles
27.07.1962	Bahrain
26.08.1962	Singapore for refit in floating dock *AFD10*
06.09.1962	Recommissioned
09.1962	Developed severe engine difficulties
27.11.1962	Destored at Singapore, place taken by *Loch Lomond*
1964	Sold for breaking up by Hong Haut Hardware
20.09.1965	Breaking up started at Singapore

HMS Loch Arkaig

The distinctive shape of the Loch class hull can be seen in this photograph of Loch Arkaig. *Designed for service in the North Atlantic the hull was built of prefabricated sections.*
(Crown Copyright/MoD)

The shipyard of Caledon Shipbuilding at Dundee received the order for a Loch class frigate on 2 February 1943. The yard themselves gave it yard number 421. Construction started on 1 November 1943 when the first steel plates were laid down and continued until launching stage on 7 June 1944 when she was given the name of *Loch Arkaig* after an inland lake north of Fort William. *Loch Arkaig* was commissioned on 1 November under the command of Lieutenant Commander P. U. Usherwood and was completed on 17 November 1945, too late to see service in the Second World War.

The standard of work on the ship meant that additional stiffening had to be added to the frigate before the ship was finally allowed to assume her duties within the Royal Navy. Many of her sister ships had also suffered from a lack of stiffness in their construction and extra metalwork had to be added to a number

of the Loch class during their early careers.

In December 1945 Lieutenant Commander C. P. Adams took over command from Lieutenant Commander Usherwood.

The start of 1946 saw the ship in shipyard hands with work being carried out on the Squid anti-submarine mortar and attention was also being placed on the Direction Finding equipment, which had been causing some problems.

Finally, out of shipyard hands in February *Loch Arkaig* took passage to Londonderry to join the rest of her flotilla and took part in Operation Deadlight, the sinking of captured German U-boats in deep water off Northern Ireland. On 16 February she sank *U-975* a Type VIIC submarine that had surrendered whilst under the command of Wilhelm Brauel and three days later *U-3514* followed her to the bottom of the ocean. *U-3514* under the command of Gunther Fritze had surrendered at Bergen in Norway and had transferred to Loch Ryan on 29 May 1945. In January 1946 she had transferred again to Molville in Northern Ireland and was held in reserve due to possible interest from Russia in the craft. On 7 February 1946 the order was received for *Loch Arkaig* to sink the German U-boat and at 0936 on 12 February scuttling charges were fired onboard. Even with scuttling charges the submarine remained afloat and 30 minutes worth of 4-inch gunfire, depth charges and Squid projectiles finally sank the submarine in a position 56°00'N 10°05'W at 1004.

The next two years were uneventful with flotilla duties and training in anti submarine procedures. The next few months were spent at Londonderry on carrying out the vital role of training new personnel in anti submarine warfare techniques.

After being in attendance at the Royal Review of the Fleet in the River Clyde *Loch Arkaig* entered 1948 with a new commanding officer in the shape of Lieutenant Commander C. F. Parker. The frigate resumed her training duties at Londonderry a role she continued whilst she took part in Operation Rusty which was a special mission to discover the standard performance of a variety of standard pieces of naval equipment in the harshest maritime environments but especially those found inside the Arctic Circle. *Loch Arkaig* sailed with the light fleet aircraft carrier *Vengeance* and the Battle class destroyers *St Kitts* and *Gabbard* on February 16 1949. The force crossed the Arctic Circle where each ship earned an unofficial 'blue nose' award. Once inside the operating areas the ships carried out a lengthy series of trials that continued until the warships returned home, in *Loch Arkaig*'s case on the 28 February to Londonderry.

Once back in Northern Ireland waters the frigate resumed her normal training role that would continue into 1950. That spring and summer was spent taking raw cadets and seamen to sea and getting them used to the demands of a life at sea. *Loch Arkaig* took part in that year's Flag Officer Submarines Summer War Exercises and also undertook a number of port visits as a member of the Home Fleet. August 1950 saw a change of command for the frigate with Lieutenant Commander M. F. de Halpert DSC assuming command.

The training programme also saw a number of foreign visits made amongst the most popular being those to Norway when the ship visited Haugensund and Nordheimsund.

In September *Loch Arkaig* arrived at Chatham Dockyard for a refit that would take until December to complete.

In January 1951 the ship was operating in the English Channel and like many of her sister ships she was heavily involved in the search for the missing submarine *Affray*. The submarine sank under mysterious circumstances somewhere in the English Channel without word and it was a race to find her and try and rescue the crew. The search continued until April when the submarine was finally discovered on the seabed many miles from her last known position. The summer months of the year saw the warship taking part in numerous fleet exercises with units of the Home Fleet.

In October she struck sister ship *Loch Alvie* whilst manoeuvring in Gibraltar Harbour. The damage was repaired within the dockyard. The following month in company with the frigates *Loch Alvie* and *St Austell Bay* she paid a visit to the Portuguese Capital of Lisbon. The visit was the last for *Loch Arkaig* as upon her return to the United Kingdom she was decommis-

sioned and laid up at Hartlepool in early 1952.

Even when laid up *Loch Arkaig* was in the news when in November 1952 she was struck by the Norwegian merchant vessel *SS Ocean Swell*. Fortunately damage to both vessels was slight. *Loch Arkaig* would remain at Hartlepool until having been placed on the disposal list she was sold in 1959 to J J King at nearby Gateshead. The frigate made her final arrival at the shipbreakers yard on 28 January 1960.

Chronology

02.02.1943	Ordered from Caledon Shipbuilding at Dundee
01.11.1943	Laid down
07.06.1944	Launched
01.11.1944	Commissioned
17.11.1945	Extra hull stiffening added
02.1946	Left shipyard hands after extreme remedial work
02.1946	Operation Deadlight and sank *U-975* and *U-3514* with gunfire
18-27.07.1947	Royal Review of Home Fleet in the Clyde
1948	Training at Londonderry
1948	Operation Rusty in Arctic Circle
28.02.1949	Londonderry in training role
Autumn 1950	Norwegian visits to Havensund and Nordheimsund
09.1950	Chatham Dockyard for refit
06.1951	Search for submarine Affray lost in English Channel
1952	Laid up at Hartlepool in reserve fleet
11.1952	Struck by merchantman SS *Ocean Swell*
1957	Disposal list
1959	Sold to JJ King for breaking up at Gateshead
28.01.1960	Arrived for breaking up

HMS LOCH CRAGGIE

The Loch class, such as Loch Craggie, *were worked hard during the war, but being relatively young ships they were retained in the postwar fleet.* *(Crown Copyright/MoD)*

Harland and Wolff laid down Job Number J3373 on 28 December 1943 and assigned it the yard number 1246. This Loch class frigate would eventually be named *Loch Craggie* when she was launched on 23 May 1944. With the launching completed the warship was towed from Belfast to John Brown's shipyard on the River Clyde for completion where extra capacity was available to complete the work. The shipyard at John Brown's fitted the ship out and *Loch Craggie* was completed on 23 October 1944 following shipbuilders' sea trials in the Irish Sea. Acceptance into the Royal Navy saw the ship assigned to the 22nd Escort Group but before she could go to war the Admiralty asked the shipbuilders to fit the new frigate with a different design of propellers and accordingly the trials of these took precedence and occupied the ship throughout November 1944.

In December the ship sailed to Tobermory where she took onboard her complement of weapons and stores for her first operational patrol.

The start of 1945 saw the frigate deploying with the sloops *Amethyst, Hart, Peacock* and *Starling* in the Irish Sea where on the 16 January the German VIIC class submarine *U-482* came under sustained attack by all the ships in the group. The submarine under the command of Kapitanleutnant Graf von Hartmut Matuschka, Freiherr von Toppolczan und Spaetgen was eventually destroyed and the five ships shared the credit for her destruction. The *U-482* had previously been responsible for the sinking of the American Jacksonville of 10,448 tons in convoy CU36 on 30 August 1944, the British corvette *HMS Hurst Castle* on 1 September 1944. Two days later *U-482* sank the Norwegian Fjordheim on convoy ONF251 and on 8 September sank two British ships *Empire Heritage* and the *Pinto* both part of convoy HX-305.

The weather in the Irish Sea and North West Approaches had caused some severe structural damage onboard the frigate that included denting and warping of metal structures and accordingly for most of February she was under repair before re-deploying on St Patrick's Day for further service in the Irish Sea based out of the Welsh port of Milford Haven. She continued in this role until selected for service in the Far East and subsequently was taken in hand for a refit which was carried out at Bailey's shipyard in Cardiff starting on 10 May. In June, just as she was completing her refit the frigate struck a tug in Cardiff Bay and had to be re-docked for repairs.

After trials were completed the frigate sailed on 20 July for the Far East routed through Gibraltar and Alexandria. At the latter she was equipped with extra Oerlikon gun mountings to deal with the growing threat posed by Japanese aircraft. Having left Alexandria in August she proceeded through the Suez Canal and into the Red Sea. It was there that on the 10 August *Loch Craggie* responded to the distress call from the British fighter direction ship *Palomares*, which was on fire. The ship had been taken up from trade at the start of the war and fitted with extra guns and radar with which to direct fighter aircraft. The *Palomares* had suffered a disastrous fire onboard in her engine rooms which had started at 0738 in the morning of Friday 17 August 1945. By 0750 the after 2 pounder gun magazine had had to be flooded to contain the blaze. Ten minutes after the flooding the fire broke out again. By 0847 the SS *Vosella* had come alongside and had taken off a number of injured crewmen from the fighter direction ship.

Loch Craggie secured alongside the starboard side of the stricken vessel at 1655 and took a further 84 ratings and five casualties from the *Palomares* onboard. The frigate remained attached until the tug *Confederate* had secured towing lines to the ship and *Loch Craggie* finally let go at just after 2300 at night and made for Massawa where those requiring hospital treatment were disembarked on 12 August.

Three days later *Loch Craggie* arrived at Aden where she stayed for a week preparing for the crossing of the Indian Ocean. The frigate finally arrived at Colombo on 29 August. It was at Colombo that the

British ship joined the East Indies Fleet and was assigned the task of defending the assault convoys bound for the planned Malayan coast landings. The force sailed in early September.

The frigate remained in the waters off Singapore and the Dutch East Indies providing support against insurgents in the region. Later she also acted as guardship at Morotai where Japanese prisoners of war were being held before their return to Japan. *Loch Craggie* remained in the Far East until July 1946 when she arrived home at Devonport. She was immediately decommissioned from service and placed in the reserve fleet where she remained for the next four years.

The pressure on the Royal Navy to provide shipping for the war effort in Korea meant a return to service for many ships in the reserve fleet and *Loch Craggie* was just one of them. She was taken in hand for a quick refit before being commissioned on 11 December 1950 at Devonport. Seven days later she was undocked and moved to No 4 Basin North Wall and secured on *Ulysses*.

On Friday 19 January 1951 the ship slipped from Devonport Dockyard and put to sea for exercises and calibration tests on her equipment. After a day and night spent at sea the following day she returned and secured on *Padstow Bay* at No 2 wharf.

After a brief visit to Bigbury Bay and further tests in Plymouth Sound, *Loch Craggie* sailed on Friday 26 January for Portland, where her work up would start. Working up the frigate would also see her extensively use the facilities at Londonderry over the course of February, only leaving Londonderry on 24 February for the warmer climes of Gibraltar and the Mediterranean to join the 5th Frigate Flotilla.

Loch Craggie remained at Gibraltar until Saturday 10 March when she went back to sea in company with sister ships *Loch Scavaig* and Loch More for anti submarine exercises en route to the fabulous city of Cannes in the South of France. The trio of British ships arrived there on Wednesday 14 March and watched the following day as the massive American aircraft carrier USS *Franklin D Roosevelt* entered the bay at 1630.

The six days at Cannes gave the ships company a

fantastic opportunity to explore ashore and sample many of Cannes' delights, but after six days in the French community *Loch Craggie* returned to sea with the rest of the ships bound for Taranto in Italy. Taranto is one of the Italian Navy's premier naval bases and from there the British ships exercised with their Italian counterparts during anti submarine exercises. Taking part in the exercises were the Italian ships *Caliope, Orsa, Aretusto, Pamonia* and the tanker *Stromboli* and a motor torpedo boat, as well as the British submarines *Toredo* and *Tabard*.

Upon completion of the first phase of the exercise the group sailed on Tuesday 27 March for Augusta. After the final phase of the exercise *Loch Craggie* and the rest of the British ships returned to Malta on Sunday 1 April. Throughout the month *Loch Craggie* remained off the Maltese coast exercising with, amongst others, *Loch More* and the destroyer *Chequers*.

Just after 1000 on Monday 14 May *Loch Craggie* sailed for Port Said with sister ship *Loch More* arriving at the Egyptian port three days later. Having joined a southerly convoy the frigate made for Aqaba via the Suez Canal the following morning. The frigate finally arrived at Aqaba in the evening of Saturday 19 May and prepared the ship for a round of official visits from VIP's. The following Monday saw the Captain ashore undertaking an official visit of his own to the Mudir of Aqaba, whilst the ships guard was paraded for the visit of the Colonel of 'O' force in Aqaba. During his visit to the Mudir, the Captain extended an invitation to visit the warship, which was accepted and saw the Mudir tour *Loch Craggie* for half an hour the next day.

Back at sea after his visit, *Loch Craggie* took part in a number of small exercises with local forces over the next few days before joining a north bound Suez Canal convoy. *Loch Craggie* made for Alexandria where she secured to No 13 buoy on the last day of May. The Captain again made official representations to the Senior Naval Officer of the Egyptian Navy who was invited to a cocktail party on the ships quarterdeck later the same evening.

After five days at Alexandria, it was back to business for the British frigate with her next destination being the Turkish port of Izmir, where the ship was opened to many hundreds of curious Turkish eyes throughout the ships three day stay in the city. From Izmir, *Loch Craggie* sailed for the Greek island of Kios, where again she was opened for public inspection. The ships company meanwhile organised a long series of sporting events including polo, shooting and swimming competitions.

After a week at Khios, *Loch Craggie* moved onto the island of Milos where she, *Loch More* and *Loch Scavaig* staged a flotilla regatta over the next six days. Prizes were awarded to the ships with the best rowing, swimming and shooting teams.

On Thursday 28 June *Loch Craggie* returned to sea and made for Marmarice in company with the depot ship *Forth* and the submarines *Tabard* and *Toredo*; all the vessels arriving safely on Saturday 30 June. During the stay men from *Loch Craggie*'s relief fire parties were landed to assist the local authorities with a local blaze. Having earned the praise and thanks of local firefighters the British ship slipped early on Monday for Malta. After refuelling at sea from RFA *Fort Duquesne* the frigate arrived at Malta on Friday 13 and secured in Sliema Creek.

She would remain at Malta for sometime undertaking a period of self maintenance finally emerging on Wednesday 29 August when she sailed for Cyprus to undertake an anti-submarine exercise around the island. After almost two weeks the frigate left Cyprus and headed north for Athens arriving after two days steaming on Thursday 13 September. The men onboard the British ship spent the first hours of her visit smartening up the vessel in anticipation of the hundreds of local Greek's who had expressed a wish to tour a modern Royal Navy warship. Once her stay was complete the ship resumed her normal operational tempo with night exercises with Greek naval units in Suda Bay. On Wednesday 19 September *Loch Craggie* returned to Athens Bay and was joined by the Greek warships *Dosca* and *Terpolitas*, with whom she exercised frequently over the course of the next few days.

At just after 1700 of Sunday 23 September *Loch Craggie* entered the Dardanelles en route to visit the Turkish capital of Istanbul, where she anchored in

Post-war most of the Loch class spent long periods in reserve. Loch Craggie *is seen here before she spent time in mothballs.*
(Crown Copyright/MoD)

twenty fathoms the following morning. She was joined the next day by the British cruisers *Liverpool* and *Euryalus*. *Loch Craggie* was dressed overall for his Excellency the President of Turkey as he received the Turkish Fleet for Turkey Navy Day.

The itinerary of the frigate allowed for a few days at the Turkish capital and most of the ships company were allowed leave to explore the remarkable cityscape with its mosques and ancient streets. All too soon the visit was over and *Loch Craggie* slipped on Saturday 29 September for Golfe Juan for exercises with the aircraft carriers *Ocean* and *Magnificent*.

On Sunday 6 October the ship arrived at Villefranche and arrangements were made with the French Navy for the frigates use as a dummy target for submarine attacks together with *Peacock*. The exercises lasted until the following Saturday when *Loch Craggie* anchored at Mentone. Three days later she sailed back to Malta where she would spend the rest of the year undertaking crew training. At the end of the year the frigate sailed for home with a well

received port visit to the Portuguese capital city of Lisbon en route.

On Sunday 2 December 1951 *Loch Craggie* sailed from Lisbon and made her way to sea and the onward journey back to Sheerness Dockyard. After three days steaming the ship turned into the Thames Estuary and at 2250 secured to No 4 buoy and remained at four hours notice for steam. The following morning the ships company disembarked ammunition and excess fuel into waiting lighters before sailing up the River Medway to secure within Chatham Dockyard.

After three days of hectic work, on Monday 10 December *Loch Craggie* was briefly accepted into the reserve fleet at Chatham, with Lieutenant Commander Plummer taking command of the frigate. The following day the ship was paid off only to re-commission soon thereafter.

Lieutenant Commander Plummer and his ships company set course for the Mediterranean and spent Christmas at Malta. On 2 January 1952 *Loch Craggie* sailed for Port Said passing the USS *Matthew Maurey*

bound for the United States. After four days at sea the frigate arrived in Egypt and secured on the tanker RFA *Black Ranger*. Later the same day the warship entered the Suez Canal as part of a southerly convoy. *Loch Craggie* made the passage to join Egyptian warships for exercises in Suez Bay that started on Thursday 10 January. The exercises lasted a fortnight and upon completion the frigate returned to Malta on 30 January. Once at rest the frigate was soon a scene of activity with a planned self refit taking place onboard. The work would occupy the ships company and contractors until Tuesday 18 March when at 1235 she slipped and secured alongside *Cygnet* at Hamilton Wharf. *Loch Craggie* remained at or off Malta until the end of the month conducting a lengthy series of trials and exercises.

On Friday 4 April *Loch Craggie* left Sliema Creek bound for Messina in Sicily and then back to Malta with *Fort Duquesne*, *Loch Scavaig* and *Peacock* in company. She was back at Malta on Thursday 10 April and anchored in berth Q4. Training occupied the ship until she sailed for Gibraltar on Saturday 26 April. For this passage the frigate was towing *MMS 1602* and accordingly was only making slow progress, eventually the passage would take six days. The tow of the minesweeper was then thankfully given over to local tugs. *Loch Craggie* meanwhile had her ammunition landed on Friday 2 May in preparation for a docking within Gibraltar Dockyard's No 3 dock. She would remain there until Mid June with the post refit trials being completed in early July.

The return passage to Malta was undertaken from Friday 11 July and upon her return *Loch Craggie* was kept busy with training and local exercises off Malta. When she sailed on Wednesday 3 September she headed south to Port Said and remained there for a fortnight before conducting an anti-submarine exercise off Famagusta with the submarine *Teredo*. On Friday 26 September the frigate returned briefly once more to Port Said before she headed back to her base at Malta at the end of the month.

October started on 5th with a transit to the French Naval Base at Toulon where she arrived after two days steaming. *Loch Craggie* secured at No 2 Berth at Appointements Milhaud. The officers went ashore to discuss with their French counterparts the rules of the planned major exercise that would take place for the following ten days. Vessels taking part in the exercise included the French ships *Berbere*, *Malgache*, *Senegalais*, *Arabe*, *Zede* and the cruisers *Gloire*, *Montcalm* and *George Leygues*.

On the final day of the exercise the British ship slipped away to visit the port of Leghorn for five days. From Leghorn *Loch Craggie* returned to Malta for a brief three days before continuing onto Augusta for more exercises with French warships including the aircraft carrier *Lafayette* and Greek warships *Niki*, *Doxa*, *Aetos* and *Panther*.

By Sunday 16 November *Loch Craggie* was back at Malta safely secured to No 10 Buoy in Sliema Creek. At the beginning of December the ship entered a period of self maintenance.

The New Year of 1953 saw *Loch Craggie* still undergoing self maintenance at Malta. Ten days later, however, her paying off pennant was raised on the masthead at 0800. An hour and a half later the Commander in Chief Earl Louis Mountbatten of Burma along with FOF and Captain of the Second Flotilla came onboard the frigate to address the ships company before leaving after a quarter of an hour onboard.

Finally on Friday 16 January *Loch Craggie* slipped from alongside sister ship *Loch More* and made for Gibraltar, which was reached after four days steaming. By 0822 the frigate was safely secured alongside 41 Berth in the dockyard at Gibraltar. Two days were spent there, which allowed the ships company the briefest of opportunities to buy the special gifts for loved ones back at Devonport, which came into view on Monday 26 January. After navigating through Plymouth Harbour the ship finally was home and secured alongside No 6 Wharf.

Preparations for taking the Loch class frigate into reserve were well in hand and after two weeks at No 6 Wharf *Loch Craggie* was moved by tugs on Wednesday 11 February to the Upper Tamar Group, whilst the ships company enjoyed foreign service leave with their families.

Loch Craggie remained with the Upper Tamar

Group until Monday 16 March when she was towed to No 4 Berth alongside the cruiser *Belfast*. During Plymouth Navy Days, held over the weekend of 23 May, *Loch Craggie* was open to the public with many hundreds of people clambering over the ship as she represented the reserve fleet.

On Thursday 28 May *Loch Craggie* was finally accepted into the reserve fleet at Devonport.

The future for the frigate seemed assured when it was announced that she would be modernised, but this plan never came to fruition. In 1954 she was mothballed at Liverpool and then transferred to Gibraltar to join the Reserve Fleet Division housed there mostly because she was offered for sale to Portugal. The proposed sale never materialised and in 1961 *Loch Craggie* was on the disposal list. Stripped of all useful equipment the frigate was finally broken up for scrap in 1963 in Lisbon by Dantops Leal and arrived there under tow on 25 October 1963.

Battle Honours

ATLANTIC 1945

Chronology

28.12.1943	Ordered from Harland and Wolff
23.05.1944	Launched and towed to John Brown's on Clydebank for completion
23.10.1944	Completed
10.1944	Joined 22nd Escort Group
11.1944	Special propeller trials
16.01.1945	With *Amethyst, Hart, Peacock* and *Starling* sank *U-482*
02.1945	Under repair
17.03.1945	Irish Sea
10.05.1945	Refit at Bailey's Shipyard in Cardiff
20.07.1945	Sailed for Far East
10.08.1945	Aden
29.08.1945	Colombo and joined East Indies Fleet
06.1946	Sailed for United Kingdom
07.1946	Devonport and reserve
11.12.1950	Recommissioned
19.01.1951	Calibration tests
26.01.1951	Work up at Portland and Londonderry
24.02.1951	Sailed for Gibraltar and joined 5th Frigate Flotilla
10.03.1951	Sailed with *Loch Scavaig* and *Loch More* to Cannes
16.03.1951	Left Cannes for Taranto for exercises
27.03.1951	Augusta
04.1951	Malta
14.05.1951	Sailed for Port Said with *Loch More*
19.05.1951	Aqaba
31.05.1951	Alexandria
06.1951	Izmir, Khios, Milos and Marmarice
13.07.1951	Malta
29.08.1951	Sailed for Cyprus and ASW exercise
13.09.1951	Athens
23.09.1951	Istanbul for Turkish Navy Day
29.09.1951	Exercises with *Ocean* and *Magnificent*
06.10.1951	Villefrance
11.1951	Malta for training

02.12.1951	Left Lisbon for Sheerness
05.12.1951	Sheerness
06.12.1951	Chatham
25.12.1951	Malta
02.01.1952	Sailed for Port Said
10.01.1952	Exercises with Egyptian Navy in Suez Bay
30.01.1952	Returned to Malta
04.04.1952	Sailed to Sicily
10.04.1952	Malta
26.04.1952	Towed *MMS1602* to Gibraltar
02.05.1952	Arrived Gibraltar and docked in No 3 dock for maintenance
11.07.1952	Sailed back to Malta
05.10.1952	Sailed for Toulon for exercises
17.10.1952	Sailed for Leghorn and Augusta
16.11.1952	Malta
10.01.1953	Paying off pennant raised
10.01.1953	Visited by Earl Louis Mountbatten of Burma
16.01.1953	Sailed for Gibraltar
26.01.1953	Arrived Devonport for the last time
23.05.1953	Plymouth Navy Days
28.05.1953	Reserve at Plymouth
1954	Announced she would be modernised
1954	Mothballed at Liverpool
1954	Transferred to reserve at Gibraltar and offered for sale to Portugal
1961	Disposal list
25.10.1963	Arrived Lisbon for breaking up by Dantops Leal

HMS LOCH DUNVEGAN

Seen at Malta Loch Dunvegan *had a long career with the Royal Navy that saw her operating across the globe.*
(Syd Goodman Collection)

As the Loch class programme gathered steam, construction times of the ships steadily decreased with *Loch Dunvegan* being constructed in just 274 days with the use of prefabrication adding greatly to the time saved. The frigate, named after a sea loch on the Isle of Skye, was laid down on 29 September 1943 having been ordered from the Bristol shipyard of Charles Hill. *Loch Dunvegan* was launched on 25 March 1944 by the wife of the shipyard owner a Mrs G Luckwell. Three months later on 25 June she completed her final fitting out.

At the end of June after contractors sea trials *Loch Dunvegan* was commissioned for service with the Royal Navy under the command of Commander E Wheeler RNR. Soon thereafter she joined the other units attached to the 10th Escort Group that operated out of the Clyde areas.

It was here on the 12th August that the new frigate collided with the destroyer *Bulldog* whilst operating together near Gourock Bay. The destroyer was badly damaged but *Loch Dunvegan* less so, but still requiring some remedial work to correct the damage.

After the repairs were completed the frigate sailed on the 15 August for convoy defence duties of the Russian bound convoy JW59 that comprised of forty merchantmen and nineteen escort vessels, starting at Loch Ewe. *Loch Dunvegan* was part of this heavy escort that also included the Russian battleship *Archangelsk* (formerly HMS *Royal Sovereign*), the cruiser *Jamaica* and the aircraft carriers *Striker* and *Vindex* plus the destroyers *Keppel*, *Whitehall* and the sloops *Cygnet*, *Kite*, *Mermaid*, *Peacock* and a number of flower class corvettes.

Nine days later the force detected submarines and attacked targets sinking the German Type VIIC submarine *U-354* under the command of Oberleutnant Hans Jurgen Sthamer. The submarine had, on 22nd August, successfully attacked and sank the corvette HMS *Bickerton* and the escort aircraft carrier HMS *Nabob*. The attack on *U-354* saw no survivors. The next day the convoy arrived at Kola Inlet and *Loch Dunvegan* detached from the convoy in preparation for the return journey to the Clyde with convoy RA59A with nine merchantmen protected by 19

escorts, which sailed on 28 August. On 1 September aircraft from *Striker* and *Vindex* detected and sank *U-394,* a Type VIIC U-boat under the command of Kapitanleutnant Wolfgang Borger, again there were no survivors. Three days later RA59A arrived safely and without loss at Loch Ewe.

On 5 September *Loch Dunvegan* sailed to Londonderry for operations in the North Atlantic together with the frigates *Helmsdale, Braithwaite, Baytun* and *Foley.*

In November it was revealed that the ship would enter refit on the Tyne on 11 December. With the refit completed in January 1945 *Loch Dunvegan* resumed her role in the North Atlantic and South West Approaches based out of Scapa Flow.

On 14 February whilst operating with sister ship *Loch Eck, Bayntun* and *Braithwaite, Loch Dunvegan* took part in the sinking of the German Type VIIC submarine *U-989* under the command of Kapitanleutnant Hardo Rodler von Roithberg. A search confirmed that there were no survivors from the enemy vessel. Such was the severity of the attack that *Loch Dunvegan*'s commanding officer was awarded the Distinguished Service Cross. The following month she sailed south to operate in the English Channel after which she continued operations in the Irish Sea based out of Milford Haven until early May. With the cessation of hostilities in Europe *Loch Dunvegan* was ordered to intercept any surrendering German U-boats and escort them into Londonderry. The frigate failed to discover any and returned to Londonderry on 13 May for repairs.

Seven days later the frigate sailed around the North of Scotland to join the Rosyth Escort Force before operating in the North Atlantic on air sea rescue missions for transatlantic flights. Later in June the frigate was off Norway where she transferred stores and mail for the re-occupation forces.

In August she was back at Londonderry, this time operating as a training ship under the auspices of the 1st Anti Submarine Training Flotilla. She also had a new commanding officer in the form of Commander G W McGuinness RNR.

Towards the end of the year the Government announced its intention to sink all captured German

U-boats in what was given the name Operation Deadlight. *Loch Dunvegan* was selected to take part but her participation ended when the frigate accidently grounded in Loch Foyle and was taken for repairs at a Belfast shipyard.

The start of 1946 saw the frigate still under repair at Belfast. Upon completion in April she spent the next few months undertaking post refit trials and training at Londonderry as part of the 4th Training Flotilla. In August 1946 she was supposed to have been reduced to category C reserve but this was delayed due to the late running of the refit of sister ship *Loch Tralaig. Loch Dunvegan* was therefore kept active with the 4th Flotilla around Londonderry with a new commanding officer in the shape of Lieutenant Commander V C F Clarke DSC.

She was finally paid off into reserve in April 1947 at Devonport where she remained until January 1949, when she was towed to Penarth for a refit that was completed in May. Upon completion of post refit trials the frigate was once again placed in reserve, this time at Portsmouth. In June she was transferred to Devonport where she remained in the reserve fleet. She would stay there until March 1950 when her new commanding officer Commander R F Nicholson was appointed. The refit continued until 1 May 1950 when the frigate was re-commissioned for service with the 2nd Frigate Flotilla. Her departure for a planned deployment to the Mediterranean was, however, delayed due to some damage inflicted to the machinery by a malcontent member of the crew. Finally, after spending June working up, *Loch Dunvegan* sailed for Malta on 26 June.

The summer months were spent exercising with the flotilla whilst in August the crew were rewarded for their hard work with a visit to the port of Messina. In September she assumed the role of Aqaba Guardship. During this time the crew and officers welcomed onboard his Highness King Abdulla of Jordan to witness weapon training together with sister ship *Loch Scavaig* on 17 September. In the autumn the frigate rejoined the flotilla and visited Leghorn and Tripoli with *Loch Scavaig* before returning to Malta.

The New Year of 1951 found the frigate operating with Loch Lomond during a visit to Dragonasti and in

February the Spring Cruise saw the ship exercising with units of the Mediterranean fleet. Her participation in the cruise ended abruptly with machinery failure. Such was the extent of the defects that *Loch Dunvegan* had to be towed back to Gibraltar where she arrived on 24 February. The damage meant that the frigate could not return to Malta for her planned refit instead arrangements were made at Gibraltar to undertake the work on the Rock instead. It was during this period that the officers and crew of the frigate became involved in one of the worst post war disasters to affect the Royal Navy. The supply ship RFA *Bedenham* exploded on 27 April after a barge alongside loaded with depth charges caught fire. Eighteen people lost their lives and the crew of the frigate tended to the injured and dying.

The refit and repairs were completed in May and after initial sea trials *Loch Dunvegan* made for Malta to resume her role with the 2nd Frigate Flotilla. *Loch Dunvegan*'s run of bad luck continued however, when she grounded on the entrance to Mellehia harbour. The Commanding Officer was dismissed his ship at a court martial. The damage caused resulted in the loss of propeller blades, scraping of the hull bottom and more time in dockyard hands. In total she would spend the next three months under repair, only in August did the frigate commence post repair trials.

Again the frigate's reputation as accident prone preceded it in September when the frigate was involved in a series of collisions in Sliema Creek in Malta; on one occasion hitting the destroyer *Saintes*.

On 21 November *Loch Dunvegan* re-commissioned at Malta under the command of Commander R N Rycroft. She then joined sister ship *Loch Scavaig* and the sloops *Mermaid* and *Magpie,* whose commander was HRH Duke of Edinburgh, as part of the 2nd Frigate Flotilla.

In January 1952 *Loch Dunvegan* sailed to Port Said, where she assumed the role of Guardship. At the time there was a great deal of tension with Egyptian threats to nationalise the Suez Canal. Men from the ship were sent ashore to bolster the ranks of the Army in trying to keep the peace. The frigate remained at Port Said until 27 February when she sailed to Benghazi to rejoin the flotilla.

In the spring of 1952 the frigate made visits to Algiers, Malta and Messina. Whilst in June *Loch Dunvegan* was part of the Mediterranean Fleet Summer Cruise that included a seven day visit to Corfu on 21 June. The next month proved to be an eventful one with a pleasant port of call paid to Dragonasti on the 3rd and a Fleet Regatta at Navarino with sister ship *Loch Lomond* on the 14th July. Six days later the frigate returned to Malta.

In the first week of September 1952 *Loch Dunvegan* took part in the Mediterranean Fleet's Summer Cruise, together with the aircraft carrier *Glory*, the cruiser *Cleopatra*, destroyers *Daring, Armada, Chequers, Chieftain, Chivalrous, Gravelines, Vigo* and *Saintes*, the frigates *Loch Lomond, Meon, Mermaid* and the despatch vessel *Surprise, Manxman* and the submarines *Sanguine, Sentinel* and *Sturdy*. The exercises started in the Western Mediterranean when the force operated with the French Navy off the naval base at Toulon.

With the large number of fast modern anti-submarine frigates and destroyers in commission or under construction, the decision was taken in the autumn of 1952 to decommission *Loch Dunvegan* the following year. After serving as guardship at Port Said again for a while in September, *Loch Dunvegan* sailed for the United Kingdom in October where she paid off into reserve at Devonport.

The prospect of further service emerged in March 1953 when Flag Officer Commanding Reserve Fleet suggested a refit for the frigate. This proposal was, however, not acted upon and *Loch Dunvegan* remained laid up at Plymouth. She did, however, receive a refit in January 1954 before spending the rest of the year laid up. In March 1955 the frigate was taken to her original builder's yard of Charles Hill in Bristol for an extensive eight month refit. After this work was complete *Loch Dunvegan* returned to Reserve status, only this time at Penarth in January 1956.

The frigate remained there until being declared surplus to requirements in 1960 and sold for scrapping to BISCO; she arrived under tow at the yard of T W Ward on 24 August. Within a year the ship was gone.

Battle Honours

ARCTIC 1944   NORTH SEA 1945

Chronology

29.09.1943	Laid down at Charles Hill shipyard Bristol
25.03.1944	Launched
25.06.1944	Completed
06.1944	Joined 10th Escort Group
12.08.1944	Collided with destroyer *Bulldog*
15.08.1944	Escort for Russian convoy JW59
24.08.1944	Sank *U-354*
05.09.1944	Londonderry area
11.12.1944	Refit on the River Tyne
14.02.1945	Sank *U-989* with *Lock Eck, Baytun* and *Braithwaite*
.06.1945	Re-occupation of Norway
.08.1945	Joined 1st ASW Training Flotilla at Londonderry
Late 1945	Operation Deadlight: Destruction of German U-boats
Late 1945	Grounded in Loch Foyle
Early 1946	Joined 4th Training Flotilla at Londonderry
04.1947	Reserve at Devonport
01.1949	Refit then reserve at Penarth
05.1949	Reserve at Portsmouth
06.1949	Reserve at Devonport
01.05.1950	Recommissioned into 2nd Frigate Flotilla
26.06.1950	Sailed to Malta
Summer 1950	Mediterranean Service
29.02.1951	Towed to Gibraltar following engine failure onboard
27.04.1951	RFA *Bedenham* exploded nearby
05.1951	Refit completed returned to Malta
01.1952	Port Said Guardship
10.1952	Reserve at Devonport
03.1955	Towed to Charles Hill at Bristol for 8 month refit
01.1956	Reserve at Penarth
1960	Disposal List
24.08.1960	Arrived T W Ward for breaking up

HMS Loch Eck
(HMNZS HAWEA FROM 1948)

Despite only having a short career with the Royal Navy Loch Eck *participated in the successful destruction of the German U-boat* U-1279 *on 3 February 1945.*
(Crown Copyright/MoD)

Smith's Dock in Middlesborough received an Admiralty contract for the construction of a Loch class frigate on 25 January 1943. This was confirmed and construction started on 25 October the same year when the first steel plates were laid down on the slipway. The building to launching stage was swift with the vessel entering the water under her new name of *Loch Eck* on 25 April 1944. Seven months later on 7 November her construction was completed and she commenced her builders and Royal Navy trials program. Upon completion she joined the 10th Escort Group under the command of Lieutenant Commander R C Freaker DSO, DSC RNR.

First stop for the new frigate was at Tobermory where she stored with ammunition and supplies and carried out a brief work up prior to joining the rest of the 10th Escort Group at Londonderry in December. *Loch Eck* spent the remainder of the month on patrol in the South West Approaches before spending

Christmas at Liverpool where the opportunity was taken to carry out some maintenance.

After spending the New Year at Liverpool 1945 started with *Loch Eck* transferring to Scapa Flow so that her advanced anti-submarine equipment could be brought to bear on German U-boat activities in the North West Approaches. During January she regularly operated with sister ship *Loch Dunvegan* and the frigates *Bayntun* and *Braithwaite*. It was whilst working with these ships that the German Type VIIC/41 submarine *U-1279*, under the command of Oberleutnant zur see Hans Falke, was attacked on the 3 February and sunk. Four days later, with no new kills, the group returned to Scapa Flow. It was not long, however, before another U-boat fell victim to the Hedgehog and Squid attacks from the British ships. On Valentine's Day *U-989* was intercepted and attacked. The submarine was a Type VIIC and was under the command of Kapitanleutnant Hardo Rodler

von Roithberg, holder of two Iron Crosses and a German Cross in Gold. Only two of the submarines crew were rescued, but they died of exposure having been in the cold North Sea off Shetland for too long to be saved.

The group's lucky streak continued when on the 17 February German Type VIIC/41 *U-1278* under the command of Kapitanleutnant Erich Muller-Bethke was attacked and sunk again off the Shetland Islands. Having taken part in the destruction of three U-boats *Loch Eck* made for Londonderry and then onward to Liverpool. The following month the frigate sailed south to bolster the forces in the English Channel operating out of Portsmouth and Plymouth.

Loch Eck sustained damaged when she grounded during operations in the English Channel and damaged her Asdic Dome. The repairs were undertaken at Portsmouth Dockyard until April. April also saw a new commanding officer take command of the frigate. Lieutenant Commander W Molness RNR supervised the final stages of the repairs and took *Loch Eck* back to sea for further service in the English Channel and Western Approaches.

On 4 May she returned to Londonderry where she was allocated for extended service in the Far East. *Loch Eck* would first enter refit to equip her with air conditioning and extra anti-aircraft weapons.

The frigate was on the 23 May at Rosyth Dockyard in Scotland where she joined the forces being assembled for Operation Doomsday, the re-occupation of Norway. When *Loch Eck* sailed she slipped with the warships *Papua*, *Bahamas* and *Bayntun* and together the four ships operated off Norway. On 1 June *Loch Eck* rendezvoused with the German submarine *U-2529* and escorted her from Kristiansand to Loch Eriboll in Scotland. Interestingly this submarine would later briefly serve in the Royal Navy as *N 28* before transferring to the USSR in 1945 where she was given the number *B28* until December 1955. After two years alongside as a power station she was broken up in 1958.

Five days later the frigate escorted the convoy of ships taking King Haakon VII back to Oslo. The Norwegian King has been in exile in Great Britain since 1940 when his country had been invaded by

Germany. Upon the frigates return to British waters *Loch Eck* was taken in hand for a refit conducted by Charles Hill Shipyard in Bristol. The refit was completed in August and after a courtesy call at Cardiff *Loch Eck* sailed for service in the Far East.

Loch Eck sailed through the Mediterranean and Suez Canal finally arriving at Colombo on 20 September. During the next few months *Loch Eck* provided a police role in the Dutch East Indies and visited many diverse ports of call including Padang, Penang and Port Swettenham before arriving at Singapore on 6 October.

The pressure on warships for the Batavia operations meant that *Loch Eck* only spent a couple of days alongside before returning to sea. The Borneo campaign of 1945 would prove to the last major Allied confrontation of World War Two in the South West Pacific. Between 1 May and 21 July American and Australian forces launched a major assault against the island of Borneo. The Allies were led by General Leslie Morshead, whilst his opposite Japanese commanders were Vice Admiral Michiaki Kamada and Lieutenant General Baba Masao.

The Allies planned to launch a six stage operation against Borneo all under the codename of OBOE. OBOE 1 would be an attack against Tarakan, OBOE 2 against Balikpapan, OBOE 3 against Banjermasin, OBOE 4 against Surabaya or Batavia, OBOE 5 against the eastern Netherlands East Indies and OBOE 6 against British Borneo. In the event only the first three stages were put into action. After providing support at Batavia the frigate continued the work of repatriating British and Commonwealth personnel by taking them back to Singapore.

Loch Eck after almost a fortnight in Singapore sailed on 6 November to continue finding and relocating military personnel from places such as Brakit and Manokawi. From 9 November the British ship assumed guardship duties at Sabang where she stayed until the 22nd.

At Singapore *Loch Eck* had a change of command ceremony in December when Lieutenant Commander P J H Hoare assumed command. On 7 December the warship slipped to sea for operations around the island of Java and Batavia. There over the next weeks the

frigate was tasked with intercepting any craft suspected of carrying illicit goods such as arms and weapons for the insurgents. She remained in the vicinity of Sourabaya until taking passage to Semerang on 14 January 1946 and from there onto Singapore.

After a fortnight's leave whilst alongside *Loch Eck* sailed back to Sourabaya on 8 February to relieve sister ship *Loch Scavaig*. Onboard the frigate was reporters and newsmen to record and report on the formal surrender of Bali, which also saw Japanese officers onboard the ship.

On 24 February the formal surrender ceremony took place onboard the frigates quarterdeck. Once the media and Japanese officers had disembarked *Loch Eck* continued to operate around Sourabaya and Bali until taking the official surrender of forces stationed at Lambok on 18 March.

Upon completion the ship sailed for Singapore via Macassar and Sourabaya. On 1 April the frigate tied up alongside at Singapore naval base where seven days leave was granted to the ships complement.

On 8 April *Loch Eck* returned to patrolling duties off Batavia, which continued over the next few months.

After stopping at Palembang on the island of Sumatra *Loch Eck* returned to Singapore on 18 May.

Loch Eck was then declared for the reserve fleet and the ship returned to the United Kingdom from Singapore on 20 May. A week later on her arrival at Colombo the frigate was in collision with the cutter Landguard creating some damage to both ships. *Loch Eck*'s requiring a period under repair before resuming her homeward journey on 6 July with sister-ship *Loch Craggie* and the light fleet aircraft carrier *Vengeance*.

On 8 August the frigate sailed from Gibraltar for Devonport with *Loch Craggie*. Four days later she arrived at Plymouth and paid off into reserve. The following month was spent de-storing before being laid up at Devonport where she remained until January 1948. The sale of the frigate to New Zealand was agreed for a price of £230,050 that included the cost of a refit before the transfer was complete. The work was carried out at Plymouth and in September 1948 she was christened as HMNZS *Hawea* by Lady Burnett, wife of Admiral Robert Burnett, Commander in Chief, Plymouth. The frigate was named after an

inland lake North West of Dunedin in the Southern Alps of New Zealand. Her new commanding officer was Lieutenant Commander A C B Blomfield DSC RN. With the work on the frigate completed she commissioned for service on 3 October and took passage to the Mediterranean for her work up based at Malta.

Together with the other five Loch class frigates bought by New Zealand *Hawea* was worked up throughout November and the following month saw the ships sail through the Suez Canal and Red Sea en route to Singapore where the crew's of the frigates enjoyed Christmas and New Year.

The New Year started with her passage from Singapore to her home port of Auckland where she joined the 11th Frigate Flotilla. On the last day of the month of January 1949 saw a change of command with the new commanding officer being Lieutenant Commander Bryce Harben Clinkard. Clinkard had been born on 23 January 1921 and joined the Royal Navy as a cadet on 1 May 1939 onboard the training cruiser *Vindictive*. He would stay with cruisers for his first proper posting to the *Hawkins* where he remained for the next thirteen months until selected for advancement training back in the United Kingdom. After his promotion he was appointed to the cruiser *Manchester* in the Mediterranean and was onboard when she was struck and sunk by torpedoes fired from an Italian motor torpedo boat off Tunisia. He was subsequently captured by the Vichy French at Algiers and interned until March 1943. Upon his release from captivity Clinkard was appointed as first lieutenant of the frigate *Bann*.

A number of desk jobs followed by Clinkard transferred to HMNZS *Tamaki*, the New Zealand Navy's training establishment at Motuihe Island near Auckland. After a short period there Clinkard finally got his first command as Commanding Officer of the frigate *Hawea*. For the next nine months the frigate operated in New Zealand waters as well as in the wider South Pacific region with visits paid to Fiji and Samoa.

In October the frigate entered the dry dock in the dockyard in Auckland where major reconstruction work was carried out on the ship. Work included improvements being made to her command and con-

HMNZS Hawea *and* Rotoiti *seen in September 1951 during a break in operations off Korea.*
(Ken Kelly Collection)

trol systems as well as updating her outdated communications suite. A great leap forward for the Royal New Zealand Navy was the installation onboard the *Hawea* of an Operations Room where all information was sent to be processed by the ships command before actions were ordered. Another alteration made during the time the frigate spent in dockyard hands was the fitting of escape scuttles for the lower mess decks.

During the course of the refit, Lieutenant Commander Clinkard was succeeded in command by Lieutenant Commander T W Stocker RN in January 1950. The work, however, continued until March when the *Hawea*'s refit was finally completed and she began a series of trials.

In the early 1950's the Royal Navy and the Royal New Zealand Navy operated a system whereby ships from both navies would transfer into the respective navies fleets for a period of time and *Hawea* along with sister ship *Taupo* joined the 2nd Frigate Flotilla

in the Mediterranean whilst the Royal Navy ships *St Austell Bay* and *Veryan Bay* transferred to New Zealand waters.

After sailing via Singapore and Aden *Hawea*, upon arrival in the Mediterranean conducted a series of anti-submarine exercises and joined the rest of the flotilla on the summer cruise between May and July. Indeed the sailors from the Kiwi ship won the Whalers Cup during the fleet regatta held at Marmarice in Turkey. Before the pair of New Zealand vessels left the 2nd Frigate Flotilla for the return journey to Auckland at the end of September a very successful visit was paid to the port of Messina in August. Hawea arrived home in Auckland in November and spent the rest of the year in home waters.

The year of 1951 would prove to be an extremely busy one for the Loch class frigate with the ship deployed to serve off Korea in support of the United Nations action there.

January saw the ship sailing towards the Korean peninsula with pre-arranged stops at Port Moresby, Hong Kong and Kure in Japan on 26 April under the command of Lieutenant Commander Francis Nigel Featherston Johnston RNZN who had joined the ship in February.

Lieutenant Commander Johnston was born in Wellington on 28 June 1919 and joined the Royal Navy as a special entry cadet in 1937 with his midshipman training carried out onboard the cruiser *Vindictive*. In the year before war broke out Francis Johnston served onboard the battleship *Barham* in the Mediterranean but transferred to the cruiser *Manchester* in 1940. Soon after he spent time onboard the Bangor class minesweeper *Rhyl* and her sister ship *Parrsborough* as well as five months on the Tribal class destroyer *Ashanti*.

In February 1943 he transferred again to the destroyer *Wishart* whilst his wartime posting was on the destroyer *Troubridge*. In 1947 he transferred from the Royal Navy to the Royal New Zealand Navy and took command of the corvette HMNZS *Kiwi* and in 1951 took command of the frigate *Hawea*.

Upon arrival off the Korean coastline *Hawea* relieved *Tutira* on station before commencing bombardment of enemy positions on the 18 May. This action proved to be the first attack by a Kiwi ship on enemy positions during the Korean War. It would not be the last for two days later when patrolling with the Royal Navy six-inch cruiser Ceylon, *Hawea* provided support when a landing by Royal Marine Commando's raided shore installations operated by the enemy forces.

For the remainder of the year she operated under United Nations control and attacked numerous targets of opportunity throughout her operational deployment.

Bombardment duties continued into the early months of 1952 a period when a BBC documentary team boarded the warship and recorded reels and reels of film of life onboard the frigate for later transmission back in Great Britain. In February the welcome sight of sister ship *Rotoiti* meant that *Hawea* could be stood down from the frontline and make for Kure for a period of R&R. En route to Auckland the ship called

at Hong Kong on the 9 February where the ship remained until early March.

On 8 March *Hawea* returned home to Auckland to a hero's welcome having been away for many months. The wharf was lined with friends, families and wives and girlfriends and made for a very happy homecoming.

Commander Johnston was soon thereafter awarded a DSC and from the American's a US Legion of Merit medal, but on the 25 March he handed command of the frigate over to her next captain, Lieutenant G R Herring RN who would command the vessel throughout her planned refit.

Upon completion Lieutenant Herring was succeeded in command by Commander G R Davis-Goff DSC RN. With the ship's sea trials successfully completed work up for the frigate focussed on the very particular challenges presented by the work off Korea and on 7 July *Hawea* was officially re-commissioned into service.

On 4 August the frigate sailed from Auckland to join the warships patrolling the waters off Korea, the route chosen was via Hong Kong and then onto Sasebo in Japan where she arrived on 1 October. The next day she sailed for duties under the United Nations flag with bombardments of enemy positions being a priority. She continued her patrols until November when she was taken off the gunline for leave in Kure, where she was visited by the New Zealand Defence Minister.

With leave completed the frigate quickly resumed her patrol duties until the end of the year that included spending the festive season alongside at Sasebo.

1953 started as the previous year had finished with patrols in support of land activity where strategies were pushing the enemy forces back towards the 39th Parallel. On 4 March *Hawea* fired her main armament at Yang-Do Island where the Allied garrison was being attacked by enemy forces that had landed by boat. The usefulness of the Loch class design was shown to great effect during this operation as *Hawea* also controlled the air strikes that had been called in to assist the garrison repel the enemy attack. Later in March she moved to the Han River area and continued to attack targets of opportunity as they arose.

The remainder of the year saw the frigate continue

the cycle of active patrols and leave time spent between Kure and Hong Kong. It was at the latter city that on 2 June the ships company of the frigate took part in the Coronation Day Parade in Anzac Park.

The Korean War was entering its final stages and on 11 June *Hawea* positioned herself so as to evacuate Allied men from the islands north of the agreed cease-fire line. The passage back south, however, was not without further incident when the frigate fired on shore targets as the junks she was escorting with civilians onboard came under attack. The final ceasefire came on 23 July and in August *Hawea* was ordered to return to Auckland via Hong Kong. Another huge welcome celebrated the ships safe return home on 29 August.

In September the frigate was taken in hand for a refit that would take until the following January to complete. Half way through the refit a new commanding officer, Lieutenant Commander J P Tuiloch RNZN was appointed to command the warship. Upon re-commissioning into the 11th Frigate Flotilla, Hawea deployed to the South Pacific with visits to Suva, Ocean Island and Nuie. The summer months of 1954 were spent in home waters before sailing to Fiji in August with the rest of the flotilla. The flotilla stayed together for most of the autumn months with Hawea being deployed back to Auckland as the year closed.

In January 1955 after a period at Auckland the frigate spent February and March on training duties around Australia. In early April she was taken in hand for a refit at Auckland which continued until June with trials continuing until the end of July. On 29 August a change of command took place when Lieutenant Commander R T Hale RNZN took command of the frigate and soon took the ship on another training cruise around the South Island of New Zealand and ports in Australia and the South Pacific. In December the frigate had returned to home waters.

1956 started with the ship deployed around Auckland prior to being taken in hand for a six-month refit lasting until July. When re-commissioned the ship was under the command of Lieutenant C D W J Brown of the New Zealand Navy. In August after trials and work up the frigate sailed for Dunedin and Chatham Island. Later in the year *Hawea* had the honour to escort the Royal Yacht *Britannia* with HRH The Duke of Edinburgh onboard during a visit to New Zealand. The occasion was spoilt slightly by the news that the frigate had been nominated for the reserve fleet. Once her duties as Royal escort had been discharged the frigate sailed to Bluff on the South Island where she rendezvoused with the *Endeavour*, the New Zealand Navy's Antarctic Support Ship and sister ship *Pukaki* on 20 December.

Onboard the *Endeavour* was Sir Edmund Hilary and a team of explorers who were attempting to make a transpolar crossing to coincide with the International Geophysical Year. *Hawea* encountered a large amount of pack ice near McMurdo Sound, where she carried out scientific experiments.

Upon her return to Auckland, she was paid off into reserve in January 1957. For a while she was used as a static harbour training ship before being sold for breaking up in September 1965 in Hong Kong.

Battle Honours

ATLANTIC 1945   NORTH SEA 1945   KOREA 1951-53

Chronology

25.01.1943	Ordered from Smiths Dock
25.10.1943	Laid down
25.04.1944	Launched
07.11.1944	Completed and joined 10th Escort Group
03.02.1945	Joined in successful attack on *U-1279*
14.02.1945	Attacked *U-989*
17.02.1945	Attacked and sank *U-1278*
02.1945	Refitted with extra anti-aircraft guns
13.05.1945	At Rosyth for Operation Doomsday – reoccupation of Norway
01.06.1945	Escorted *U-2529* from Kristiansand to Loch Eribol in Scotland
06.06.1945	Operation Doomsday
06.1945	Refit at Charles Hill Shipyard in Bristol
20.09.1945	Colombo
06.10.1945	Singapore before service in Batavia
09.11.1945	Guardship at Sabang
08.02.1946	Formal surrender of Japanese at Bali
01.04.1946	Singapore
08.04.1946	Returned to Batavia
18.05.1946	Singapore
20.05.1946	Sailed for the United Kingdom
27.05.1946	Collided with cutter *Landguard* at Colombo
06.07.1946	Resumed passage to United Kingdom with *Loch Craggie* and aircraft carrier *Vengeance*
08.08.1946	Sailed from Gibraltar for Plymouth
12.08.1946	Plymouth
09.1946	Destored ahead of lay up
09.1949	Renamed HMNZS *Hawea*
03.10.1949	Commissioned for service in Royal New Zealand Navy
10.1949	Arrived in New Zealand
10.1949	Major refit at Auckland
03.1950	Refit completed
Summer 1950	With Royal Navy's 2nd Frigate Flotilla in Mediterranean
11.1950	Returned to Auckland

January 1951	Start of Korean War service
18.05.1951	Bombarded enemy positions for 1st time
02.1952	From frontline to Hong Kong for R&R
09.02.1952	Hong Kong
08.03.1952	Continued home to Auckland for refit
07.07.1952	Recommissioned
04.08.1952	Took passage back to Korea for UN service
11.06.1953	Evacuated Allied troops from Korean ceasefire line
08.1953	Ordered home to New Zealand
29.08.1953	Auckland for a refit
1954-1956	Home waters off New Zealand
20.12.1956	With *Pukaki* and *Endeavour* sailed for Antarctica for International Geophysical Year
01.1957	Laid up in Auckland and used for harbour training
09.1965	Sold for breaking up in Hong Kong.

HMS Loch Fada

HMS Loch Fada *was the first of class to commission and spent the early part of her career on trials for the rest of the Loch class.*
(Crown Copyright/MoD)

Loch Fada was ordered from the shipyard of John Brown on Clydebank on 19 January 1943. She was laid down on the slipway on 8 June the same year. Her hull was completed to the launching stage on 14 December with the ceremony being conducted by Miss Patricia Piggott. Completion of the frigate took another four months with *Loch Fada* finally being accepted into Royal Navy service on 14 April 1944.

The remainder of the month was spent undergoing contractors sea trials before sailing to Liverpool where she joined the 2nd British Escort Group under the command of Lieutenant Commander Ben A. Rogers, who would, in later life, command the British India Steam Navigation Company School ships *Dunera, Devonia* and *Nevasa*.

In mid April 1944, the ship sailed north to Tobermory where the crew busied themselves filling every last space onboard with stores, ammunition and food. As the first of the Loch class to commission into service *Loch Fada* would spent a great deal of her early career carrying out first of class trials to assess just how good the Loch class design would be. The trials conducted in Scottish waters and the North Atlantic proved to be most satisfactory. In June the frigate sailed into Plymouth for the first time before sailing into the Bay of Biscay on the search for enemy submarines in conjunction with Royal Air Force aircraft and a flotilla of Royal Navy vessels including sister ship *Loch Killin* and the sloops *Wren, Wild Goose* and *Starling*. One unfortunate enemy submarine, *U-333* entered the zone and was attacked and sunk by *Loch Killin*.

In August, whilst *Loch Fada* was still operating in the Normandy area two further Type VIIC submarines were sunk, the *U-736* under the command of

Oberleutnant zur see Reinhard Reff who was rescued along with eighteen of his crewmates West of St Nazaire and *U-385* under the command of Kapitanleutnant Hans Guido Valentiner West of La Rochelle.

Following the successful D-Day invasion of the 6 June 1944 and the subsequent anti submarine campaign in the English Channel many of the Royal Navy warships were released from the area and *Loch Fada* was dispatched for duties in the North West Approaches based at Londonderry. She continued to operate in this role for the next few months before cracking was discovered in her hull. Extra strengthening was added to the ship's hull by the end of 1944.

1945 started with the frigate conducting operations in the South West approaches. The German Type VIIC/41 submarine *U-1018* attacked convoy BTC081 and sank the Norwegian steam vessel *Corvus* about seven miles off the Lizard in Cornwall. Within two hours *Loch Fada,* under the command of Commander B A Rogers RNR, attacked and sank *U-1018,* which had been under the command of 26 year-old Kapitanleutnant Walter Burmeister. Later the same day *Loch Fada* shared the honours with *Wild Goose* and *Labuan* in the destruction of another Type VIIC/41 U-boat *U-327,* under the command of Kapitanleutnant Hans Lemcke, all sailors onboard the U-boat being lost.

The next few months saw the frigate continue operations off the west coast of Great Britain before being part of the force assigned the role of the re-occupation of Norway. On 6 May 1945 *Loch Fada* sailed into Norwegian waters before going on to visit Kristiansand. In July the frigate was back at Rosyth undertaking anti-submarine training before sailing the following month for Germany via Kristiansand. *Loch Fada* would go on to visit the shattered city of Hamburg and her crew assisted in the reconstruction programme. Upon her release from this mission the frigate returned to the River Clyde for further anti-submarine training duties.

The closing months of 1945 saw the frigate continue her training programme for officers and seamen based at Londonderry, but *Loch Fada* did venture as far afield as Iceland during a visit to the capital of Reykjavik.

In December a change of command took place when Lieutenant Commander W P Hart took over the vessel. *Loch Fada* was detailed to take part in Operation Deadlight, the sinking of captured German U-boats in deep water off the Londonderry coast as such she escorted submarines from Loch Ryan in Scotland to the sinking zones. The operation started on 8 December and saw a number of U-boats safely disposed of by the end of January 1946. The following month *Loch Fada* resumed her role as training ship until sailing for a refit at Devonport on 18 March.

She remained at Devonport until June but re-commissioned under the command of Lieutenant Commander P C S Black DSC. After sea trials were successfully completed *Loch Fada* returned to Londonderry where in September she was part of the newly formed 4th Escort Flotilla.

Christmas leave was taken at Devonport and in January 1947 the frigate returned to Londonderry for a series of exercises with units of the Home Fleet. Upon completion the frigate spent June conducting anti submarine training during which she had a minor collision at sea that required the damage to be repaired at Rosyth dockyard.

During this period the frigate was fitted with Type 271 radar and new communications equipment. The work continued until 7 January 1948 when the ship under the command of Lieutenant Commander F J Rand, commenced post refit sea trials. Upon completion she returned to Londonderry.

The New Year of 1949 saw *Loch Fada* continuing her role of training seamen in the techniques necessary to combat submarines. She also transferred to the 3rd Training Flotilla. In March 1949 Lieutenant Commander Peter Ashmore assumed command.

Peter Ashmore was born in Saltash in Cornwall on 4 February 1921 and educated at Western Province Predatory School in South Africa and at Yardley Court School in Tonbridge in Kent. He had been born into a naval family being the son of Vice Admiral Leslie Halburton Ashmore CB, DSO and it was almost a formality that he would follow his father into the Royal Navy. Peter Ashmore entered the Royal Naval College at Dartmouth on 1 May 1938 and spent his first time

at sea onboard the cruiser *Vindictive*.

In 1939 as war broke out in Europe Midshipman Ashmore was serving on the County class cruiser *Dorsetshire* on the China and Indian station and remained with the ship until April 1940 when he returned to Greenwich for advance training. Ashmore ultimately chose to specialise in anti-submarine warfare. Later that year on 28 December he was mentioned in dispatches during an attack on an enemy submarine off Tobruk whilst serving onboard the destroyer *Kipling*. Five months later the same ship was sunk by German dive bombers off Crete.

Ashmore would later serve onboard the destroyer *Melbreak* and the cruiser *Royalist* before returning to the Far East as First Lieutenant of *Tartar*.

In 1946 he was appointed as equerry to the King, a post he held until given the role of executive officer of the destroyer *Zephyr* on 16 March 1948. Ten months later he was given his own command that of *Loch Fada*.

Ashmore would eventually rise to the rank of Vice Admiral on 16 October 1969 and be knighted by HRH Queen Elizabeth II

In April the ship arrived at Rosyth and was taken in hand for a refit that lasted until August. After working up, the frigate again continued her primary role of anti submarine training in the Londonderry areas. With a reduced crew due to manpower shortages afflicting the whole of the United Kingdom armed forces, but particularly the Royal Navy, the ship continued in this role for the remainder of the year.

After ten months in command, Lieutenant Commander Ashmore passed the baton to his colleague Lieutenant Commander T F Page in January 1950, who continued to operating in the Londonderry areas on anti submarine training until September.

In that month she was again in the hands of the dockyard workers at Rosyth who supervised a three month refit returning the ship to service in November. During her work up in the North Sea, *Loch Fada* found and towed the trawler *Lettid*, which had suffered a mechanical breakdown, into Leith harbour on the 3 November.

On 18 December Lieutenant Commander R J E Cundall RN assumed command of the frigate and con-

tinued the anti submarine training in Northern Irish waters into the New Year.

When news reached the Royal Navy of the loss of the submarine *Affray* many ships were detached to the area of the English Channel where the boat had last been seen. *Loch Fada* was sent to search with her powerful sonar. The search continued throughout June after which the frigate returned to Londonderry.

In September the frigate took part in Home Fleet exercises before representing the Royal Navy during visits to Horsa and Kiel in Germany. Upon release, in November, *Loch Fada* and the other units of the flotilla continued anti submarine warfare training from Londonderry, which continued until March 1952 when she was relieved by the destroyer *Tyrian*. *Loch Fada*, meanwhile, made her way to Portsmouth.

In April 1952 *Loch Fada* returned to Portsmouth where she was soon reduced to reserve status awaiting a modernisation programme. The wait continued until October 1953 when she was taken in hand for a refit at Portsmouth Dockyard.

In 1954 *Loch Fada* commenced her post refit trials, but any thoughts of a return to active duty were short lived when she was towed to Barry in South Wales in July, where de-humidification equipment was installed onboard as the ship was prepared for another spell in reserve with all of the equipment on the upper deck covered in cocoons.

Loch Fada's stay was a brief one, in January 1955 she was selected to be returned to active service and the following month was towed back to Portsmouth to have herself brought up to operational readiness. On 21 June 1955 she was re-commissioned into service under the command of Commander Michael Lindsay Coulton Crawford DSC.

He joined the Royal Navy as a midshipman on 1 May 1935 and trained onboard the cruiser *Exeter* on the America and West Indies Station. Upon promotion to Acting Sub Lieutenant Crawford transferred to the battleship *Malaya* in 1937 for one month before moving onto the battlecruiser *Revenge* for just two months. In 1938 he took the submarine course at HMS *Dolphin* in Gosport and after briefly serving on the depot ship *Maidstone* in the Mediterranean transferred to submarines full time firstly in *Sealion*, but in 1940

as First Lieutenant of *Upholder* where he stayed until December 1941. During this time he earned the first of his two DSC's awarded for his heroism during the war patrols against Italian forces. In June 1942 he took command of *P51* (later renamed *Unseen*) before later commanding *Oberon* and *Tireless*.

Postwar he commanded *Artemis* before joining the staff of Commander in Chief, Home Fleet onboard the battleship *Vanguard*, a post he held for two years from 1953.

After a shakedown in late June and work up at Portland throughout July, *Loch Fada* returned to Portsmouth on 22 July to give leave to her crew - fourteen days to each watch. Upon their return in August the frigate sailed for Invergordon to exercise with the Home Fleet where exercises were conducted with the cruiser *Glasgow* in early September. When not conducting training exercises the ships at Invergordon carried out a series of sporting challenges amongst themselves including an improvised Highlands Games with many of the ships company attempting to toss a caber or two. On 18 September the frigate took passage to Portland to take part in a NATO exercise held in the English Channel.

The following month *Loch Fada* sailed north to visit the Norwegian capital of Oslo on 3rd October. After three days steaming the British ship arrived in the city and berthed alongside the Australian frigate HMAS *Queenborough* within sight of the Town Hall. The visit was a huge success with hundreds of local people touring the British and Australian warships. Many coming back late at night to see the pair floodlit against the staggering beauty of the darkened fjord. After four days *Loch Fada* prepared to leave Norway. The British Ambassador to Norway was embarked from the aircraft carrier Eagle along with his naval attaché as the two ships were joined by the depot ship Tyne on the return passage to the United Kingdom. *Loch Fada* took the Ambassador and his staff to Drombak where they disembarked.

At Drombak the passengers were landed and the frigate continued with her program. These were interrupted by a serious machinery defect caused by blocked condensers that resulted in *Loch Fada* being withdrawn from planned Running Tide Exercise and a visit to Ipswich instead the ship limped into Portsmouth for repairs to be undertaken. After some days of fevered work by the dockyard *Loch Fada* sailed on 9 November into rain clouds en route to the Middle East. The Bay of Biscay lived up to reputation with a strong gale blowing before arriving at Gibraltar. The men were given some shore leave whilst some minor repairs were made to the Cemetex covering on her quarterdeck which had suffered at the hands of the gale. The crossing to Malta started on the 15 November but the ship rediscovered the gale which made for a rather unpleasant crossing. On arrival at Malta a 17 gun salute was fired to Commander in Chief Mediterranean, Admiral Sir Guy Grantham KCB, CBE, DSO before berthing in Sliema Creek. On her night passage through the Suez Canal on 24 November she anchored in Bitter Lakes and cheered ship as the sloop *Flamingo* sailed past and relieved her on station with the latter returning to the United Kingdom.

On the final day of the month she arrived at Aden only staying there for two days before resuming her passage to Bahrain. The seven day passage was used by those onboard the frigate to practice their .22 rifle shooting as well as staging a tug of war competition onboard before finally arriving on 9 December. After a month in transit the week following *Loch Fada*'s arrival was spent painting and cleaning the ship.

When she next put to sea *Loch Fada* and sister ship *Loch Killisport* had teamed up and started patrolling the Persian Gulf. The ship visited Yas and Dalma on a summer cruise with the Senior Naval Officer Persian Gulf embarked. With this completed course was set to head back to Bahrain but not before rendering medical aid to the supply ship RFA *Wave Master* on 21 December which had a sick officer onboard who needed urgent medical attention. After reuniting with the medical officer at Bahrain, the frigate made the short passage to Kuwait where *Loch Fada* was alongside in Kuwait for Christmas. Officers and men received numerous invitations to dances and parties as well as sporting competitions too. Sadly the ship did not win any silverware for the ward room. Two days after the celebrations the warship slipped and sailed back to Bahrain.

January 1956 started with the ship providing a guard for the Annual New Year reception given by the Ambassador to the Ruler of Bahrain His Highness Sheikh Sir Sulman Bin Hamid al Khalifa. Whilst there the ship took part in soccer matches played against teams from sister ship *Loch Killisport* and the Portuguese sloop *Bartolomieu Diaz*. Two days later the frigate sailed to the North of the Persian Gulf for a patrol that also included a visit to Basra as guests of the Basra Petroleum Company who took the men on a very informative visit to the oil installations at Zubair and Rumaila, some forty miles into the Iraqi Desert. At Bandar Mashur in Iraq, entertainment was varied with visits to a dairy farm and the Agha Jira oilfields, whilst others visited the ancient Persian trading town of Bushehr before the ships football team lost a football match to a local side. The frigate remained there until leaving on the 20th to resume her patrol and visit Bandar Abbas where walking and climbing expeditions were made into the hot dusty interior of the country.

After a brief stop at Khor Kuwair for maintenance to the shore facilities to be undertaken, *Loch Fada* continued onto her base port of Bahrain arriving there on 26 January. After her annual inspection the frigate sailed in company with her sister ship *Loch Lomond* and patrolled the Persian Gulf with the usual round of courtesy and official visits. In March, however, her planned departure for Colombo was postponed due to a disturbance in the form of a demonstration when the British Foreign Secretary, Selwyn Lloyd visited the country. The Captain took the decision to land a platoon of men to assist the local law enforcement officers ashore in restoring law and order in Bahrain.

Loch Fada's planned programme was soon in disarray as on the 4 March instead of heading for Colombo the frigate sailed for Aden and again a change of itinerary occurred on passage when she was diverted for a second time to Mombasa at best speed. The reason for the change in plans was to transport Archbishop Makarios, Bishop of Kyrenia Cyprus to Male in the Maldives for detention there. The Archbishop had been responsible for a large amount of the troubles on the island of Cyprus that had consumed so much attention of the Royal Navy over the previous few years.

After refuelling at Mombasa on 11 March, *Loch Fada* rendezvoused with the East African Ship Rosalind out of sight of land in Wasin Channel and transferred the Archbishop for transit to Male, where they arrived three days later. *Loch Fada* stayed in the Seychelles for three days before resuming the postponed visit to Colombo where she entered dry dock on the 17 March for a much needed maintenance period. Upon her arrival the ships company experienced the first of many tropical storms with thunder, lightning and sheets of rain pouring in torrents from the sky.

Loch Fada's work package resulted in the frigate remaining in Colombo until 2 May with the ships company taking station leave at Diyatalawa rest camp. During her time in dry dock the ship received onboard Admiral Louis Mountbatten when he spoke to the Captain and made a brief tour of the ship. The ship's sea trials were not totally satisfactory as on one occasion the main bearing overheated and had to be repaired.

On 2 May *Loch Fada* slipped out of the dockyard and made her way to Trincomalee a short one day passage away. En route a signal was received onboard telling the frigate that she would no longer be needed for the Atomic Tests at Monte Bello Islands. This news came as a disappointment to the ships company who had been looking forward to a cruise to Singapore, Christmas Island and possibly Fremantle in Australia. Upon arrival at Trincomalee *Loch Fada* berthed alongside Saigang Jetty.

For most of the month the fleet exercised in the waters around Trincomalee testing machinery and weapons and men to their fullest, sometimes in the company of the cruiser *Superb*. In addition there were several sporting fixtures laid on and visits were made to the ancient city of Anuradhapura and to the site of the former fort and Royal Palace at Sigiriya Rock. Upon release from the exercises *Loch Fada* sailed into the South West monsoon with its accompanying strong winds, heavy rains and great humidity to Cochin for a visit to the Royal Indian Navy Training Establishment there on 1 June.

The opportunity was taken to meet and greet Indian officers whilst the men found that a large number of entertainment packages had been arranged ashore.

Indeed a party of four officers and sixteen ratings spent a weekend at the High Range Club in Munnar. The reception given them by the tea planters high in the hills 120 miles from Cochin was said to be stupendous. A great visit was had by all onboard but after four days the British ship sailed onto her next destination - Bombay. The voyage was marred by a heavy monsoon swell which left many onboard feeling unwell. After three days at sea *Loch Fada* entered the harbour at Bombay for a five day visit. The British community in the city extended the hand of friendship to the ship inviting them to many dances and parties and the ships water polo team played a successful match against the local Breech Kandy Swimming Club.

Next on the programme for the frigate was Karachi where again a large number of runs ashore had been organised for the men to enjoy. A team from the frigate took on the challenge of competing for the Mauritius Cup against teams from the Karachi Yacht Club narrowly missing out on the silverware. Unfortunately at the end of the visit forty percent of the ships company had complained about upset stomachs. The medical officer suspected that the local water might be the culprit. After another successful visit *Loch Fada* returned to more familiar surroundings in the Gulf arriving at Aden on 20 June. Six days later she rendezvoused with sister ship *Loch Alvie* en route for the United Kingdom.

No such luck for the officers and crew of *Loch Fada* as her sister ship sailed away she was left to contend with severe sandstorm conditions across Aden. Such concerns were soon forgotten when on 6 July a distress signal from the merchantman SS *Corabank* was intercepted. The civilian ship reported that she was running low on fuel whilst off the coast of Socotra. *Loch Fada* intercepted the ship and escorted her to Bandar Delisha where the pair anchored in the safe anchorage there. A few days later the Royal Fleet Auxiliary tanker RFA *Wave Sovereign* arrived and pumped fuel into the civilian ships tanks. *Loch Fada* meanwhile had returned to patrolling the Persian Gulf.

On 14 August crews from *Loch Fada* took down equipment at Khor Kuwair and loaded it into the frigate for transfer back to Bahrain. Two days later she

was deployed in support of the authorities at Um Said to restore civil power if required following suspected local civil unrest due to the Suez Canal crisis.

Finally she returned to Bahrain to carry out a Trucial coast patrol where she visited Um Said and Kor Kuwai again on 23 August. Three days later she continued her patrol and made further visits to Dubai, Yas and Damar. On 2 September *Loch Fada* was back alongside at Bahrain for eight days. Leave was granted to some of the crew but once they were back onboard the ship slipped to again on 10 September for a patrol that included visits to Hallul, Yas and Sir Abu Nair. The crew were astonished at the warmth of the welcome they received at each of the ports of call. Only three days were spent at Sir Abu Nair before the patrol was resumed in the Persian Gulf.

Loch Fada's crew had for some time been made aware that the frigate would be returning to the United Kingdom at the end of her latest commission and this drew closer when, on 14 September, *Loch Fada* arrived at Bahrain. On 15 September the frigate made a week long visit to Basra, in Iraq - the last of the commission.

After another two days at Bahrain *Loch Fada* started her journey home when she sailed to join sister ship *Loch Killisport* at Khor Kuwai. *Loch Killisport* assumed the Persian Gulf patrols from her sister and allowed *Loch Fada* to sail for Mombasa on 27 September.

On 5 October the frigate arrived at Mombasa for a short two day stopover before sailing onto Zanzibar, Dar-es-Salam and eventually arrived at Singapore on the 16th. After a period alongside she resumed her voyage home and on 28 October arrived at Freetown to replenish her fuel tanks. She remained at the African port overnight and sailed for the United Kingdom the next morning. The sights of Portsmouth welcomed the crew on 8 November. There followed a refit period and she recommissioned on 5 December under the command of Commander D A Loram MVO.

Loch Fada's refit continued until 18 February 1957 when the crew started to return onboard. Her sea trials commenced on 4 March. Five days later the frigate sailed from Portsmouth for Portland where she was steadily worked up to active service over the follow-

ing weeks. On the 8 April HRH Prince Michael of Kent spent five days onboard before the ship took passage to Bahrain on 17 May via the Cape of Good Hope in South Africa. The ship, however, did not get too far before a machinery repair was necessary and the decision was taken to return to Portsmouth where she remained until 19 May.

The remainder of the journey south to South Africa was uneventful and on 29 May the frigate sailed into the harbour at Freetown. Leave was granted to the ships company who found many bars in which to spend their pay. When they left, the frigate made a scheduled visit to the naval base at Simon's Town on 11 June before sailing back up the east coast of Africa making landfall at Das-es Salam on 21 June. There she rendezvoused with the heavy cruiser *Ceylon*, which had onboard the Commander in Chief East Indies Squadron. The CinC made an inspection tour of the frigate and was said to be satisfied with the condition of *Loch Fada*.

The British frigate sailed onto her next destination at Khor Kuwai having endured a rough voyage from Das-es-Salam and arrived in port at the start of July. Two sister ships, *Loch Alvie* and *Loch Fyne* arrived the next day and as a squadron the three ships deployed in the Persian Gulf making ports of call to Bahrain and Basra. At the latter *Loch Fada* was placed in quarantine due to an outbreak of a virulent strain of Asian Flu on board. Once cleared to proceed the frigate sailed for Bahrain on 14 July.

The stay alongside lasted only four days before the frigate slipped to sea with a cargo of ammunition which was being delivered to Trucial Oman Scouts in Dubai. Once this duty was completed the frigate assumed the role of searching for and intercepting dhows suspected of carrying illicit merchandise.

The month of August started with the ship off Bahrain during civil unrest ashore caused by the recent Suez Crisis. The ship's Royal Marine detachment was landed to assist the police force ashore together with contingents from the other Loch class frigates. Once the crisis was calmed *Loch Fada* was allowed to resume her normal Batina coastal patrol, which also included a much needed visit to Dubai.

The patrols continued into September with ports of

call made to Muscat and Um al Quawain. The latter port saw quite a distraction for the Captain and Officers of *Loch Fada* when they were invited to dine with the sheik. The following month proved to be an active one for the British ship when she stood by to assist the *SS Adlai* which had run aground off the coast of Oman, suffering severe flooding as a consequence. *Loch Fada* remained with the merchantman until a local tug arrived to pull the ship free and tow her to the Pakistani port of Karachi.

During a visit to Umm Said in Qatar the ships company were entertained by the men building an oil field at Dakhan. The oil field was at the time of the visit under construction and *Loch Fada*'s crew learnt a great deal about oil extraction and refining before returning to Bahrain.

The final months of the year saw the frigate at the northern end of the Persian Gulf with a visit to the port of Fao in early November which was followed by a large scale CENTO exercise in the Indian Ocean entitled Exercise Crescent. Other ships taking part in the exercise included the cruiser *Gambia* and *Loch Alvie* plus numerous ships from America, Turkey, Pakistan and India. The aim of the exercises was to improve interoperability between the navies as well as anti-submarine and anti-surface warfare training. The exercise continued until early December when *Loch Fada* was scheduled to go to Trincomalee where the men of the frigate expected to enjoy a somewhat tropical festive season. This proved to be a short lived hope when the warship was required off Oman following an outbreak of civil unrest. *Loch Fada* sailed north on 10 December having returned from Karachi. The civil unrest also meant that *Loch Fada* would not take part in the planned naval review in Karachi harbour of the ships taking part in Exercise Crescent.

Upon her arrival she immediately started patrolling, together with the cruiser *Gambia*, the waterways around the Batina coast.

January 1958 saw some very unusual passengers onboard the frigate, but before they embarked *Loch Fada* visited Djibouti in then French Somaliland for two days from 7 January after which she relieved the cruiser *Gambia* at Berbera in neighbouring Somaliland. Her arrival co-incided with civil unrest in

the territory and the Royal Marines onboard the frigate were once again landed to aid local defence forces. After two days ashore the marines re-embarked on *Loch Fada* and the ship proceeded to sea. On 12 January the officers of the ship received a strange communication requesting that the ship sail for Aden to collect two unusual passengers plus their food for passage to Bahrain. The two passengers were prize heifers and they were being added to the Ruler's herd of cows. The cows stayed onboard until the ship docked at Sitra on the 16th. Once unloaded, the ship sailed onto Karachi where she was taken in hand for a period in dry dock. The extended break from operations allowed the ship's company time to devote to pastimes and entering competitions such as the Mauritius cup for sailing dinghies. *Loch Fada*'s team eventually won the cup on the last day of January.

The maintenance on the frigate was completed on 10 February and *Loch Fada* sailed from Karachi back to the Persian Gulf where she resumed her normal duties off the Batina coast with numerous stopovers at Bahrain until 11 March.

Loch Fada completed her sea inspection in company with sister ship *Loch Ruthven* whilst the pair operated off Muscat. Upon completion the frigate made for Mombasa after a brief stop at Muscat for a medical emergency. Her journey was further interrupted when signals were received that the Norwegian merchant-man Skaubryn was on fire in the Indian Ocean. The ship was loaded with almost 1300 people bound for Australia from Germany. When *Loch Fada* discovered the ship the crew and passengers had abandoned her and been rescued by the SS *City of Sydney*. The British frigate took the Skaubryn under tow but two days later on 4 April passed the tow to the Dutch tug *Cyclops*. News reached *Loch Fada* that the stricken vessel finally sank on 6 April.

Loch Fada, meanwhile, arrived at Mombasa on 8 April where she landed security personnel to assist local authorities in calming another state of civil unrest. Later in the month when the frigate had returned to Aden two of the ship's company ERA Spreadborough and LM(E) Williams were attacked whilst ashore and received injuries when caught in the blast of a hand thrown bomb in Aden.

On 23 April the ship was released from her duties at Aden and headed for home routed through the Suez Canal, Malta and Gibraltar. On her arrival at Portsmouth on 14 May the frigate was taken in hand for a refit which lasted until 6 August. That day also saw the arrival onboard of her new commanding officer Commander D E P George. Her trials programme was undertaken as usual off Portland and upon completion she sailed for the Persian Gulf again on 17 November. The frigate was routed through the Mediterranean and Red Sea with further stops made at Aden before finally arriving at her base port of Bahrain on 8 December. The ship and crew quickly settled into the routine of patrols in the Persian Gulf before arriving at Abadan on 23 December where the ships company celebrated Christmas. Three days after the big day she sailed back to Bahrain.

The new year of 1959 started with the ship deployed off the Batina coast before returning to Bahrain on 15 January. The following month saw visits paid to Horeamz and Banda Mashur. Whilst alongside at Mina al Amadi in Kuwait from the 18 February the ship's company were allowed a period of rest and recuperation before the patrol was continued with visits to Ganneveh and Kharg Island in Iran. On 24 February the frigate once again secured alongside at Bahrain where she remained until early March.

March saw the frigate continue her operations off Batina with port visits to Das, Muscat and Abu Dhabi. On 23 March *Loch Fada* arrived back at Bahrain and spent a few days preparing the warship for a planned docking period at Karachi on 29 April. After sailing across the Gulf she docked down and remained there until 27 May when the frigate returned to service to resume her Persian Gulf patrols.

The month of June was as busy as any previous month with official visits paid to ports as diverse as Abadan, Kisim in Iran and Khor Kuwai. It was whilst she was at the latter that a faulty propeller shaft first came to light and saw the ship being withdrawn from a planned exercise and instead made for the dry dock back at Karachi to affect repairs.

The assessment by engineers at the dockyard found *Loch Fada*'s damage to be extensive and immediately called for the frigate to sail back to the United

Kingdom for full repairs to be undertaken. *Loch Fada* was made sea worthy and sailed soon after routed through Aden, Suez and Gibraltar.

On 9 September *Loch Fada* arrived back at Portsmouth where she was taken into the dockyard for full repairs to be undertaken. The work would be completed on 19 January 1960 when she re-commissioned under the command of Commander R R Whalley RN who had joined the ship the previous month. After working up in Portland throughout February *Loch Fada* sailed on 19 March for the stormy waters around Iceland to take part in a Fishery Protection Patrol during the first Cod War with Iceland.

Loch Fada battled fierce seas and Icelandic gunboats until relieved on 9 April. April was spent in British waters before starting her preparations for foreign- service in the Middle East. *Loch Fada* sailed from Portsmouth on 10 May and was routed through Gibraltar to Messina where she arrived ten days later. The ships company enjoyed four days at the resort with long sunny days and copious amounts of alcohol

consumed. After leaving Messina *Loch Fada* sailed through the Suez Canal and entered the Red Sea. On 2 June the frigate was at Perim where the wartime destroyer Khartoum was wrecked on the beach on 23 June 1940 following an explosion onboard.

A fractured pipe on *Loch Fada* had been causing the warship some difficulty and the opportunity was taken to repair the pipe whilst alongside the heavy repair ship *Hartland Point* when the frigate arrived at Aden.

Loch Fada, once repaired, set sail on 7 June for a dhow patrol but this was cut short following a steering gear defect the following day. Such was the extent of the problem that the ship reverted to using hand pumps to steer the ship and flags were hoisted which told other shipping that *Loch Fada* was not under control. Eventually the engineers corrected the problem and the frigate resumed her planned participation in CASEX with other squadron vessels at Darsait in Oman. By the 13 June she was back at Bahrain and soon took onboard Commodore Arabian Sea and Persian Gulf. With the Commodore onboard, *Loch*

HMS Loch Fada *passing through the Suez Canal enroute to Aden on 24 October 1962.*   *(Ken Kelly Collection)*

Fada visited Little Qioin Island, Muscat and took part in Exercise Mudlark 7 before sailing back into Bahrain harbour on 30 June.

Much of July was spent at Mina al Amadi in Kuwait for a crew rest and recuperation period ahead of more coastal patrols off Batina and repeat visits to Dubai and Muscat. At the former the ships company witnessed the construction of the new harbour.

August started in a similar vein but on the 4th the warships port engine main bearing developed a major fault leaving the ship with only one shaft. In this condition she was not the best to try and assist the stricken SS *Steel Recorder* which had run aground. Fortunately, the merchantman did not request any help from the British frigate.

At Bahrain the troublesome port engine and bearings were fixed just ahead of exercises with sister ship *Loch Lomond* on 15 August. A week later Flag Officer Middle East embarked for visits to Dubai and Sharjah. The following month *Loch Fada* resumed her role of patrolling the Batina coast plus visits to Muscat and Abu Dhabi.

On 3 September the frigate together with sister ship *Loch Lomond* exercised at Jebel Danna in the United Arab Emirates before returning to Bahrain a fortnight later. After a few days alongside *Loch Fada* resumed her patrols in the central Gulf area with visits paid to Dubai and also to Banda Mashur. After six days at sea the frigate once again returned to her homeport in the region of Bahrain. Repairs were made to a defective sonar recorder, which had been brought out to the Gulf onboard *Loch Ruthven.*

October started with a joint exercise with *Loch Lomond* before deploying to Batina coast for another patrol and further exercises entitled Exercise Mhunk IH at Karachi again with *Loch Lomond* and local forces. November saw further manoeuvres including Exercise Midlink III. Upon completion of the exercises *Loch Fada* sailed for an official six day visit to Bombay.

Later in November *Loch Fada* paid visits to Cochin and Karachi for a routine docking period that continued until 27 December when the British frigate sailed back to Bahrain.

1961 started with a major naval exercise codenamed Aspex 7 together with units of the amphibious warfare squadron and escorted by *Loch Fada*, *Loch Fyne* and *Loch Ruthven*. The exercise took place off Bahrain and lasted for ten days with marines storming a number of beaches from landing craft. The exercise was followed by a most official function - to be present at the enthronement of the new ruler of Dubai on the 17 January. For the visit the ship was dressed overall and the captain and his senior officers made a number of official calls ashore.

Upon completion the frigate sailed onto Sharjah on the 20th and assumed the role of air sea rescue ship in the Arabian Sea. *Loch Fada* had been detailed to a position on the known flight path of the aircraft carrying HM Queen Elizabeth II and the Duke of Edinburgh on a state visit to India. Fortunately the flight arrived safely and *Loch Fada* was dispatched back to Bahrain for a self maintenance period from the 25 January, which continued into February. By 10 February the frigate was back in service and assumed the onerous task of Batina coast patrol which was enlivened by towing a Rhino ferry from Bahrain to Muscat where the frigate rendezvoused with the Commando Helicopter Carrier *Bulwark* and handed over charge of the ferry to the larger ship. The remainder of February saw visits paid to Mombasa and Tanga in Tanzania on the 25 February where she anchored offshore.

Tanga was an interesting visit because the ships company ventured inland and saw a number of projects including a logging company and an inland malaria control centre.

March proved to be just as eventful with visits to Lindi, Mtwara and Das-el-Salaam in Tanzania before returning to Mombasa on the 7th March where station leave was granted to the ships company.

On 16 March *Loch Fada* set sail for Aden but called on the small community of Larnu the following day for an informal visit. Seven days later the frigate arrived at Aden where she rendezvoused with sister ship *Loch Alvie.*

Loch Fada then started a series of visits in the region with one of the most interesting being to the Ethiopian Naval Base at Masawa. The visit was a somewhat subdued affair as it followed an Army coup

in the capital of Addis Ababa. Also of note was that the Red Sea appeared to full of naval activity with numerous Russian vessels, which *Loch Fada* shadowed from a distance. On 2 April the British frigate, called at Port Sudan and were hosted by the local oil company. Six days later *Loch Fada* entered the Suez Canal at the start of a northerly transit of the waterway.

On 10 April *Loch Fada* made an official visit to Tobruk to mark the 20th anniversary of the siege of the city during World War Two. The frigate anchored in the harbour whilst men were sent ashore in the sea boats to rehearse for the official parade through the city streets. On the 14 April the frigate, in the harbour, was joined by RMS *Orantes* with Australian veterans onboard for the occasion. The day of the parade also saw a flypast by an RAF Vulcan bomber.

Soon thereafter *Loch Fada* resumed her passage calling at Gibraltar before finally arriving home at Portsmouth on 27 April.

After a brief period of leave *Loch Fada* sailed around the Southern coast to Chatham Dockyard arriving on 5 May. She paid off and entered into a long refit to improve the habitability as well as to upgrade her weaponry and sensors. This refit started on 24 May and was not completed until May 1962.

After trials *Loch Fada* re-commissioned at Chatham Dockyard on 26 June for service in the Far East under the command of Commander W H Hart AFC. July was spent working up in the Thames Estuary before transferring firstly to Portsmouth and then at Portland, a pattern that continued until 3 October.

She sailed from Portsmouth on 8 October on the first leg of her journey to the Far East calling at Gibraltar, Malta and Aden before arriving at Colombo on 8 November.

Political unrest on the Maldives caused the frigate to be diverted there two days later. The residents were protesting over the use of the islands as American bases and in particular the use of Diego Garcia – still a contentious issue to this day. *Loch Fada* assumed the role of guard ship to try and stem outbreaks of civil unrest on the usually peaceful islands. The unrest caused the remainder of the frigates program to the Far East to be cancelled.

Upon release *Loch Fada* sailed to Singapore on 7 December and started a period of repair upon her arrival six days later. The frigates arrival was fortuitous due to the start of the 'Konfrontasi' operations in Borneo on the 8 December. *Loch Fada* started her first patrol on 1 February 1963. The island of Borneo was in 1961 divided into four separate states, Kalimantan, the Sultanate of Brunei, Sarawak and British North Borneo. The conflict grew out of a British desire to withdraw from its colonies in South East Asia after the Second World War and the British Government proposed combining its three colonies with the new Federation of Malaya.

Many local's protested against the proposal and eventually took up arms against it. The North Kalimantan National Army (TNKU) sparked the conflict on 8 December 1962 when they staged an abortive insurrection and seize oil fields and capture the Sultan of Brunei. The insurrection failed faced with a superior British force comprising of amongst others Gurkha troops. Operations to capture the remains of the TNKU took until May 1963 to complete.

After sixteen days the frigate returned to Singapore and prepared for a deployment in the Pacific Ocean in March. The route chosen took in visits to Manus, Suva and she also undertook an Air Sea Rescue duty at Phoenix Island. *Loch Fada* was positioned on the expected flight path of a Royal flight in early April.

The flight arrived at its destination without incident and *Loch Fada* resumed her passage to Guam. At the island the ships company were entertained by the US Navy based there. After three days she slipped and headed for Hong Kong for a self maintenance period alongside at HMS *Tamar*.

Loch Fada's itinerary resumed on 9 May when she set sail for a tour of Japanese ports starting four days later at the port of Moji on Kyushu Island. The ships company were amazed by the warmth of the greeting they received from the locals, which was duplicated at Marzuru and also at Muroran. On 28 May she left Japan bound for Tawau.

At Taway *Loch Fada* provided support to the anti piracy patrols in the region before returning to Hong Kong after two weeks of patrolling off Borneo. Most of July was spent in Hong Kong waters before returning to the conflict off Borneo until the end of August.

After a brief stop at Hong Kong, *Loch Fada* took part in Exercise Dovetail off Singapore for four days from 16 September that also saw the participation of two Australian warships the Daring class destroyer HMAS *Vendetta* and the frigate HMAS *Quiberon*. The following months saw the frigate once more searching for insurgents in the waters off Borneo. After a whole month on this mission *Loch Fada* returned to Singapore on 28 October.

In November the crew of *Loch Fada* started work preparing the ship for the refit ahead. They de-stored the vessel and assisted the local dockyard when it came to getting the ship into the dry dock at Singapore. On 18 November *Loch Fada* re-commissioned into Royal Navy service as part of the 3rd Frigate Squadron; her latest commanding officer, Commander M C Evelegh taking command.

The refit continued until January 1964 but on the 29th *Loch Fada* started her post refit trials programme, which proved satisfactory. By February with

any last minute problems having been ironed out the ship was accepted back into service and started her preparations for her next deployment. First though the frigate joined numerous Royal Navy vessels and a number of foreign warships from Australia, the United States and New Zealand for Exercise Jet on 28 February. The exercise took place in the Indian Ocean and was a huge success. Upon completion *Loch Fada* resumed her normal duties in and around Singapore on 19 March.

The following month the frigate was despatched to the Indian Ocean and for a while became Gan Guard ship before crossing the Indian Ocean and visiting the African port of Mombasa on the 14 April for a lengthy stay during which the crew spent time ashore at Safari parks whilst the ship received a period of maintenance.

On 26 April *Loch Fada* resumed her patrols off Zanzibar and later embarked men from the Kenyan Police force together with vehicles for an exercise

This aerial view of Loch Fada *clearly shows the ships layout with the main 4-inch gun in B position, the open bridge, mainmast and funnel and the open quarterdeck.* (Crown Copyright/MoD)

held at Lamu. After four days the frigate headed out to sea to rendezvous with the new frigate *Gurkha* and together the two ships returned to Mombasa on 2 May. After a further spell at Mombasa, *Loch Fada* carried out a series of independent exercises from the 14 May including firings of her Squid anti-submarine weapon system. On one occasion the missile failed to fire due to faulty mortars.

Two weeks later the ship took part in exercises centred on the aircraft carrier *Centaur* together with the destroyer *Cavendish* and the tanker RFA *Tidereach*. Upon completion of which, *Loch Fada* made for Aden to embark Squid projectiles from the supply ship RFA *Fort Langley*.

After five days the frigate slipped her moorings and set course back to Bahrain after topping up her fuel tanks during a replenishment at sea from the tanker RFA *Wave Chief*.

After arriving at Bahrain she operated locally until 22 June when she took part in the naval exercise Fomex 18. During one aspect of these exercises *Loch Fada* experienced a steering gear defect on 28 June, which was sorted out by the engineering staff by the next day in time for naval serials with the submarine *Aeneas* and later the Tribal class frigate *Mohawk*.

The next set of exercises commenced in July with the frigates pitted against Royal Navy submarines. At the end of the serials on 3 July the force returned to Bahrain for a few days. Three days later *Loch Fada* was back at sea for the amphibious warfare section of the exercises with 3 Para at Yas Island. Upon completion she returned to Bahrain where for eleven days she was under repair in the dockyard.

The following months saw the frigate undertake the usual mixture of dhow patrols and exercises around Yas Island, but all the while the ship was increasingly experiencing troubling machinery problems that required more and more time alongside at Bahrain to fix. On 3 August *Loch Fada* was once again at Bahrain with engineers assessing the nature of the latest machinery failure. Such was the extent of the breakdown that the frigate was placed at extended notice for steam. A week later with her latest problem solved *Loch Fada* sailed to resume her patrols off the Batina coast. After only four days at sea, however, the

nagging mechanical problems arose once more requiring yet more time alongside at Bahrain.

When she did get back to sea on 20 July *Loch Fada* visited Das before returning two days later to Bahrain where three days later there was a families day organised at HMS *Jufair* and the ship was opened to visitors.

On 26 August *Loch Fada* sailed in company with the frigate Gurkha to Bombay where machinery defects were corrected. The frigate remained there until 7 September when she sailed for Gan to assume guardship duties at the British territory. After a week *Loch Fada* sailed onto Singapore where she was taken in hand for a major rectification programme of her defects to be addressed. *Loch Fada* arrived at Singapore on 16 September but only entered the dry dock there on 28 October. Workers at the dockyard spent the next six weeks assessing the problems and finding solutions to the growing list of defects on the ship.

On 13 December 1964 *Loch Fada* finally sailed for Hong Kong where she spent Christmas and New Year.

On 2 January 1965 *Loch Fada* sailed from Hong Kong bound for the waters off Borneo to undertake a 'Konfrontasi' patrol, which lasted for the next three weeks. On 25 January she took passage to Singapore where she arrived four days later. Upon her arrival the crew were kept busy cleaning the ship in preparation of her re-commissioning planned for 4 February. At the ceremony her latest commanding officer, Commander D Mansell officially took over from Commander Evelegh.

Loch Fada spent the next week alongside undertaking a period of self maintenance before sailing for Hong Kong on 13 March. From there she continued onto the ongoing Borneo patrols. These patrols continued until 21 April when *Loch Fada* returned to the familiar surroundings of Singapore Dockyard.

The following month the frigate slipped from Singapore with other units of the Royal Navy to take part in a series of naval exercises in the Gulf of Thailand with American, Australian and Thai warships.

On 4 May the British ship visited Bangkok before sailing onto Hong Kong for a six day visit and arrived on 13 May. Upon completion the frigate returned to

Singapore and was taken in hand for a refit on the last day of the month.

For four months the workers in Singapore Dockyard repaired, cleaned and overhauled faults on the ship, which finally put back to sea on 5 September for initial trials. When she re-commissioned she joined the 26th Escort Squadron.

On 7 October *Loch Fada* resumed her usual pattern of operations when she sailed for Hong Kong arriving there after five days at sea. Further repairs were made before the frigate once again returned to Singapore. *Loch Fada* arrived back on 30 October and throughout November operated in local waters in preparation of another Borneo patrol.

Throughout December the frigate continued her patrols continued into 1966. On 8 January her final 'Konfrontasi' patrol ended when *Loch Fada* took passage to Hong Kong. Upon her arrival at HMS *Tamar* the ship undertook a twelve day self maintenance period before returning to Singapore on 29 January. She operated locally before entering dry dock for repairs on 28 February.

Upon completion in April the ship re-commissioned into the Royal Navy with Commander W H Barnard RN appointed to command the frigate. In May she returned once more to shuttling between Hong Kong and Singapore where she returned to on 27 May.

The summer months were spent operating with her squadron around Singapore. August saw *Loch Fada* taking part in a lengthy series of exercises before sailing on 3 September to Hong Kong where she again arrived after five days at sea.

After *Loch Fada* spent the next thirteen days at the colony enjoying the many varied sights, sounds and flavours, the crew sailed back to Singapore. The following month was a varied one with a four day visit to Penang from the 8th. On the last day of the month *Loch Fada* returned to her home base and was soon taken in hand for another short refit.

At the start of 1967 *Loch Fada* remained in refit and only resumed squadron duties on 12 January. After working up locally the frigate sailed from Singapore for a planned return visit to Penang. The visit was a poignant one for the ship and crew as it was to be the last visit to the city before she sailed home to decom-

mission from service. *Loch Fada* arrived at Penang on 18 February and remained alongside for four days allowing the crew time ashore and to allow VIP's to tour the ship. In March and April *Loch Fada* resumed duties with the rest of the squadron. On 29 April the ships arrived at Hong Kong for a brief three day visit before sailing onto Japan and a tour of Japanese ports.

On 6 May the first of five visits were made to Simizu on the island of Honshu, this was followed over the course of the next eighteen days with visits to Yokohama, Shiogama, Qninato and finally Hakodate. On 24 May *Loch Fada* slipped and sailed from Japanese waters back to Hong Kong where she arrived five days later.

The stay was a brief one and on 3 June *Loch Fada* was once again at sea bound for Singapore where the ship was given an extensive self maintenance period alongside until 10 July. The frigate slipped from Singapore Naval Base that day and made for Hong Kong on her final visit to the colony, where she arrived on 25 July.

On the first day of August the frigate was in Castle Peak Bay and the day was spent conducting the standard swimming tests for the ships company. The next day she had moved to Long Harbour and then on into Hong Kong itself on 3 August. In the early hours of Friday 4 August the ship was dressed overall and a 21 gun salute was fired to mark the birthday of HM Queen Mother.

In what could have been a much more serious incident the next day saw a bomb explode in HMS *Tamar* near to the survey ship *Dampier* on the South Wall in a suspected terrorist attack.

On Wednesday 9 August *Loch Fada* started her return journey to the United Kingdom and an uncertain future and took passage to Singapore, where she arrived after four days steaming. The officers and men welcomed onboard a number of VIP's from Singapore for the ships official farewell cocktail party on Friday 18 August and three days later the ship slipped to sea. For the return passage home Lieutenant Commander M J Rogerson RN took command of the ship. From Singapore the frigate called at Gan to top up her fuel tanks and at Port Louis in Mauritius on Saturday 2 September. Four days were spent there, allowing the men runs ashore and access to the local beaches.

Finally *Loch Fada* left and started the final leg of her homeward journey. Calling at Gibraltar for two days from 4 October it was only a short distance to Portsmouth where she arrived on Tuesday 10 October and anchored at Spithead. The following day after customs officials had boarded the frigate and checked everyone's possessions the port tug *Griper* came alongside with family members onboard. Just after eleven in the morning of Wednesday 11 October *Loch Fada* started her final entry into Portsmouth harbour with her paying off pennant flying.

The frigate was de-ammunitioned on Friday 13 October and on Monday 23 October the final crew members left the ship and marched to the Royal Navy Barracks.

Loch Fada was soon reduced to reserve status with-in the dockyard but was, in 1968, loaned to the British Aircraft Corporation to use in the programme to develop the Seawolf missile system. She was fitted with numerous systems necessary to launch and track the system but on 5 November 1968 she broke free from her moorings in Luce Bay. Soon she was drifting in the Irish Sea but was recovered and towed back to safety at Pembroke Dock. An inspection of the vessel was undertaken and it was found that the sea or weapons had caused numerous cases of damage and rendered the ship unsuitable for further trials work.

The final years of the *Loch Fada* story saw the abandoned frigate laid up at Pembroke Dock before being finally sold to BISCO for demolition by Metal Industries at Faslane where she arrived on 28 May 1970.

Battle Honours

NORMANDY 1944 - ENGLISH CHANNEL 1945 - ATLANTIC   1945

Chronology

19.01.1943	Ordered from John Brown shipyard
08.06.1943	Laid down
14.12.1943	Launched
14.04.1944	Completed
04.1944	Joined 2nd British Escort Group
04.1944	First of class trials
06.1944	Bay of Biscay
31.07.1944	Attacked *U-333* with *Loch Killin, Wren, Wild Goose* and *Starling*
06.08.1944	Attacked *U-736* and *U-385*
09.1944	Londonderry area
11.1944	Belfast for hull stiffening
27.02.1945	Sank *U-1018* and shared in destruction of *U-327*
06.05.1945	Reoccupation of Norway and visited Kristiansand
07.1945	Hamburg
Late 1945	Training in Londonderry
12.1945	Operation Deadlight. Destruction of captured German U-boats
18.03.1946	Refit at Devonport
06.1946	Recommissioned into 4th Escort Flotilla at Londonderry
04.1952	Reduced to reserve at Portsmouth
1954	Towed to Barry in Wales to join reserve ships there
02.1955	Towed to Portsmouth
21.06.1955	Recommissioned
08.1955	Invergordon
03.10.1955	Oslo
09.11.1955	Sailed for Middle East
03.1956	Transported Archbishop Makarios to Maldives for detention
17.03.1956	Refit at Colombo
02.05.1956	Sailed for Trincomalee, Cochin, Bombay and Karachi
06.07.1956	Went to aid of merchantman SS *Corabank*
15.09.1956	Basra
05.10.1956	Mombasa
08.10.1956	Portsmouth for refit
05.12.1956	Recommissioned
18.02.1957	Refit completed

08.04.1957	HRH Prince Michael of Kent onboard
17.05.1957	Sailed for Middle East via the Cape of Good Hope
21.06.1957	Das es Salaam with cruiser *Ceylon*
07.1957	At Basra. Ship quarantined due to Asian flu outbreak
08.1957	Civil unrest in Bahrain. RM detachment landed
10.1957	Went to aid of merchantman SS *Adai* off Oman
12.1957	Civil unrest in Oman. RM detachment landed
01.1958	Visited Djibouti and Berbera
01.1958	Transported pair of prized heifers to Karachi
03.1958	Went to aid of Norwegian *Skaubryn* on fire in Indian Ocean
14.05.1958	Portsmouth for refit
06.08.1958	Refit completed
17.11.1958	Sailed for Persian Gulf
06.1959	Faulty prop shaft required repairs in United Kingdom
09.09.1959	Portsmouth for repairs and refit
19.01.1960	Recommissioned
19.03.1960	Fishery Patrol off Iceland
10.05.1960	Sailed for Middle East
02.06.1960	At Perim for repairs to fractured pipes
07.06.1960	Dhow Patrol in Persian Gulf
04.08.1960	Port main bearing failed leaving ship with only one propeller
10.1960	Exercise MIDLINK III at Karachi
11.1960	Visited Bombay, Cochin and Karachi
01.1961	Exercise Aspex 7
17.01.1961	Enthronement of new ruler of Dubai
10.04.1961	At Tobruk for 20th anniversary of WW2 siege
27.04.1961	Portsmouth
24.05.1961	Long refit started at Chatham Dockyard
26.06.1962	Recommissioned for service in Far East
08.10.1962	Sailed from United Kingdom
08.11.1962	Colombo
11.1962	Civil unrest on Maldives and Diego Garcia
07.12.1962	Singapore for Konfrontasi operations in Borneo
01.02.1963	First Borneo Patrol
04.1963	Visited Guam and Hong Kong
09.05.1963	Sailed for Japan. Visited Mogi, Marzuru and Muroran
28.05.1963	Sailed for second Borneo Patrol
28.10.1963	Singapore for refit
18.11.1963	Recommissioned into 3rd Frigate Squadron
29.01.1964	Refit completed
28.02.1964	Exercise JET64
04.1964	Guardship at Gan and also visited Mombasa
05.1964	Exercised with *Centaur* and *Cavendish*
06.1964	Returned to Persian Gulf
26.08.1964	Sailed for Bombay for repairs to machinery

16.09.1964	Continuing mechanical problems were addressed at Singapore
13.12.1964	Sailed for Hong Kong
02.01.1965	Third Borneo Patrol
04.02.1965	Recommissioned at Singapore
13.03.1965	Sailed for Hong Kong
03.1965	Fourth Borneo Patrol
04.05.1965	Visited Bangkok
13.05.1965	Hong Kong
31.05.1965	Singapore for a four month refit
05.09.1965	Sea trials and then recommissioned into 26th Escort Squadron
07.10.1965	Sailed for Hong Kong
12.1965	Fifth Borneo Patrol
29.01.1966	Singapore for refit
04.1966	Refit completed
18.02.1967	Visited Penang
29.04.1967	Hong Kong
06.05.1967	Visited Simizu, Yokohama, Shiogama, Qninato and Hakodate
25.07.1967	Final visit to Hong Kong
09.08.1967	Sailed on first leg to United Kingdom via Singapore
08.1967	Routed home via Gan, Mauritius and Simonstown
04.10.1967	Gibraltar
11.10.1967	Portsmouth to pay off
1968	Used to test new Seawolf missile system
05.11.1968	Broke free of moorings in Luce Bay during storm. Recovered and towed back to Pembroke where she was, due to damage sustained, declared unsuitable for further trials.
28.05.1970	Arrived Fasland under tow for breaking up by Metal Industries

HMS LOCH FYNE

The Loch class, Loch Fyne *is seen here, retained the open bridge until all of the class passed from service. The open bridge, it was thought, offered much better all round vision for the commander.*　　(Crown Copyright/MoD)

On 8 December 1943 the first steel for *Loch Fyne* was laid down at Burntisland Shipbuilding and construction progressed swiftly to the launching stage. The frigate was duly named and sent into the water on 24 May 1944. Final fitting out was completed by the 9th November. Lieutenant Commander H H D MacKillican RNR was appointed as *Loch Fyne*'s first commanding officer and he took her through her initial sea trials programme; once completed the frigate joined the 18th Escort Group at Tobermory on 14 November.

Loch Fyne, like many of the Loch class, suffered from a lack of stiffness in heavy seas and it was decided to add extra stiffness to *Loch Fyne* immediately the work being carried out at Dunstaffnage near the Scottish town of Oban from 4 December. The modifications were completed just before Christmas and on

22 December *Loch Fyne* sailed for her first operational patrol between the United Kingdom and Gibraltar.

The New Year of 1945 saw *Loch Fyne* continuing her escort protection duties with the 18th and 22nd Escort Groups before transferring to Force 38 on February 27 in the North Atlantic. The following month *Loch Fyne* made a series of anti-submarine patrols but without success. In April the frigate operated in the English Channel and also visited Cherbourg.

The frigate sailed North at the end of the month for a boiler clean on the Clyde arriving there on 29 April. Once the boiler work had been completed the frigate continued northwards and participated in the re-occupation of Norway based out of Scapa Flow.

Loch Fyne was operating in the frozen Norwegian

Sea when news reached the ship that she had been designated for service in the Far East. Before that, however, the frigate's attention was focussed on the demands of Operation Deadlight: the destruction of captured German U-boats. She visited Trondheim and shepherded a number of U-boats back to Loch Ryan in Scotland for eventual sinking in deep water. On the return passage members of the ships company sailed onboard the German U-boats in company with HM ships *Keats* and *Kempthorne*. The ships leaving the Norwegian port on 29 May.

Upon her arrival in British waters *Loch Fyne* continued onto Milford Haven where she was taken into dockyard hands at Pembroke Dock for a refit to enable her to serve in the Far East. *Loch Fyne* was fitted with extra 20mm guns as a defence against determined Japanese aerial attack and also improved air conditioning facilities.

The last day of the month saw *Loch Fyne* sail around the Welsh coastline to Cardiff where leave was granted to the crew. From Cardiff the frigate operated in the Bristol Channel until 11 August when she headed south to Gibraltar. At the helm was her new commanding officer, Lieutenant Commander R F J Maberley RNR.

From Gibraltar the frigate crossed the Mediterranean and transited the Red Sea. A brief stop was made at Aden to refuel before *Loch Fyne* continued onto Colombo where she arrived on 24 September.

With the end of the war the frigates main duties were policing the region including visits to Cochin and Colombo and also on Air Sea Rescue missions.

Loch Fyne continued this role until nominated for return to the United Kingdom in February 1946. In late February she sailed from her base at Karachi for the harbour at Trincomalee and from there on the 20 March sailed for Great Britain.

Loch Fyne arrived back at Portsmouth in April where she was quickly de-stored and prepared for the reserve fleet where she would spend the next four years.

In April 1950 the ship was taken in hand by dockyard workers at Portsmouth to prepare the ship for further service in the 6th Frigate Flotilla. The refit lasted until the end of the year during which time the ship became a Chatham manned ship. In October the first of the new complement of men joined *Loch Fyne* and assisted in bringing the frigate back to life. The following month *Loch Fyne* started a lengthy series of post refit trials in the harbour and in December sea trials in the English Channel.

In January 1951 the frigate recommissioned with Commander C P McN Hart DSC in command. During the course of her sea trials the frigate was damaged with a depth charge exploded prematurely. The repairs were carried out at Portsmouth and took until the end of March to complete.

With the repairs completed *Loch Fyne* carried out further weapons trials with the rest of the flotilla off Portland before visiting the Cornish port of Falmouth for a few days. Falmouth proved to be one of the most popular runs ashore and the local public houses apparently did good trade during the frigates stay.

When word reached *Loch Fyne* of the loss of the submarine *Affray* somewhere in the English Channel the frigate was one of the large fleet of ships assembled to search for the submarine.

On 14 June the final resting place of the submarine had been discovered by the diving support ship *Reclaim* and *Loch Fyne* was given the duty of being wreck guardship. She remained over the wreck site for some time before being released to resume her previously planned programme of visits that included a port of call to Milford Haven. Summer leave was granted to the crew upon her return to Chatham Dockyard.

August was spent at Chatham while the following month she deployed to Portland for a series of weapons trials. A series of storms in September saw the frigate struggle to take passage to Londonderry. So bad, in fact, were the storms that *Loch Fyne* returned to Portland to ride out them out. Sadly tragedy struck when the frigate was mooring. Normal practice when mooring was to launch a whaler with a crew to attach the ships lines to the mooring buoy but due to the adverse weather conditions the crew of the mooring whaler were at great risk and Petty Officer Woods died trying to help them. When the storm abated *Loch Fyne* sailed to Londonderry for Home Fleet anti-submarine training.

In November *Loch Fyne* sailed into Gibraltar together with other units of the Home Fleet where the ships company enjoyed some leave. Upon their return onboard *Loch Fyne* slipped and returned to Chatham Dockyard for seasonal leave to be taken.

The first few months of 1952 saw the frigate exercising with the Home Fleet but news reached the ship that she would be reduced to reserve status in March. In February, however, *Loch Fyne* visited Gibraltar, Nice and Malta. Whilst off Nice *Loch Fyne* fought her way through heavy seas and strong winds and off Malta the frigate escorted five motor fishing vessels on passage to the United Kingdom.

Upon *Loch Fyne*'s arrival at Chatham Dockyard she was soon paid off into reserve with the intention to modernise the warship for further service. *Loch Fyne* was laid up until April 1953 when she was towed from Kent to the Henderson shipyard in Glasgow for her modernisation to commence.

The frigate was in refit until June 1954 when *Loch Fyne* commenced her harbour trials before commissioning for sea trials in the Clyde areas. With machinery trials complete *Loch Fyne*'s weapons trials took place off Portland. Upon completion *Loch Fyne* sailed north via the Irish Sea for Henderson's shipyard for preparations to be made prior to another period spent in reserve at Devonport from January 1955.

Finally, in July, *Loch Fyne* was towed from Devonport to Southampton to commence another refit to equip the ship for service in the Middle East. The frigate also changed home port from Chatham to Devonport. On Valentine's Day 1956 *Loch Fyne* recommissioned at Southampton under the command of Captain H S Baker who worked the ship up at Portland through February and March. Foreign service leave was granted to the ships company in preparation for her planned extended deployment, which started in May when *Loch Fyne* sailed from Plymouth

HMS Loch Fyne *spent most of her career East of Suez in the Persian Gulf where she undertook frequent showing the flag missions and dhow patrols intercepting local vessels for inspections.* (Crown Copyright/MoD)

for the Middle East via Gibraltar and Aden.

By June the frigate was at Bahrain and started her preparations for the usual pattern of patrols in the Gulf. The first of these started the following month in the southern region of the Persian Gulf and off the coastline of Oman. Whilst some distance offshore of Oman *Loch Fyne* received a distress call from the Swedish oil tanker MV *Julius* on 8 July, which had suffered a series of engine defects that had left the ship without power. MV *Julius* had successfully anchored and upon arrival the British warship sent over a team of engineers to assist in repairing the merchantman's machinery. After initially towing the MV *Julius* engine power was restored but only for a very slow speed. *Loch Fyne* stayed in convoy with the Swedish vessel but the British frigate received another distress call and had to break company and made at speed for second distress call from the American vessel SS *Steel Worker*.

Onboard the SS *Steel Worker* an officer had abdominal pains and needed medical treatment. He was transferred to the frigate who took him to hospital at Bahrain. The officers and men of *Loch Fyne* must have felt that their Samaritan work was over but when the repairs to the MV *Julius* broke down again they rushed to be with the merchantman once again taking her in tow into Bahrain.

By August *Loch Fyne* was back on Dhow patrol and during this time intercepted a number of the vessels to search for illegal cargoes or arms. She also paid visits to Ra-al-Khaimar and Sharjah. In the autumn the frigate returned to the Northern Gulf and exercised with the Iranian Navy before spending the winter months off Bahrain. By December *Loch Fyne* was to be found off the Batina coast and also off Aden.

1957 started with a return journey to Bahrain where on 16 January she assisted the Norwegian flagged oil tanker *Gilda*, which had run aground off the Iranian coastline. *Loch Fyne*'s ship company had attached tow lines to the stricken ship and attempted to pull her clear. The initial attempts met with little success until the cargo and water ballast of the *Gilda* had been jettisoned.

The dhow patrols continued for *Loch Fyne* and in March they proved to be successful when a German

yacht was seized and found to be carrying a cargo of explosives whilst off Perim Island. After this success the frigate made for the Seychelles as the first stop on her return journey to the United Kingdom. With the Suez Canal closed the frigate would have to make the long voyage round the Cape but this did afford the ships company the opportunity to visit a number of ports rarely visited by Royal Navy vessels in recent years.

Loch Fyne finally arrived at Devonport in June and was soon in dockyard hands for a short refit, which was completed by the end of July. She re-commissioned into service on 30 July under the command of Captain B S Pengelly DSC RN. She also embarked a detachment of Royal Marines whose role would be to board suspicious vessels in the Gulf upon their return to the Middle East.

On 7 September 1957 *Loch Fyne* was recommissioned at a formal commissioning ceremony at Devonport. Six days later the frigate was off Portland at the start of her work up. Part of this was exercising the embarked Royal Marines when the left the ship to invade Portland island. The three day Exercise Standfirm occupied the ship from 24 September before completing her work up period on 8 October. The next day *Loch Fyne* returned to her berth within Devonport and was visited by Flag Officer Flotillas - Home Fleet.

Loch Fyne next put to sea for Londonderry where in the stormy Northern Irish waters she practiced the skills and techniques necessary to combat the ever more complex tactics being employed by submarines. This anti-submarine exercise was concluded on 18 October and two days later it was a chance to reacquaint the ship with her namesake Scottish loch. The frigate arrived at Ardrishaig on *Loch Fyne* for a four day stay with the locals.

Next on the agenda was a return to Devonport where General Service Leave was granted to the ships company ahead of the planned deployment to the Middle East. Finally on 20 November *Loch Fyne* sailed from Plymouth and made for the Persian Gulf via Gibraltar, Malta, Port Said and Aden where she topped up with fuel. The frigates next port of call was on 18 December when she pulled into Socotra before con-

tinuing onto Muscat on 20 December. After a five day patrol of searching for gun running dhows *Loch Fyne* arrived at uninhabited desert island of Daimaniyat for Christmas Day. *Loch Fyne* contested that she was the only warship in peacetime and wartime to spend Christmas on a desert island. With the festivities over the ship continued her journey onto Khor Kuwait where she relieved *Loch Alvie*, which in turn sailed for home. The closing days of December saw the British warship fuel at Bahrain before leaving on 3 January 1958 on another patrol off Batinah.

After landing an interpreter at Sur *Loch Fyne* patrolled around 20 miles of coastline before returning to Sur where the ship stayed all day and night fixing a cracked main bearing on one of the ships big ends. Later in the day the interpreter was re-embarked along with numerous Arab VIPs who were taken to sea to witness for themselves the Royal Navy's gunnery skills. At the same time a PO Yeoman became seriously ill with heart trouble. Upon the ships arrival at Bahrain he was taken off the ship and transferred to the Royal Naval Hospital at HMS *Jufair*. Whilst alongside Sitra oiling jetty fresh supplies of oil, water and food were embarked into the frigate. Once loaded, the ship slipped to Bahrain anchorage where she was visited on 14 January by C-in-C East Indies Vice Admiral H W Biggs CB DSO.

Four days later the ship sailed for Khor Kuwait arriving within twenty four hours and met sister ship *Loch Ruthven*. By the end of January *Loch Fyne* would have paid official and courtesy calls upon Muscat and Sur before being relieved by Loch Fada on 22 January. This allowed *Loch Fyne* to return to Bahrain and secure on *Loch Ruthven* the next day. Three days were spent alongside before sailing at 1030 on the 26 having first embarked Political Resident Persian Gulf Sir Bernard Burrows KCMG and Lady Burrows for a visit to Das and Abu Dhabi.

On the morning of 27 January the ship arrived at the floating oil rig off Das before proceeding onto Das itself. Many amongst the ships company managed to get ashore to enjoy the splendid hospitality and fabulous food on offer by the local population despite the fact that the city was in mourning over the death of their ruler. After two days *Loch Fyne* returned to sea

bound for Dubai early in the morning at 0400. The passage was marked by numerous swordfish jumping out of the water as the ship sailed along. At Dubai the ship anchored at 1430 and remained in the vicinity for the next couple of days. On 30 January *Loch Fyne* proceeded down Persian coast on tanker route before starting a Batunah patrol off Muscat the next day.

The final day of the month also saw one crewmember struck down with a suspected appendicitis. Full speed was ordered for Muscat where the patient was whisked away by a waiting RAF plane. After five hours at Muscat, *Loch Fyne* set sail again at 1800 bound for Christmas Isle where she anchored on 2 February at 2300. She was underway again by 0800 the following morning and started on a routine patrol. On the 3rd the frigate was operating off Khor Kuwait and rendezvoused with sister ship *Loch Ruthven* and operated with her for the entire day before continuing onto Bahrain. The passage was noted for the rough sea conditions encountered but by 1330 on 6 February the frigate let go her anchor having first refuelled at Sitra oiling jetty.

After a night at anchor *Loch Fyne* slipped and made the short passage to Bandar Markur. The passage was again marked by an unsettled sea but the ships company were pleased to find that free beer had been laid on for the two day stay in the Persian oil town. On the 10th February she proceeded down river for Bandar Shapur and then onto the mouth of the Euphrates. Over the course of the next two days the British warship ventured further inland eventually arriving at Margil on 13 February and secured alongside the jetty at the RAF Camp there.

Terry Soar, a stoker on *Loch Fyne* recalls the ships movements. "*Left Margil bound for Sitra and patrol. We refuelled then patrol all day on the 17th en route for Little Quoin. Arrived and repaired a diesel before leaving at 0730 for Muscat and patrol. Got to Muscat at 0700 on the 20th and sailed again at 1800 for patrol. On the morning of the 21st exercised radar gun firing and closing ship down to ABCD state 1A gastight. In the afternoon landed sports teams on island. Sailed at 1700 and conducted night encounter exercise with* Loch Fada - *patrol all night. 22nd on patrol off Trucial Oman and on 23rd anchored in*

Muscat Harbour for mail - leave 1400 and patrol up coast. Arrived off Dibba on 24th and left at 1230. On patrol all day 25th laying off coast all morning for dhows. On 26th refuelled from RFA Wave Premier *and then proceeded to Muscat.*

Left Muscat 1000 on 3rd and refuelled from RFA Wave Premier *in company with* Loch Fada *and* Loch Ruthven. *Transferred gear from* Loch Fada *and then anchored off Dimaniyat for 48 hours stand off.*

Sailed 1330 on 5th for patrol; called at Muscat for 1 hour and left again. We called at a small place to board dhow on the 6th. At sea all day 7th and had a suspicious dhow alongside 2300 - 2359. On patrol all day 8th. Laid to from 2200 - 0600 off coast. We arrived at Muscat 1000 on 9th - Divisions in No6's. Sail at 1700, patrol all night at slow ahead. On 10th ordered to Doha at 15 knots as trouble us flaring up there. On 11th trouble is over and we are redirected to Bahrain where we stay until 17th fixing the evaporators. We left for Bayanh coast at 1000 on 17th. Exercise at sea with Venoms on the 18th. Anchored at Khor Kuwait for fix condensers - work finished on

19th. Remain at Khor Kuwait all night and met Loch Ruthven *at 1000 on 20th."*

The frigate transferred stores from sister ship *Loch Ruthven* before leaving Khor Kuwait at midday on 20 March and resumed her patrol.

The frigate anchored for two hours off Christmas Isles on 21 March before again resuming her patrols and rendezvousing with sister ship *Loch Ruthven* for the transfer of the all important mail just ahead of visiting Muscat. After further ports of call to Dimaniyat, the warship returned to Muscat in company with *Loch Fada* and *Loch Killisport* on 29 March. Following the visit *Loch Fada* sailed for Mombasa, *Loch Killisport* to Bahrain and *Loch Fyne* remained at Muscat until 2 April when the frigate once again resumed her patrol duties.

Information is received that the leader of the bandits, a man called Talib, is on the move and *Loch Fyne* is sent to try and locate him, with sadly no success. The ship returns to Muscat on 6 April.

She was back at sea six days later for a short patrol. By 17 April she along with *Loch Killisport, Loch*

HMS Loch Fyne *seen departing Gibraltar flying her paying off pennant. In the background is the aircraft carrier* Ark Royal *alongside the South Mole.*
(Crown Copyright/MoD)

Ruthven and RFA *Wave Premier* took part in a series of manoeuvres that also saw the men of the frigate manhandle three months supplies of stores from the supply ship.

On 16 April the body of Corporal Hodges, who had been killed on active service, was brought onboard *Loch Fyne*. The ship sailed the following morning at 0630; flags were at half mast as the Corporal's body was committed to the deep two hours later. Following the funeral the frigate continued on her assigned patrol duties. Intelligence had indicated that an arms shipment for the bandits was en route. The next few days would prove to be hectic ones with refuelling from RFA *Wave King* and patrols with *Loch Killisport* taking up most of the time. On 29 April news reached the ship that a ship had run aground and best speed was made to the scene, on one boiler as the other had been taken off line to be rebricked. As *Loch Fyne* neared the incident, news was received that the merchantman had managed to refloat herself without assistance. *Loch Fyne* continued onto her berth at Sitra.

On 6 May after sailing and transferring mail to *Loch Killisport*, *Loch Fyne* continued on to Ceylon, mooring to buoys in the harbour for a short while until preparations had been completed to receive the frigate in the dry dock at Diyatalawa. *Loch Fyne* would spend most of the month in dry dock being repaired and repainted until she was refloated on 25 May.

At 0800 on 27 May *Loch Fyne* sailed for Trincomalee for exercises with the Indian and Pakistani Navies that included the former British cruisers *Mysore* and *Delhi*. The first set of exercises continued 13 June when all the crews were given two days rest. On 16 June it was back to sea to take part in Exercise Foamite, which saw the ships encounter stormy seas brought on by the strong south westerly monsoon winds. Amongst the ships taking part were the carrier *Bulwark*, the cruiser *Newfoundland* and *Cavalier* and *Ulysses*. The poor weather made the exercises hard work for the various ships companies but particularly so for small ships such as *Loch Fyne*. Finally on 26 June the exercises were completed and *Loch Fyne* spent three quiet days at Trincomalee.

On 1 July the frigate sailed for Bahrain and headed into stormy seas that slackened considerably as *Loch Fyne* approached the Persian Gulf. Tension in the Gulf was at fever pitch on 14 July following the assassination of the Crown Prince of Iraq and the disappearance of the King and Prime Minister. *Loch Fyne* is ordered to proceed, at best speed, to Iraq to ensure the safety of any British nationals in the country. She arrived at Shatt al Arab and anchored. Nearby the supply ship RFA *Wave Commander* and the American frigate USS *Greenwich Bay* were also at anchor.

On 1 August *Loch Killisport* relieved her sister ship and *Loch Fyne* returned to Bahrain securing alongside the newly arrived *Loch Insh*. She would remain there for a fortnight. On 14 August she took on board supplies from the supply ship RFA *Fort Charlotte* before carrying out another anti-piracy patrol that finished on 9 September when she returned to her berth at Sitra having been relieved by *Loch Alvie*.

Loch Fyne proceeded to sea on 15 September bound for Mombasa flying her paying off pennant as she headed out of port. King Neptune and his court arrived onboard the frigate on 24 when she crossed the Equator and the traditional Navy custom was observed with everyone onboard receiving a dunking, shave and brought up before King Neptune's Court on usually trumped up charges. Two days later she arrived at Mombasa and anchored in the harbour.

On 3 October the ship embarked Mr John Profumo MP OBE, the under secretary of State for the Colonies, and sailed for the Seychelles, where the frigate arrived four days later. *Loch Fyne* remained at anchor in Port Victoria, Mahe, until leaving for Aden on 14 October. The frigate was routed through Aden and Aquaba in Jordan where she refuelled from RFA *Wave Regent* on 25 October. The next day two coastal minesweepers, *Houghton* and *Dartington,* tied up alongside the frigate. The warship remained at Aquaba until 2 November. During her time in port the ships company enjoyed a movie night with screenings of the films 'Picnic', 'Richard III' and 'Cockleshell Heroes', whilst on 2 November King Hussein of Jordan visited the ship during the forenoon as British troops withdraw from the country. A 21-gun salute was fired and the cruiser *Ceylon* left at 1200 followed by LCT's bound for Kenya. *Loch Fyne* and the minesweepers were the last British warships to leave Jordan.

Loch Fyne proceeded up the Suez Canal and made for Great Britain via Malta and Gibraltar before finally anchoring in Plymouth Sound at 2359 on 17 November. After customs officials had done their work in the early morning of the 18th November, the ship was prepared for a ceremonial entry into harbour. *Loch Fyne* got underway at 1020 and fired a 15-gun salute to the Admiral before berthing alongside 6 Wharf at Devonport at 1100. The frigates entry had been made all the more memorable because two members of the ships company, Chief Shipwright E L Shaw and Able Seaman B Olsen were dressed as two Arabs and a camel.

Loch Fyne remained in refit at Devonport until 27 January 1959 when she re-commissioned under the command of Commander C R Barratt. Finishing touches to the works package continued until March when the frigate started her trials programme off Portland and Plymouth. Once cleared for foreign-service duty the ship sailed in June for the Middle East where she arrived the following month and quickly assumed the role of dhow patrols.

July also saw the frigate taking part in Exercise Mad Dog, an exercise designed to test the defences of the oil fields at Dubai. The remainder of the summer was spent on patrol in the Gulf before sailing for Karachi in October for a routine docking period. When the work was completed the opportunity was taken to exercise with the local Pakistani naval units before returning to the Gulf.

1960 started with a series of visits to Banda Masnur and towards the end of the month to the Indian port of Bombay where the frigate was to take part in the annual Exercise Jet. This multinational exercise took place with Indian, British and Pakistani warships over a wide stretch of the Indian Ocean and tested all the ships abilities with interoperability, anti-submarine, anti-surface and gunnery routines. The exercise ended in March and *Loch Fyne* sailed for Trincomalee and then onto the Seychelles Island chain. These were the first two stops en route home to the United Kingdom with further stops arranged at Mombasa and Aden.

On 8 April 1960 *Loch Fyne* arrived back at Devonport having sailed via Mombasa, Aden and the Red Sea. A few days later she took passage to Rosyth

Dockyard where she was taken in hand for a short refit that lasted until September. *Loch Fyne* re-commissioned on 15 September for service with the 9th Frigate Flotilla under the command of Commander P J H Shevlin. The commissioning ceremony was conducted by the Reverend J F Walmsley MA, and Vice Admiral R H Wright, CB, DSC.

After working up around Portland *Loch Fyne* visited Cherbourg in October for a non official visit. On 3 November the frigate arrived at Portsmouth Dockyard and once secured alongside foreign-service leave was granted to the crew. Those remaining onboard were tasked with making repairs to the ship.

Just prior to departure for the Middle East the crew busied themselves storing ship. One unusual item loaded was an Army Officers yacht that would be unloaded when *Loch Fyne* reached Aden.

On a cold 23 November *Loch Fyne* slipped from alongside and with the men lining the ships sides sailed down Portsmouth harbour. She passed the famous Round Tower and headed out into the English Channel en route to Aden.

The frigate stopped at Malta on 3 December to refuel and to grant some limited shore leave. Unfortunately for one Able Seaman leave was cut short when he was seriously injured in a road traffic accident and had to be hospitalised. *Loch Fyne* sailed on without her injured crewman arriving at Aden on 16 December. There the yacht and other Army supplies were offloaded and extra fuel and food was taken onboard. After twenty four hours at Aden, *Loch Fyne* sailed for her first dhow patrol of the deployment. Four days later news reached the ship that the injured sailor at Malta had died from his injuries. Two days later the ship arrived at Bahrain in time for Christmas.

Loch Fyne put to sea on 10 January 1961 for an anti-submarine exercise but found a fault in her sonar equipment that required repairs at Karachi. On 11 January the frigate left the exercises in the southern Gulf and set course for Karachi.

After a two day passage *Loch Fyne* was docked at Karachi for a replacement sonar dome to be fitted. The repairs took six days to complete. On 19 January the British frigate sailed back to the Persian Gulf having first stood by on air sea rescue duties for a Royal

Flight to Delhi with HM Queen Elizabeth II onboard. The ship had sailed with some Somali ratings onboard that were kept under guard suspected of gold smuggling. The men were being transported to Bahrain to face trial. They were disembarked upon arrival on the 23rd. After five days alongside the ship resumed her dhow patrols but time was also found for visits to Kuwait and Bahrain in early February.

On 22 February the ship sailed for anti-aircraft exercises before arriving at Aden six days later. At Aden *Loch Fyne* joined with a large number of Royal Navy warships for a major naval exercise called Roulade. Central to the exercise was the assault carrier *Bulwark*. The exercises lasted for nine days until 10 March. After a four day break at Aden *Loch Fyne*'s crew were once again being exercised in Fleet Exercise Sea Sheik where she operated as part of the escort for the aircraft carrier *Victorious*. After four days of hard work the exercise finished once again at Aden. After the high adrenalin rush of the exercises spread over a fortnight *Loch Fyne* returned to dhow patrols plus a visit to Muscat on 22 March.

On 4 April *Loch Fyne* rendezvoused with sister ships *Loch Alvie* and *Loch Ruthven* for a series of exercises. Onboard the frigate was a number of Army personnel who were onboard to gain experience of operating with the Royal Navy and to learn some of their procedures. Four days into the group exercises the trio of British ships were ordered to assist in rescue operations of the passenger ship MV *Dora* which was on fire 250 miles west of the British frigates.

Upon arrival the next day, the frigates fought the fire with their hoses and later landed a boarding party onboard. *Loch Fyne* then towed the drifting hulk away from shallow waters until the tow was transferred to the tug *Ocean Salvor* on 10 April.

During the tow MV *Dora* finally succumbed and sank. The death toll on the merchant ship was later ascertained to be 238 dead.

The three British frigates resumed the exercises that were completed on 14 April when they returned to Bahrain. *Loch Fyne*, however, hit the fuelling jetty at Sitra Depot causing some damage. Once secure the safe from MV *Dora* was handed over to the lost ships' owners. After a few days alongside *Loch Fyne* sailed independently on 24 April for a dhow patrol in the coastal waters off Qatar.

Loch Fyne made an unofficial visit to Mina-al-Ahmadi in Kuwait three days later before returning to Bahrain on 2 May for a fortnight long maintenance period. On 14 May she started a short patrol that culminated in a brief visit to Doha before once again returning to her base of Bahrain on 17 May.

On 18 May *Loch Fyne* and sister ship *Loch Ruthven* ventured to sea for the latter's Sea Inspection before going on to land a party of men at Jebel Dhanna in Abu Dhabi with the aim of the removal of ordnance and explosives from a firing range at the site of a future oil production plant. The wok was very dangerous and amongst the party were experts in the clearance of such explosive devices. With the men ashore there was little need for the frigates to remain nearby and after five days at Jebel Dhanna, *Loch Fyne* resumed her journey on 28 May and went onto pay a port of call to Sharjah.

On 2 June *Loch Fyne* returned to pick up the men at Jebel Dharra and sailed upon their return to the ship to Abadan. En route the Flag Officer Middle East was embarked for a flag visit in company with sister ship *Loch Alvie*.

The ships company manned the ships sides as the frigate arrived at Abadan on 8 June and three days later on the occasion of the Queen's Birthday Royal Marines and seamen were landed to parade through the city. Later the same day the frigate sailed bound for Bahrain.

Late June was given over to a routine docking in Karachi but after the frigate had arrived on 18 June the refit was cancelled with immediate effect and the ship recalled to the Gulf. The reason soon became apparent with the forming of Task Force 317 designed to defend Kuwait from an invasion from neighbouring Iraq to the north. Britain had promised to defend Kuwait from any such attack and *Loch Fyne* was part of a large naval presence quickly assembled in the Gulf for the protection of Kuwait.

Loch Fyne loaded live ammunition at Bahrain before joining the Task Force off Kuwait on 5 July for Operation Vantage. *Loch Fyne*'s role was to seek out and intercept any Iraqi naval vessels trying to make

for the Kuwaiti coastline. The tension lasted the whole of July and into early August but when the frigate was finally released from Operation Vantage duties she was dispatched to Karachi to resume her previously planned programme and the interrupted refit.

On 9 August with the refit completed in quick time *Loch Fyne* was once again allocated to Task Force 317 but three days later was relieved by sister ship *Loch Insh*. Operation Vantage came to an end on 14 August after an international agreement was reached over the dispute.

If anything the rest of the year was a lot quieter for *Loch Fyne* with the usual flotilla duties and dhow patrols together with a number of exercises and on 15 September the frigate's Sea Inspection at Bahrain.

Having successfully passed this test the British warship sailed for a tour of East Africa with visits paid to Zanzibar and Mombasa. At the latter she collected the minesweeper *Bassingham* and took her in tow. The minesweeper was being relocated to Malta and a tow from a frigate saved on fuel. The two ships arrived at Aden on 16 October, but *Loch Fyne* had an unfortunate incident with the fuelling buoy when she struck it.

After three days at Aden, *Loch Fyne* set sail for the Red Sea and Suez Canal.

On 6 November *Loch Fyne* arrived at Malta and handed over the minesweeper *Bassingham*. After five days on the island the frigate continued her journey back to the United Kingdom via Gibraltar. On 6 December *Loch Fyne* took passage from Gibraltar to Plymouth where she arrived four days later for a short refit. *Loch Fyne* re-commissioned under the command of Commander P R O Kimm on 18 January although the refit was not completed until March 1962. In March and April the frigate carried out her post refit trials off Plymouth and Portland.

On 11 May the work up was complete and *Loch Fyne* started her final deployment when she sailed from Portsmouth on 19 May. The passage to the Middle East was eventful with strong winds and heavy seas off Gibraltar and a machinery malfunction at Malta. The frigate limped into dock at Malta on 28 May and remained there until the last day of the month when she resumed her passage to Aden via the

Suez Canal. On 9 June she arrived at Aden and two days later after a lot of spit and polish from the ships company the Crown Prince of Ethiopia was welcomed onboard the British ship. The next day *Loch Fyne* sailed for Bahrain where on the 18th she joined sister ships *Loch Lomond* and *Loch Ruthven*. On 23 June the trio undertook an exercise FOMEX12 that continued until 4 July when the ship returned to Bahrain.

The following day the ship sailed to Muscat where the Captain was presented with a silver coffee pot by the Sultan. *Loch Fyne* remained at the historic city for four days before resuming her journey to Bahrain. En route the opportunity was taken to exercise with some of the Sultan's armed forces and particularly with aircraft from his air force.

Upon her arrival at Bahrain the ship welcomed onboard the 2nd Sea Lord for a brief visit who told the captain of the ships planned deployment on the dhow patrols in the Southern Gulf. *Loch Fyne* sailed five days later on the 18 July and remained on this necessary but boring task until the 30 July. The embarked Royal Marines were buoyed by the prospect of a major amphibious exercise at the beginning of August called AWEX8.

The frigate together with a number of other Royal Navy warships practised the skills to get a heavily armed but mobile force of Marines ashore as quickly as possible over the course of four days. On 5 August *Loch Fyne* was back alongside in Bahrain.

The rest was only temporary as after two days the ship was once again at sea on her next dhow patrol which also included a visit to Abu Dhabi. The frigate continued in this fashion for much of the summer. Only in September did the routine change with visits to Tumb and Bu Musa in early September and exercises in the waters off Bahrain to hone the skills of the crew in anti-submarine and anti aircraft warfare.

These were but a prelude to a much larger exercise entitled Exercise Duffel that saw *Loch Fyne* operating with the assault carrier *Bulwark*, the destroyer *Carysfort* and sister ship *Loch Ruthven*. The exercises started on 24 September and were completed three days later with a return to Bahrain with her sister ship. October also saw the frigate undertaking a significant amount of training starting from the 1st of the month.

Ten days later a large scale anti submarine exercise saw three Loch class vessels, *Loch Ruthven*, *Loch Alvie* and *Loch Fyne* determined to locate the submarine *Taciturn*.

On 13 October the frigate sailed independently to Karachi for a routine docking period which lasted until 3 November. Upon completion she sailed back to join the rest of the fleet for exercise Midlink V that ended off the coast of Bahrain where she arrived on 29 November in company with the submarine Andrew. The following month saw participation in another major exercise given the name ASWEX II and at the end of this event the frigate paid a courtesy call to the Iranian naval base at Bandar Abbas on the 8 December.

Four days later she sailed for a survey tasking to Ras-al-Khamai and also to carry out another dhow patrol in the region. During this period *Loch Fyne* paid calls to Dubai and Qatar before returning to Bahrain in time for Christmas to be celebrated.

Bahrain traditionally stages an annual Ruler of Bahrain parade on the 1st January and in 1963 *Loch Fyne* was requested to provide a guard of honour. The men marched through the streets on the traditional route used for hundreds of years. Eight days later *Loch Fyne* herself slipped to sea and resumed her dhow patrols together with a series of naval exercises and visits. Amongst the interesting places called upon were Umm Said, Dalma and Yaz.

After a maintenance period at Bahrain, the British frigate sailed in February for the Annual Sea Inspection carried out by the Flag Officer Persian Gulf. On Valentine's Day having successfully completed the inspection the ship visited Yaz Island to rest and recuperation.

On 18 February *Loch Fyne* together with other units of the flotilla joined the amphibious warfare squadron and undertook a number of staged landings of beaches to hone the Royal Marines skills. With the training completed the frigate sailed back once again to Bahrain on 21 February. She stayed only long enough to refuel and replenish the stores before sailing the next day bound for Bombay. After six days steaming she arrived at the bustling metropolis. The sights and sounds of the city were staggering to many onboard who had never visited Bombay. Many of the ships company sampled local food and drink and went sightseeing during the visit. Meanwhile Flag Officer Middle East had joined ship for an official visit to the chief of the Indian Navy.

Loch Fyne's final deployment was proving to be an eventful one. In March after a four day dhow patrol the frigate visited Hallaniya Island in the Kuria Maria Group of islands. She followed this with a port of call to Salalah the next day. Another final visit was made to Mombasa where maintenance was carried out on the ship and station leave was granted to the crew. On 29 March *Loch Fyne* sailed into the port of Tanga in Tanzania, which proved to be a most extraordinarily successful visit with sporting events and challenges between the locals and the ships company proving quite an attraction.

On 4 April the frigate sailed from Tanga for Aden and called at Socotra on passage. On 11 April *Loch Fyne* pulled into Aden, where two days later the ships company was assembled on deck to hear an address from the Flag Officer Middle East, thanking them personally for all their hard work during the deployment. Three days later the ship resumed her voyage back to the United Kingdom. During her passage of the Red Sea *Loch Fyne* encountered the brand new Tribal class frigate *Nubian* on the 20 April. Identities were exchanged and the newer frigate took over from the Loch class vessel the duties of the Royal Navy presence in the Middle East.

After navigating through the Suez Canal, *Loch Fyne* refuelled at Tobruk on 23 April and rendezvoused with the Royal Yacht *Britannia* before both ships entered Gibraltar on 28 April.

The final leg of her journey started on the morning of 2 May when *Loch Fyne* slipped form Gibraltar and started the four day passage to Devonport where she arrived wearing her paying off pennant. Soon the ship was inside the dockyard and was quickly de-stored and reduced to reserve. *Loch Fyne* remained at Devonport until sold for breaking up in 1970 to BISCO. The work was carried out by J Cashmore at Newport in Wales who started work immediately upon her arrival on 20 August 1970.

Chronology

08.12.1943	Laid down at Burntisland Shipbuilding, Ltd, Fife
24.05.194	Launched
09.11.1944	Completed
Early 1945	Escort protection duties with 18th and 22nd Escort Groups
19.04.1945	Clyde
Summer 1945	Operation Deadlight
06.1945	Refit at Pembroke Dock
08.1945	East Indies
06.1946	Reduced to reserve at Portsmouth
10.1946	Refitted for service in 6th Frigate Flotilla Home Fleet
04.1950	Refitted at Portsmouth
01.1951	Damaged by faulty depth charge
04.1951	Searched for sunken submarine *Affray* in English Channel
31.03.1952	Care and Maintenance at Sheerness awaiting modernisation
04.1953 – 06.1954	Modernised at D & W Henderson Ltd, Glasgow then to Harland and Wolff, Southampton for semi tropicalisation for service in East Indies.
14.02.1956	Re-commissioned at Southampton
04.05.1956	Left Devonport for East Indies/Persian Gulf patrol
16.01.1957	Assisted tanker Gilda aground of Iranian coastline
20.07.1957	After refit at Devonport sailed for Bahrain
02.1958	Batinah Coast Patrol
07.1958	Guardship at Shatt-El-Arab, Iraq.
01.06.1959	After refit left United Kingdom for Persian Gulf
18.04.1960	Arrived Devonport, then to Rosyth for refit
23.11.1960	Rejoined 9th Frigate Squadron in Persian Gulf
09.10.1961	Left Mombasa towing minesweeper *Bassingham* to Aden and the Suez Canal
10.11.1961	Arrived Devonport for a refit
19.05.1962	To Persian Gulf
02.05.1963	Sailed from Gibraltar to Devonport for the last time.
06.05.1963	Arrived Devonport to pay off for disposal
20.08.1970	Arrived Newport to be broken up by John Cashmore Ltd

HMS LOCH GLENDHU

On 12 April 1945 Loch Glendhu *encountered the German U-boat* U-1024 *and captured documents and information from the submarine before it foundered in heavy seas.* (Crown Copyright/MoD)

Job number J11832 was awarded by the Admiralty on 2 February 1943 to Burntisland Shipbuilding. Having been laid down on 29 May 1943 over the next year and a half the shipyard quickly assembled the complex jigsaw of steel and material to fashion a Loch class frigate that was given the name of an inland loch in Sutherland, *Loch Glendhu.* Construction was rapid and the ship was launched on 18 October 1944.

Construction was completed on 18 October 1944 and following builders trials she entered service with the Royal Navy as one element of the 8th Escort Group under the command of Lieutenant Commander Edric Guy Bromfield Knaption RN.

Loch Glendhu's first few months of service proved to be interesting ones, especially whilst on anti-submarine and escort duties in the North West

Approaches and Irish Sea on 12 April. On that day the frigate detected the submerged Type VIIC/41 *U-1024* under the command of Kapitanleutnant Hans-Joachim Gutteck and together with other Royal Navy units attacked the U-boat forcing it to the surface. *U-1024* had sailed on her only mission on 3 March and had attacked and badly damaged two American merchantmen the James W Nesmith and the Will Rogers, both of which had to be beached. *U-1024* was quickly abandoned by the German crew, 37 of which were rescued by the attacking British ships amongst the nine dead was the U-boats commanding officer. The German submarine, whilst still afloat, was boarded by a party from *Loch More* who discovered valuable information and documents onboard and was taken in tow but floundered in heavy weather and sank.

With the end of the war in Europe the frigate was

assigned the task of escorting surrendered German U-boats between Scapa Flow and Stranraer during Operation Deadlight before being allocated to the East Indies Fleet to continue the fight against the Japanese. On 8 June she arrived at Troon where she was given a short refit to prepare her for the Far East, this included the addition of extra 20mm anti-aircraft guns and improved ventilation and air conditioning. The work was completed towards the end of July and on 23 July she sailed from British waters. She was routed through the Mediterranean and arrived at Aden on 15 August. Two days later after storing the ship with food, water and oil fuel *Loch Glendhu* sailed north to Massawa in Africa to rendezvous with the damaged fighter control ship *Palomares*. The *Palomares* had been severely damaged by a fire onboard and was making her way at slow speed to Aden.

Upon her arrival back at Aden, a change of command took place when the latest commanding officer, Commander H L Hayes OBE took command. On 23 August *Loch Glendhu* resumed her interrupted passage to join the East Indies Fleet, finally arriving at Colombo seven days later.

In September the ship was heavily involved in Operation Zipper, the amphibious landings in the Port Swettenham area sailing on 6 September. Operation Zipper had been conceived as an operation to capture either Port Swettenham or Port Dickson and in so doing allow the British forces a staging post from which to recapture the all important port city of Singapore. The end of the war in the Pacific, however, meant that most of the plans were never put into practice. After the recapture of Singapore the warship remained based in the area and supported the work of liberating prisoners of war and escorting the transport ships that carried them to safety.

The following November saw *Loch Glendhu* deployed as Sourabaya guardship before returning once again to Singapore on 9 December. On Boxing Day the frigate embarked a complement of Royal Marine Commandos who took passage to Morotai in the Moluccas Islands in Indonesia. After seven days at sea the warship arrived off the port and landed the commandos who quickly took over control of the town. Australian soldiers were already at Morotai

guarding the Japanese prisoners of war captured during the retaking of the community.

After four days as guardship *Loch Glendhu* sailed back to Singapore via Karaurota in Indonesia before finally arriving back at Singapore on 12 January.

On 2 February *Loch Glendhu* was assigned the task of being guardship at Batavia where ten days later she escorted the surrendered Japanese U-181) to be sunk by gunfire from *Loch Glendhu* and sister ship *Loch Lomond*. The Type IXD2 U-boat was under the command of one of Germany's more decorated submarine Commanders Kapitan zur see Kurt Freiwald. The boat had sailed from Bordeaux in France on 16 March 1944 and arrived at Penang on 8 August. On 31 August she was at Singapore and made another three war patrols sinking the last of the boat's 27 victims, the American *Fort Lee* on 2 November 1944. She was taken over by the Japanese in May 1945 following the end of the war in Europe and officially entered service as *I-501* on 15 July. *I-501* was captured by the Allies when Singapore was recaptured and the decision was taken to scuttle the submarine offshore. Once complete the frigate took passage to Colombo for a month long refit. Upon completion of the refit the ship returned to Singapore to resume her guardship duties at Batavia.

It was whilst she was performing this task that *Loch Glendhu* intercepted two former Japanese subchasers that had fallen into the hands of insurgent forces from Segal in Java. The two vessels eventually surrendered to the British warship and were escorted back to Singapore with the aid of officers from the Imperial Japanese Navy onboard under British guard.

On 6 June *Loch Glendhu* hosted a meeting with the Indonesian insurrectionist forces at which an agreement was reached on the future direction of the country. This was finalised at another meeting again held onboard the frigate on 26 June. With her diplomatic role completed the frigate was free to return to her usual patrols of the Indian Ocean and in July arrived at Trincomalee. All too soon the tropical paradise was left behind as the unrest in Abadan in the Middle East threatened to spill over into a crisis. *Loch Glendhu* and the cruiser *Norfolk* were sent from Trincomalee to quell the unrest. The two ships arrived at the port on

23 July having battled through severe weather. Onboard the frigate many compartments had suffered flood damage due to the severity of the storms encountered in the Indian Ocean. Those onboard the cruiser did not fare much better as she was suffering from a partial breakdown of her air conditioning units.

Having landed some personnel to assist the local authorities at Abadan *Loch Glendhu* was in late July and August deployed on patrolling the Persian Gulf, with visits paid to Khor Kuwait and Muscat.

A long overdue refit was stared on 23 September at Colombo that lasted until November when the post refit trials commenced. Later in the month the dangerous work of removing Japanese explosive devices on the approaches to the Andaman Islands fell to *Loch Glendhu*'s explosive disposal team. Upon completion of this task the frigate went onto visit a number of ports in the region including Port Blair, Port Stewart, Katar and Port Nicobar before returning to Singapore.

The frigate remained in port until January 1947 when she was stationed in and around Singapore before heading out into the Indian Ocean where she visited many British dependencies before carrying out a similar operational role on the East Coast of Africa. In March *Loch Glendhu* headed north for the Persian Gulf finally arriving at Abadan on 22 March.

The following month the frigate took passage to Karachi as escort for five motor launches operated by the newly created Royal Indian Navy finally arriving at the port city on 27 April. Having successfully delivered the craft *Loch Glendhu* carried on to Singapore where she was taken into a dry dock for a two-month works package to be undertaken.

Upon completion of the work *Loch Glendhu* carried out a humanitarian task when in July she was loaded with a cargo of rice that was urgently needed in the Nicobar Islands where a combination of bad weather and a failed harvest had left the islands desperately short of food.

Loch Glendhu returned to the Persian Gulf upon delivery where she was to take part in the recovery operation of a BOAC Plymouth flying boat that had crashed at Bahrain. To the ships company of *Loch Glendhu*, fell the grisly task of recovering eight of the ten people killed in the tragedy on 23 August. The

frigate remained in the Gulf until November when she sailed to Colombo for a maintenance period that continued until the end of the year.

In January 1948 *Loch Glendhu* operated out of Trincomalee while the following month saw her returning to the Persian Gulf. It wasn't long, however, before she would once again be in the Indian Ocean taking part in a large naval exercise (details) with the Royal Indian Navy in April. At the completion of the exercises *Loch Glendhu* paid a visit to Cochin before sailing onto Singapore ahead of a planned refit. During the refit, which lasted until November, the ships command was transferred to Commander D J A Heber-Percy RN.

After post refit trials in November the frigate sailed from Singapore on 2 December bound for Trincomalee where she arrived after six days steaming. The end of the month saw the frigate operating in the Indian Ocean along with a visit to Aden. January 1949 started with a resumption of patrols in the Indian Ocean that occupied the ship until the beginning of March. During the three months the British frigate made ports of call to numerous cities in the region including Djibouti, Mombasa, Zanzibar, Kilwa, Kisiwani in Tanzania, Landi and the Seychelles.

On 8 March *Loch Glendhu* arrived at the wide natural harbour at Trincomalee where she stayed for the following month. Whilst at Trincomalee, the ships company carried out self maintenance on the ship along with jungle training. Finally on 7 April the warship sailed for the west coast of India before arriving at Colombo on 26 April. It was at Colombo that the ships company welcomed onboard the frigates latest commanding officer Commander H B Acworth OBE.

Loch Glendhu having left Colombo in late April arrived back at Trincomalee on 5 May where she was informed of a change in program following the Yangtze River incident involving the sloop *Amethyst*. The *Amethyst* was a Black Swan class sloop and on 20 April 1949 was en route to replace *Consort* as guardship for the British Embassy at Nanjing during the Chinese Civil War. The sloop came under fire from Chinese Communist forces and eventually grounded on Rose Island in the river. At 0930 the ship was hit by numerous shells that killed Lieutenant Commander

B M Skinner. The Royal Navy ship would remain grounded and under almost constant attack for the next ten weeks until 30 July 1949 when she successfully extricated herself from the Yangtze River finding the destroyer *Concord* there to greet her. The *Amethyst*'s signal to the fleet being '*Have rejoined the fleet off Woosung…God save the King.*"

For a while *Loch Glendhu* was to be based at Singapore on detached duty and she arrived at the naval base there on 21 May. *Loch Glendhu* remained at Singapore for the next month before sailing on 27 June to resume her interrupted program.

The following month the frigate carried out a lengthy patrol in the Indian Ocean and made some notable port visits including Penang, Nancowry, Car Nicobar, Port Blair and Port Cornwallis before returning once again to the familiar surroundings of Trincomalee on 16 July.

Autumn was spent operating out of Colombo on exercises whilst on 1 October *Loch Glendhu* arrived at Mogadishu where members of the ships company were landed to provide assistance to the local authorities as the ship stood offshore to act as guardship, whilst law and order were restored ashore. *Loch Glendhu* remained off the former Italian colony until 24 October when she resumed her previous itinerary.

On 3 November the warship took passage to the Seychelles where a fantastic time was had by all. Her

HMS Loch Glendhu *arriving at Plymouth in December 1953.*   *(Syd Goodman Collection)*

next destination proved to be just as idyllic, Trincomalee for a fortnight. On 21 November the frigate sailed back to Singapore where a week later she was taken in hand for a refit. The refit lasted until April 1950 when after post refit trials she sailed, on 6 April, for Trincomalee once more.

Loch Glendhu spent the summer in the Indian Ocean only returning to Colombo on 12 August. She returned to sea for Exercise Jet with the Indian Navy in September. At the end of the exercise the frigate visited Karachi and Bombay.

In December the frigate returned to Karachi ahead of a major deployment in the Bay of Bengal in January 1951. Work was carried out onboard the warship upon her return to Singapore in February; the refit taking until April to complete. Upon its completion the ship toured the Indian Ocean with both official and unofficial ports of call made to destinations as diverse as Zanzibar, Cocus Islands and the Seychelles throughout the summer months.

After another dry docking in Colombo in August the frigate returned to the Persian Gulf having first honoured a request to visit the port of Karachi. The passage to Bahrain was undertaken with a water lighter picked up at Bombay under tow, so the passage was, understandably quite slow.

In December a change of command took place when the frigates latest commanding officer, Lieutenant Commander R S Brookes DSC RN took command.

Loch Glendhu started 1952 in the Persian Gulf with a number of forays into the Indian Ocean planned throughout the year. The first of these occurred in February when the frigate sailed to Trincomalee at the start of a major naval exercise involving a number of Royal Navy ships and a flotilla of Indian Navy vessels. These exercises continued throughout March and upon their completion the ship returned to Singapore where she was taken in hand for a refit.

The work was quite extensive and continued until July. Upon completion of her post refit trials *Loch Glendhu* resumed her duties in the Bay of Bengal with a visit laid on for the ships company to Madras. She remained in the area throughout the summer months of 1952 making visits to British colonies in the region including Mauritius and Diego Garcia before sailing for a docking period in December.

1953 started with the frigate operating in the Indian Ocean before transferring to the Persian Gulf in February. She would remain based at Bahrain until June when she sailed out of the Gulf to visit Colombo for a maintenance period. Upon completion *Loch Glendhu* carried out a patrol in the Bay of Bengal and along the West Coast of India that saw the ship besieged by large crowds at every port of call including Madras and Cochin.

The future for the frigate, however, had already been decided in London and it was that *Loch Glendhu* was to return to the United Kingdom and be placed in the Reserve Fleet.

In October the frigate patrolled the Persian Gulf for the final time before making her way to Karachi and then onto Aden. On 17 November *Loch Glendhu* sailed from Aden for the journey home. For this voyage she had a new commanding officer in the shape of Lieutenant Commander V C Freeland. The frigate arrived back at Portsmouth on 7 December and was soon placed in the reserve fleet in early 1954. Two years later she was on the disposal list and was demolished by Clayton and Davie at Dunston with the ship arriving there under tow on 14 November 1957.

Battle Honours

ATLANTIC 1945

Chronology

02.02.1943	Ordered from Burntisland Shipbuilding
29.05.1943	Laid down
18.10.1944	Launched
23.02.1945	Completed and joined 8th Escort Group
12.04.1945	Attacked *U-1034*
06.1945	Operation Deadlight
08.06.1945	Arrived Troon for a refit to fit extra AA guns
23.07.1945	Sailed for Far East
17.08.1945	Rendezvoused with damaged *Palomares* and escorted her to Aden
30.08.1945	Colombo
09.1945	Operation Zipper off Malaya
06.09.1945	Amphibious landings at Port Sweetenham
11.1945	Sourabaya Guardship
09.12.1945	Sailed for Morotai and Moluccas Islands
12.01.1946	Singapore
02.02.1946	Guardship at Batavia
12.02.1946	Escorted *U-181* to be sunk by gunfire
02.1946	Month long refit at Colombo
06.06.1946	Hosted meeting with Indonesian insurrectionists
Summer 1946	Indian Ocean and Persian Gulf
23.09.1946	Refit at Colombo
03.1947	Persian Gulf
04.1947	Escorted 5 motor launches for Royal Indian Navy
27.04.1947	Karachi
07.1947	Humanitarian relief work in Nicobar Islands
07.1947	Recovery of crashed BOAC Plymouth flying boat at Bahrain
11.1947	Sailed for Colombo
01.1948	Operated out of Trincomalee
04.1948	Cochin
05.1948	Refit at Singapore
01.1949	Indian Ocean until March
08.03.1949	Trincomalee for a month
07.04.1949	Sailed for Colombo

26.04.1949	Colombo
05.05.1949	Trincomalee
21.05.1949	Singapore
07.1949	Indian Ocean
16.07.1949	Trincomalee
01.10.1949	Mogadishu due to civil unrest
24.10.1949	Sailed for the Seychelles
28.11.1949	Singapore for refit
Summer 1950	Indian Ocean
Early 1951	Visits to Zanzibar, Cocus Islands and Seychelles
08.1951	Docking at Colombo
01.1952	Persian Gulf
02.1952	Trincomalee for exercises
Summer 1952	Visits to Mauritius, Diego Garcia and Colombo for docking
01.1953	Indian Ocean
02.1953	Persian Gulf
10.1953	Final Persian Gulf patrol
17.11.1953	Left Aden for United Kingdom
07.12.1953	Portsmouth
1954	Reserve fleet
1956	Disposal List
14.11.1957	Broken up by Clayton and Davie at Durtson

HMS Loch Gorm

A good three quarters view of Loch Gorm *showing the layout of the stern of the ship; the Loch class's quarterdeck was frequently awash in heavy seas.*
(Crown Copyright/MoD)

Harland and Wolff in Belfast received confirmation of an order for a Loch class on 2 February 1943. The Admiralty had given the contract Job Number J3397. The shipyard themselves gave it a yard number of 1247. Construction started three days after Christmas the same year. Six months later on 18 June the hull was ready for launching and was given the name *Loch Gorm*.

In October 1944 final fitting out was nearing completion but the ship was transferred to the fitting out base at Dalmuir on the River Clyde. Nine days short of a full year since work began *Loch Gorm* was completed on 19 December 1944 under the command of Lieutenant Commander R Johnston DSC. She commissioned into the 23rd Escort Group following successful completion of her sea trials in mid December. *Loch Gorm* sailed for Tobermory where she took on board supplies before

crossing the Irish Sea to join the rest of her group at Londonderry. After a brief work up period *Loch Gorm* sailed in February 1945 for operations in the North West Approaches escorting vital North Atlantic convoys. The heavy pounding given to the ship by the Atlantic waves proved to be costly. *Loch Gorm*, like many of her sister ships, began to show structural weaknesses and she was taken in hand in March for hull strengthening on the River Tyne.

Upon completion of the rectification work *Loch Gorm* resumed her previous deployment on the lookout for German U-boats and protection of the convoy traffic. VE Day was celebrated onboard but soon after *Loch Gorm* was one of the ships assembled to escort Operation Doomsday. The operation was to take the official Norwegian Government back to Oslo on Convoy RN1. *Loch Gorm* went on to visit a number of Norwegian

ports on resupply missions and also to assemble the defeated German U-boats for passage back to the United Kingdom as part of Operation Deadlight.

The need for warships in the Far East to combat the Japanese saw many Loch class vessels detailed for service in the Pacific Ocean and *Loch Gorm* was one of these. To prepare the ship she was refitted at Londonderry before sailing for the Far East in July 1945. It was during this time that her second commanding officer Lieutenant Commander H Vernon RNR was appointed to the ship.

Loch Gorm's route took her through the Mediterranean with calls at Gibraltar and later at Aden. The news everyone had been hoping for reached the ship on 15 August that Japan had surrendered to the Allies following the dropping of Atom bombs on Hiroshima and Nagasaki. The end of the war did not, however, mean and end to a huge amount of work. *Loch Gorm* became part of the escort to convoys to Malaya as part of Operation Zipper based out of Trincomalee. This role continued into September with escort duties between Bombay and the

Malacca Strait near to Singapore.

October 1945 saw *Loch Gorm* taking part in the repatriation duties and 17 October saw the frigate sail from Tanjong-Priok in company with the River class frigate *Taff* and the supply ship *Glenroy*. The following day the three ships anchored off Semerang at 2300. The next morning the ship went to action stations at 0745 as the three ships closed the port and covered the area to allow assault craft to land ashore with Gurkha soldiers onboard.

For two days the ship remained at high alert until the situation ashore had been stabilised. On 19 October she landed a small party consisting of one officer, a signalman, and six armed ratings. Their mission was to establish a signals station. The next day at the request of the officer commanding the Gurkha Battalion another landing party of one officer and eight ratings was landed to repair and man two Japanese anti tank gun positions.

Another ten ratings were subsequently requested ashore the next day to assist and repair and ultimately to operate Army mortar transport vehicles. By 21 October

Seen at anchor Loch Gorm *had a very active period in the aftermath of the Japanese surrender with patrols across South East Asia.*
(Crown Copyright/MoD)

the need to improve ship to shore communications was severe and a wireless operator with a Type 67 radio was sent ashore to establish another radio link at the Battalion Headquarters.

On 22 October at nine in the morning *Loch Gorm* landed a relief food party with stores and equipment for three hundred Dutch women and children in the civilian hospital who were all suffering from malnutrition. At the same time another party from the ship carried out a survey of the port and its infrastructure.

The shore parties were relieved early on 23 October when Army reinforcements arrived in *LCI's 215, 262, 266* and *180* and in SS *Sumire Maru*. By the end of the next day all shore parties had been re-embarked onboard *Loch Gorm* and control of communications in the area had been handed over to *LCI 266*. 24 October also saw the embarkation of Japanese General Makamura under guard and under arrest. His 1,500 men travelled back to Tanjong Priok on board SS *Sumire Maru* and *LCI's 215, 262* and *181*; the force arriving at the port at 1630 on 26 October.

From Sourabaya Loch Gorm sailed to Ceylon where in December she was in involved in a minor incident when she and sister ship *Loch Lomond* were in collision with both ships receiving only minor damage.

The New Year started with a return to Singapore where she was needed for various support duties around Malaya, including calls at Batavia, Vizgapatan and Karachi. In February a new commanding officer in the shape of Lieutenant Commander T E Edwards RNR was appointed to the ship.

The following month *Loch Gorm* was one of a number of Royal Navy vessels tasked with escorting troopships carrying Gurkha soldiers to Semarang in Indonesia.

Upon completion the frigate returned to Singapore. She did not remain in port for long having embarked the Governor of the Christmas Islands and Cocas Islands on a tour of the dependencies.

Later in the month *Loch Gorm* grounded on a reef and damaged her propellers. The damage did not, however, prevent the ship from completing a planned anti-piracy patrol in the Malacca Straits off Singapore.

With the postwar run down of the Royal Navy, *Loch Gorm* was one of the ships selected for paying off into reserve and accordingly she sailed for the United Kingdom in April 1946. She was routed via Colombo, Trincomalee, Aden, Malta and Gibraltar before arriving at Devonport with her paying off pennant flying.

Loch Gorm was quickly de-stored and paid off being reduced to reserve at Plymouth by August 1946. The frigate remained there for the next five years until plans emerged to refurbish her and bring her back into service in 1951. Unfortunately the plans fell through and the frigate remained at Plymouth for another three years. In 1954 the installation of dehumidification equipment required that *Loch Gorm* be towed to Glasgow and then onto Barrow to join other ships in the reserve fleet stored there.

In 1956 *Loch Gorm* was one of the Loch class frigates offered for sale to the Government of Portugal but after they turned the offer down *Loch Gorm* was placed on the disposals list. She languished at Barrow for another five years until being sold in April 1961 to Kavounides Shipping Ltd and converted by Cammell Laird for use as a passenger ferry. The conversion was quite extensive and when completed she was renamed *Orion* and continued to serve until broken up in 1966 in the then Yugoslavia.

Chronology

02.02.1943	Ordered from Harland and Wolff
28.12.1943	Laid down
18.06.1944	Launched
10.1944	Towed to Dalmuir for fitting out
19.12.1944	Completed
12.1944	Sea trials and work up
02.1945	North West Approaches
03.1945	Hull strengthening on River Tyne
05.1945	Operation Doomsday – Re-occupation of Norway
07.1945	Sailed for Far East
Autumn 1945	Operation Zipper off Malaya
04.1946	Returned to United Kingdom to pay off into reserve
1954	Towed to Glasgow and then Barrow to join reserve fleet
1956	Offered for sale to Portugal – sale fell through
04.1961	Sold to Kavounides Shipping Company and converted into a ferry at Cammell Laird Shipyard and renamed *Orion*
1966	Broken up in Yugoslavia

HMS LOCH INSH

Amongst Loch Insh's *wartime victories was that of the destruction of the U-boat* U-297 *together with the frigate* Goodall.   *(Crown Copyright/MoD)*

The contract for the frigate that would become *Loch Insh* went to the shipyard of Henry Robb in Leith on 25 January 1943. The first steel plates were laid down on the slipway on 17 November later the same year once the slip had been cleared by the launching of the previous vessel. Construction of the hull was swift and on 10 May 1944 the frigate was launched by Mrs H C Bovell, wife of Vice Admiral H C Bovell, CB, CBE, DSO. Workers from the shipyard continued to work on the ship until she was declared complete on 20 October 1944 having already finished her contractors' sea trials in the North Sea.

HMS Loch Insh joined the 19th Escort Group under the command of her first Captain, Commander E C W Dempster, RN. Trials were completed at the end of October that saw a visit paid to Aberdeen and storing at Tobermory.

It wasn't long before the frigate saw action, after join-ing the rest of the ships of the 19th Escort Group at Liverpool. On 28 November she sailed for the North West Approaches. On 6 December following the loss of the frigate *Bullen*, *Loch Insh* and *Goodall* attacked and sank the German Type VIIC/41 submarine *U-297* under the command of Oberleutnant Wolfgang Aldegarmann off Cape Wraith. *U-297* had been preparing an attack on a carrier group in the region.

The New Year of 1945 saw the frigate deploy to the English Channel before returning to Belfast on 1 February to carry out some repairs. The next day *Loch Insh* returned to duty operating out of Liverpool and Milford Haven.

In April she formed part of the escort of the convoy of JW66 which consisted of 26 merchantmen. The convoy sailed from the Clyde for Northern Russia. Its escort was under the command of Admiral Graham and comprised of the cruiser *Bellona*, escort carriers *Vindex* and

Premier, six destroyers, four corvettes and a sloop. At 1300 on the 9 April the convoy was reinforced by three destroyers, four corvettes and sixteen Russian submarine chasers from the Faeroes. *Loch Insh* together with sister ship *Loch Shin* joined the force and had to force their entry into the Kola Inlet passed a line of U-boats. The escorting vessels recorded no less than 26 sonar contacts and expended over four hundred depth charges. The convoy would prove to be the last wartime convoy to Russia and arrived safely at the Kola Inlet a week later. Upon arrival *Loch Insh* detached from the group and joined other HM ships including the minelayer *Apollo* for Operation Tramwell, the laying of an offensive minefield which was defended by the destroyers *Obedient, Opportune* and *Orwell*.

Just prior to the departure of the return convoy RA66 to the United Kingdom, *Loch Insh* sailed on 29 April to carry out a reconnaissance mission and to search for any German U-boats. The 19th Escort Group were sent ahead at 1856 and *Loch Insh* soon obtained a sonar contact at 780 yards and 65 degrees. The frigate turned towards and attacked at 1900 with Squid. Thirty seconds later *U-307* under the command of Oberleutnant Erick Kruger surfaced and was strafed with gunfire from *Loch Insh*, *Loch Shin* and *Cygnet*. At 1903 *U-307* sank stern first. Fourteen survivors were plucked from the icy Arctic waters. The Germans struck back when Goodall was torpedoed at 1935 by the Type VIIC boat *U-286* under the command of Oberleutnant Willi Dietrich. Just prior to the torpedoes hitting the British ship she had obtained sonar contact and was preparing to attack. At the same time *Loch Shin* made contact and the submarine came under attack from *Loch Shin* and *Anguilla*. A third attack by *Cotton* sealed the fate of the submarine.

By the time that convoy RA66 left Russia for Britain the war in Europe was over and as *Loch Insh* arrived in Britain at the beginning of May she was taken in hand for a refit at Henry Robb's shipyard to fit her for service in the Far East. She arrived at Leith on 6 May and remained there until 27 July when she sailed for Rosyth Dockyard.

After working up and trials *Loch Insh* sailed on 23 August to join the East Indies Escort Force routed through Gibraltar, Malta and Aden before finally arriving at Colombo on 25 October. *Loch Insh* was based there for the next two months, a period which saw the frigate

operate in support of British forces in the region off Java and Sumatra.

On 29 November *Loch Insh* sailed for Singapore to escort POW convoys between Singapore, Padang and Colombo. December 1945 saw the frigate off East Africa with a popular visit to Kilindini in January and February 1946.

News reached the ship on 23 February that upon her return to the United Kingdom she would reduce to the reserve fleet. Before that, however, *Loch Insh* sailed to Trincomalee where she planned to meet her relief, sister ship *Loch Quoich*. On 8 March the frigate arrived at Trincomalee and anchored in the wide harbour there to await the arrival of her sister ship. When the she arrived *Loch Insh* set sail for the United Kingdom, finally arriving at Devonport in May. She was quickly de-stored and prepared for the reserve fleet.

During her long stay in the reserve fleet the ship was refitted by Brigham and Cowan in Hull in 1949. After three years of inactivity the frigate was refitted and brought back to life at Devonport in July 1950. The following month she carried out sea trials around Plymouth and Portland joining the 6th Frigate Flotilla of the Home Fleet under the command of Commander R S Foster-Brown RN on 21 September.

The closing months of the year saw her carrying out weapons training at Londonderry before sailing south to Gibraltar with the rest of the flotilla in November for fleet exercises and a visit to Bayonne.

In January 1951 she, together with the other units of the flotilla, carried out a series of Home Fleet exercises, which also saw visits paid to Gibraltar, Aranci Bay, Savona and Monaco. The exercises finished in early March with the ship returning to Devonport. 1951 was also a year of tragedy, when in April the submarine *Affray* sank in the English Channel, *Loch Insh* was one of the many warships assembled to search for the stricken submarine, a duty that continued until June.

The summer months saw the frigate make numerous ports of call to Falmouth and Milford Haven before spending some weeks under repair at Devonport in August. The autumn of 1951 saw further Home Fleet exercises and more visits to Portland and Troon.

The year closed with the announcement that *Loch Insh* had been selected as the prototype for a major recon-

struction programme, the so called Loch class frigate modernisation.

January 1952 saw *Loch Insh* in a lengthy series of flotilla and Home Fleet exercises that culminated in a trip to the Mediterranean and visits paid to Gibraltar, Nice and Malta. Upon being relieved by *Virago* in April 1952 the frigate returned to her base at Devonport and was soon handed over to the care of the dockyard pending a planned modernisation program. A care and maintenance complement was retained onboard with the remainder of the crew having been re-assigned to other vessels in the fleet.

Her modernisation programme commenced in May 1953 when she was taken in hand by Devonport Dockyard. During the refit the ships' single 4-inch gun was replaced by a twin Mk XIX 4-inch. Secondary armament was also changed with the original outfit being replaced with a single twin Mark V and four single Mark VII 40mm Bofor guns. The Mk 5 gun was also fitted with a Simple Tachymetric Director. *Loch Insh* also received a new Type 277 radar set. The refit continued until July the following year. After post refit trials *Loch Insh* was earmarked for service in the Persian Gulf to relieve her sister ship *Loch Quoich* on the station. With the successful completion of her post refit trials, *Loch Insh* commissioned on 6 September under the command of Commander A J T Harris RN.

She spent the remainder of the month on trials off Portland before sailing to Malta where further work was undertaken together with Destroyer Command Mediterranean Fleet throughout October.

Loch Insh continued onto her operating area in the Persian Gulf in the autumn months and met sister ship *Loch Alvie*. The pair operated in the Southern Gulf area in the first days of 1955.

In January 1955 having arrived at the large natural harbour at Trincomalee some leave was granted before sailing onto Colombo the following month. At Colombo the frigate entered dry dock for a period of routine maintenance. In March the frigate patrolled the East Coast of India together with visits to Nicobar, Cittagong and Madras.

Later in March 1955 *Loch Insh* returned to the Persian Gulf where she continued showing the flag and intercepting and inspecting dhows. A break from routine was

organised in April with a series of port visits to amongst others Dubai, Sharjah and Ras-al-Khaima. In May *Loch Insh* was off the Straits of Hormuz when on the 20th she joined *Loch Killisport* fighting a fire onboard the Dutch tanker SS *Argea Prim*. The Dutch vessel was ablaze following a collision with another Dutch ship the MV *Tabian*. When the frigate arrived on the scene the *Argea Prim* was under tow by the SS *Esmeralda*. *Loch Insh* stayed with the Dutch tanker and arrived at Bahrain on the 25 May, the merchant vessel having successfully restarted her engines.

Loch Insh returned to her normal pattern of patrols in June and July. August, however, saw the frigate start her return journey to the United Kingdom where she arrived to pay off into refit at Devonport.

On 11 October the frigate was commissioned with normal ceremony as she still had two months to go before the end of her refit. The day also saw Commander T E Fanshaw DSC officially take command of the frigate. Work was undertaken in improving the standard of accommodation onboard for the ships company who were accommodated in the Royal Naval Barracks.

The ship was finally ready in early January 1956 with the service of blessing conducted by the Senior Chaplain of the Royal Navy Barracks, the Reverend H W Brierly OBE, MA RN on Sunday 15 January.

Monday morning saw the start of a hectic period of sea trials that lasted until the following Friday. Upon completion *Loch Insh* secured alongside No 2 wharf at Devonport for the weekend. Next on the agenda was a period of workup at Portland and a final inspection on 9 February before arriving back at Devonport the next day. Seven days leave was granted to each watch ahead of sailing again for the Middle East.

Loch Insh left Devonport under clear sunny skies on 27 February and took passage to Gibraltar passing the cruiser *Gambia* en route to the United Kingdom in the Bay of Biscay. The frigate continued her journey via Malta and Port Suez; her arrival at Suez coinciding with the final stages of the British evacuation from the area. The Captain welcomed Port Said General Sir Richard Hull onboard for an update on progress.

After an uneventful southerly transit of the Suez Canal *Loch Insh* was ordered to fuel briefly at Aden and then procede at best speed to Bahrain where disturbances had

Bow and stern profiles of Loch Insh *clearly showing the layout. Of particular note is the clear quarterdeck.*
(Crown Copyright/MoD)

broken out and needed to be stopped. Regrettably the frigates planned itinerary was thrown into disarray with the planned visits to the Kuria Muria islands and Masirah cancelled.

When *Loch Insh* arrived at Bahrain she relieved sister ship *Loch Lomond* before refuelling at the BAPCO Jetty at Sitra. Then she sailed through the difficult channel to Khor Kaliga and found *Loch Alvie* and the American USS *Valour* at anchor.

In April the frigate visited Iraq and sailed up the Shatt-al-Arab waterway for 97 miles before securing at Margil Jetty at Basra for a most enjoyable visit before returning to Bahrain.

After sailing on 21 April the ship received a message from the lighthouse at Jazirat Tunb in Oman stating that one of the men manning the facility was seriously ill and in need of immediate medical attention. It later transpired that the man was in the nearby village with a bad case of malaria.

During the first week of May the frigate visited three small coastal towns in Southern Iran, Daiyr, Asalu and Lingeh. On her way back to Bahrain it was discovered that the Shah Allum light ship was missing from its station. *Loch Insh* carried out a search but did not find it, suspecting that the 1914 vintage craft had sunk.

Later in the month *Loch Insh* took part in a joint exercise with the forces of Oman and later visited the ancient and historic city of Muscat. The ship fired a national salute upon entering the harbour allowing the shots to reverberate around the surrounding hills and deep water. Despite temperatures of 104°C in the shade the ships company took on locals at games of tennis, badminton, hockey and swimming competitions.

The growing tensions in Egypt and along the Suez Canal caused the ship to be deployed around Aden during the summer months in addition to voyages in the Indian Ocean and Persian Gulf. July saw visits paid to Ra's-al Khairan in Oman and Sharjah in the United Arab Emirates before returning to Bahrain for a maintenance period.

In late summer *Loch Insh* sailed north to the hot and arid conditions found around the Iraqi port of Basra. The visit was a huge success with many of the ships company enjoying the hospitality of the locals whilst also exercising with the local naval forces of Iraq but it also coin-

cided with an outbreak of smallpox in the Zubaii oilfield area. The visit was cut short by the outbreak of the Israeli-Egyptian crisis with the ship getting under way in extraordinary circumstances. *Loch Insh* was undergoing repairs when she received the order to proceed as soon as possible resulting in the engine room staff virtually rebuilding the engines and re-bricking No 1 boiler in under six hours. On her return journey to her temporary base port of Bahrain she operated off the Omani coast and again visited Muscat in October. During the passage back to Bahrain at the end of her latest patrol *Loch Insh* intercepted and salvaged a derelict and abandoned ship, the MV *Hangkong*, adrift some distance south of Bahrain on 10 October. Over the course of the next two days the frigate stayed with the ship during some bad weather conditions until a party from the British warship went onboard and attached a tow line and took the vessel back to Bahrain.

The mid 1950's were a period of growing tensions between the Middle East and the Western nations with growing nationalism amongst many of the Arab States, none more so than in Egypt. On 1 November Colonel Nasser of Egypt made an appeal to the Arab world to stand against the West. This resulted in the Western forces in the region put on standby for action. *Loch Insh* was no exception, together with the cruiser *Superb* and *Loch Fyne*, the frigate stood by ready to assist if required in the Persian Gulf.

This situation continued for three days until the frigate was ordered to take over guard duties at oil installations and BAPCO owned properties on 4 November. Upon her arrival at Sitra, a general strike was in force. The ship's company quickly assumed the role of the striking dock workers and assisted in the berthing and unberthing of oil tankers in the port.

The situation in the Suez Canal Zone worsened to the point that Operation Musketeer had been initiated, a plan to seize the all important waterway with military force. French and British warships massed off the Egyptian coastline and made a series of successful strikes against Egyptian positions around the Canal and at Port Said. As a consequence of the action in the Mediterranean, *Loch Insh* was positioned in the Red Sea at the other end of the Suez Canal as a contingency and remained there until December when released from the Musketeer operations.

The time spent at Aden had proved useful as it gave *Loch Insh* the opportunity of exercising with other Royal Navy units also based at Aden.

Loch Insh, upon release, made her way back to Bahrain where she spent Christmas alongside having been joined by *Loch Lomond* on Christmas Eve. The New Year arrived and so did sister ship *Loch Ruthven* and after the exchange of responsibilities had been finalised, *Loch Insh* sailed for the United Kingdom on 28 December, sailing around the Horn of Africa, due to the closure of the Suez Canal. The extra mileage allowed *Loch Insh* to visit Mombasa, Simonstown and Freetown before finally arriving back at Devonport on 8 February 1957 for a major refit.

The refit continued until 7 January 1958 and saw major improvements made to the ships air conditioning systems, accommodation spaces and main machinery. After initial sea trials and weapon training at Portland in the winter months *Loch Insh* spent February working up prior to a visit to Londonderry for a spell of anti-submarine warfare training in the North West Approaches. Further exercises and visits to Liverpool and the French port of Le Havre occupied the frigate until late April. Easter leave was granted to the crew ahead of a planned return to the Middle East in the late spring of 1958.

The frigate sailed from Plymouth in May arriving at her regional base of Bahrain after a fortnight underway. She resumed the normal operational duties of frigates in the Persian Gulf with port visits and exercises dominating the programme for the next few months. In July, however, the schedule was abandoned following the assassination of King Faisal II of Iraq and the ensuing uncertainty in the region. Tensions were running high and the Government in Jordan asked for British assistance, particularly with the escorting of oil tankers in the Gulf and in the Suez Canal areas.

Eventually, the tensions abated and *Loch Insh* resumed her normal operating cycle. On Monday 27 October the frigate undertook a plotting exercise in company with sister ship *Loch Killisport*. The next day at 1255 both engines were stopped whilst en route to Karachi and the ships whaler was lowered to collect stores from RFA *Echodale*. Once completed, the frigate resumed her journey finally arriving at Karachi on Monday 3 November to find the Portuguese frigate *Goncalves Zarco* and

Pakistani frigate *Zulfiquar* already in port. Four days later *Loch Insh* carried out a replenishment-at-sea from RFA *Wave Sovereign* as part of the MIDLINK exercises that also included *Loch Killisport*, the American destroyer USS *Waldron* and the Pakistani PNS *Alamgir* (the former British C class destroyer *Creole)* and the British submarine *Sea Devil*. Upon completion of the exercise, on 17 November, *Loch Insh* undertook an Exercise Shop Window on Friday 21 November in company with PNS *Babur*, with the intention of selling weapon systems to the Pakistanis.

After the end of the exercise *Loch Insh* entered dry dock at Karachi for routine maintenance to be carried out on the ship's hull and equipment. Upon completion the ship went on to visit Cochin on 23 December and spent Christmas there.

1959 started with visits made to Muscat and a flotilla exercise with her sister Loch class frigates in the region after which the frigate also took time for a return visit to the ancient and historic city of Muscat. It was here that a guard of honour was landed to present a most unusual gift to the ruler of Muscat, the ships bell from the minesweeper *Welcome*. HMS *Welcome* had been associated with the ruler in 1945 and when the ship was decommissioned it was felt to be an appropriate gesture to present the ships bell to Oman. After a most enjoyable stay *Loch Insh* set sail to Mombasa.

In March 1959 *Loch Insh* was deployed off the East African Coast whilst the following month she was at Massawa in Eritrea where the ship, her departments and salesmen from the United Kingdom tried to interest the nation in the purchase of British arms during a Shop Window demonstration. Having successfully secured some lucrative business for the British arms trade *Loch Insh* sailed for Devonport where upon her arrival was taken in hand for a refit that would last until the following July. Part of the refit enabled the permanent embarkation of a Royal Marines detachment for boarding roles onboard.

Under the command of Captain T N Catlow RN *Loch Insh* carried out post refit trials in the autumn months in waters off Portland and Plymouth.

On 16 November *Loch Insh* sailed south to Gibraltar and suffered some areas of flooding onboard as the frigate battled through heavy weather especially in the

Bay of Biscay. The warship eventually arrived safely at Gibraltar where the weather damaged sections, including the Asdic sonar dome, were repaired.

The frigate resumed her interrupted passage to Aden in the Red Sea on the 24 November and met up with the cruiser *Gambia* in the Red Sea on 8 December. At Aden she took part in a further Shop Window on 17 December where she demonstrated the latest weaponry available for sale to the region with representatives from the leading defence contractors onboard. The next day she sailed for Bahrain and spent the festive season at Mina-al-Ahmadi.

1960 started as the previous year had ended with the ship in the Persian Gulf and making a series of port visits to maintain good relations with the nations that bordered the international waterway. She also carried out inspections of dhows to determine whether they were carrying illegal cargoes of weapons and ammunition. In February, together with sister ship *Loch Killisport*, *Loch Insh* undertook an anti-submarine exercise before visiting the community of Umm Said on the 11 February. After three days alongside the frigate sailed and went on to visit Dubai, Bahrain and Muscat before the end of the month.

March saw *Loch Insh* sail for Karachi where she was docked down for a short refit that also saw the ships damaged A bracket on her propeller shaft being fully repaired. Upon completion of the refit *Loch Insh* carried out a lengthy series of sea trials that culminated in her participation in naval exercises organised by the Pakistani Navy on 16 April.

Loch Insh returned to the Persian Gulf in late April and resumed her normal duties there. A major naval exercise off Kharg Island in Iran was next on the frigate's itinerary. Exercise Khargex II would involve large numbers of Royal Navy and Iranian warships and was designed to test the response of both navies to a simulated attack on Iran.

Further exercises were staged in late May at Yas and Jebel Dharsna along with the normal official port visits around the Gulf. In June *Loch Insh* called at Abadan on the 10th and two days later was alongside at Khorramshah in Iran where men from the warship paraded in the city to mark the Queen's birthday.

The next day *Loch Insh* was once again back at sea on a course back to Bahrain. After a few days in port, *Loch*

Insh was sent south to Mombasa having first exchanged a defective fan for an operational one from sister ship *Loch Killisport*. The frigate reached Mombasa on 2 July but the lingering problems with her machinery put pay to a planned visit to Zanzibar. The visit was cancelled and instead on 7 July the frigate paid a port visit to Tanga.

Five days later *Loch Insh*, together with the minesweeper *Bassingham* returned to Mombasa. The annual inspection of the islands in the Seychelles by the Governor of the region meant sailing on the 14 July for the tropical island chain and anchoring in the harbour upon arrival at the Seychelles capital of Mahe. The Captain welcomed onboard the Governor at Victoria and then took him on a tour of the islands of Bird, La Digue, Dennis and Frigate Islands.

Sadly the tour was marred by the death onboard on 22 July of Electrical Mechanic W. McCarthy during the return passage to Mahe. The next day he was buried on the island. *Loch Insh* left the Seychelles behind the next morning and sailed for Aden where she arrived after six days at sea.

On 2 August *Loch Insh* welcomed onboard the Commander British Land Forces at Aden for passage to Mombasa where the frigate arrived after seven days steaming. The facilities at Mombasa were well known to generations of sailors and the frigates ships company were granted station leave during the ships maintenance period at Mombasa, which was undertaken with assistance from the carrier *Bulwark*. The carrier was in Mombasa for a series of exercises prior to the frigate returning to the more normal surroundings in Bahrain.

The passage back to Bahrain, however, was far from trouble free with the frigates steering gear breaking down in the busy and dangerous Straits of Hormuz on 25 August. The next day with no steering available the British warship ran aground at Sitra and had to be refloated with the use of local tugs.

An inspection followed to ascertain the extent of the damage the grounding had inflicted on the frigate and upon the engineers report it was decided that it would be prudent to sail back to the United Kingdom to correct a nagging shaft alignment failure. *Loch Insh* sailed from Bahrain on 3 September and six days later whilst off Muscat took part in a two day amphibious warfare exercise before continuing her journey through the Suez

Canal and into the Mediterranean. *Loch Insh*'s only stop en route to Rosyth Dockyard was at Malta on 27 September.

On 5 October 1960 *Loch Insh* was taken in hand at Rosyth Dockyard for a refit that would take until 10 January to complete. She re-commissioned for service in the Persian Gulf under the command of Captain I G Raikes DSC RN. February was spent conducting post refit trials and rectifications before sailing south to Portsmouth in March. On 18 March *Loch Insh* arrived at Portland for her work up that continued into the summer months. The hardship of work up was broken with a visit to Southampton and Easter leave was granted whilst the ship was alongside at Devonport.

In late April and early May *Loch Insh* worked up in the waters off Portland before taking passage to Londonderry on 4 May where training continued until the end of the month. As a result of the hard work undertaken by the ships company *Loch Insh* was rewarded with a visit to the seaside resort of Bournemouth from 26 May.

The following month saw the frigate preparing for her next scheduled foreign deployment to the Persian Gulf where it was planned that she would replace sister ship *Loch Ruthven* on station. When she sailed on the 4 June *Loch Insh* was routed through Gibraltar and Malta. At the latter she was loaded with deck cargo for Operation Vantage in Kuwait. Operation Vantage had been staged rapidly due to the Iraqi threats to the nation of Kuwait and *Loch Insh* and sister ship *Loch Ruthven* were to play a significant part in quelling the impending military invasion by Iraq of her smaller neighbour.

Loch Insh sailed from Aden on 15 July together with seven coastal minesweepers which were to be utilised in the waters off Kuwait if Iraq chose to mine the sealanes off the country. Unfortunately onboard the frigate the next day the engineering department found to their horror that the frigate suffered a complete loss of power onboard, but this was quickly and expertly corrected by the same engineering staff.

Prior to *Loch Insh*'s arrival at Bahrain she rendezvoused with *Loch Ruthven*, which was headed for the United Kingdom. The two sister ships exchanged signals and then proceeded on their respective ways with *Loch Insh* arriving alongside in Bahrain on the 22 July.

The need for escort vessels for Operation Vantage was a pressing one and *Loch Insh* relieved sister ship *Loch Alvie* on the 2 August as part of Task Force 317. She remained on station for another twelve days before returning to Bahrain for the start of a series of Dhow patrols. Usually Dhow patrols were relatively mundane affairs intercepting and inspecting craft suspected of smuggling illegal goods, weapons and contraband but on 24 August *Loch Insh* went to the aid of the Spanish tanker *Mequinenza*. The merchantman had run aground on Shah Alum Shoal and the frigate assisted with the refloating of the ship. Later in the month she visited Muscat, whilst on the 3 September *Loch Insh* returned to Bahrain for a brief refuelling stop before sailing the next morning with *Loch Fyne* for Exercise FOMEX off Yas Island.

The continuing threat from Iraq to Kuwait dominated the deployment and on the 11 September *Loch Insh* and the Type 61 frigate *Chichester* undertook a patrol off the coastline of Kuwait as a deterrent against hostile actions on the part of the Iraqi Government. Finally peace returned to the region with Operation Vantage coming to an end on the 14 September, but the frigates remained off shore until near to the end of the month.

Having returned to Bahrain with *Chichester*, *Loch Insh* was alongside for over a fortnight to allow her ships company to take leave and to undertake some alongside maintenance.

On 13 October *Loch Insh* sailed for another Dhow patrol that also saw visits paid to Sir Adu Musa, Das, Bahrain and Aden. On 3 November the frigate sailed together with three coastal minesweepers for Karachi for a major CENTO exercise called MIDLINK IV. The passage was rough onboard the frigate, but onboard the little coastal minesweepers the conditions were horrific with heavy seas and strong winds battering the vessels. Indeed it might have been this heavy sea that later caused problems for *Loch Insh* when taking part in the exercise she experienced a series of significant boiler room problems including contamination that caused the engines to shut down for a while.

The exercises started on 17 November and also involved *Loch Alvie* as well as a number of Commonwealth warships. *Loch Insh*'s faulty boilers, however, restricted the frigate's participation in

HMS Loch Insh *spent much of her postwar career serving in the Middle East.*　　(*Crown Copyright/MoD*)

MIDLINK IV and on the 27 November she sailed to Karachi where adjustments and repairs were undertaken. *Loch Insh* would also, during this period, visit the Indian port city of Bombay.

On 2 December *Loch Insh* made her way to Karachi where it was planned for the frigate to be taken in hand by dockyard workers for an Interim Docking and a hull scrape. The ship would also receive a short refit. *Loch Insh* sailed into Karachi two days later and eased into the docks.

On 4 January 1962 the frigate completed her trials and sailed from Karachi bound for Bahrain. After a four day passage *Loch Insh* arrived at her homeport in the Gulf. Ten days later she sailed to take part in a major naval exercise with other Royal Navy units in the Persian Gulf and also made a series of port visits to Sharjah, Dubai,

Doha, Abu Dhabi and Yas Island. On completion she resumed her dhow patrols before arriving back at Bahrain on 1 February.

After a period alongside the frigate sailed on 13 February with Flag Officer Middle East onboard for an official visit to Bombay. The passage took six days. Upon their arrival the ship was welcomed in usual Indian style and the hospitality of the locals was said to be overwhelming. *Loch Insh* was only in Bombay for four days before she returned to Bahrain where she had been scheduled to take part in a series of naval exercises in the Persian Gulf.

Finally the frigate arrived back at Bahrain on the first day of March. The men of *Loch Insh* then spent the next fortnight making and mending and preparing the ship for her next patrol which started with a visit to Bandar

Mashur followed by more dhow patrols.

The frigate's annual inspection awaited the ship upon her return to Bahrain and after a successful sea inspection on the 12 April she sailed the next day for a tour of East African ports. The planned itinerary was changed at short notice when *Loch Insh* received orders to proceed to the island of Gan in the Maldives. The island had been struck by a series of riots and *Loch Insh* and her sailors were to provide support to the local police forces on the island and restore order. The British warship arrived on the 23 April.

On Sunday 6 May *Loch Insh* sailed from Gan to the Seychelles Island chain after refuelling from RFA *Wave Victor* and embarking Admiral Flag Officer Middle East. The frigate arrived at Port Victoria after four days steaming. Men from the ship were allowed a short period of leave to explore the island and the locals were likewise allowed onboard to tour the warship, before the frigate sailed on the 14 May for Mombasa with Flag Officer Middle East embarked. The frigate stayed just long enough at Mombasa to refuel and replenish her stores on the 17th, sailing just two hours after arriving and made for Aden, where she arrived on the 23rd. At Aden she anchored in the harbour and within two days had met the coastal minesweeper *Tarlton*. This vessel was to be towed back to the United Kingdom. The Royal Navy vessels slipped on the 25th and sailed up the Red Sea and stopped at Port Suez. *Loch Insh*'s relief had been delayed due to a machinery defect and the decision was taken to wait at Port Suez until she arrived. The frigate's northerly transit of the Suez Canal started on the 2 June and once

at Port Said the minesweeper was detached and made her own way independently back to the United Kingdom. *Loch Insh* meanwhile, made a rough crossing of the Mediterranean and arrived at Malta on the 8th.

She only stayed long enough to refuel before resuming her passage to Gibraltar. After another brief stop at The Rock, *Loch Insh* continued onto Plymouth, where she arrived on Wednesday 20 June wearing her paying off pennant. She secured alongside No 1 Wharf and two days later the frigate was formally decommissioned.

The sale of *Loch Insh* to the Malayan Navy had been agreed and in 1963 she was transferred to that Navy pending a refit, which was undertaken at Portsmouth. The whole appearance of *Loch Insh* was altered with the addition of a helicopter landing pad and substantially remodelled superstructure.

The ship was undocked from 15 Dock at Portsmouth on Friday 17 April 1964 and two weeks later on Friday 26 April stores were taken onboard the frigate. It would, however, not be until Friday 11 September when harbour trials commenced and were completed on Wednesday 30 September. The frigate was commissioned as the *Hang Tuah* and after initial sea trials in the Solent and English Channel the warship sailed for Malaysia on 12 November 1964. As the largest and most powerful ship in the Malaysian Fleet, *Hang Tuah* was also the flagship, a role she retained until 1971 when the frigate was converted into a training ship. For another six years the *Hang Tuah* served the Malaysian Navy until withdrawn from service and scrapped.

Chronology

17.11.1943	Laid down at Henry Robb shipyard
10.05.1944	Launched
20.10.1944	Completed and joined 19th Escort Group
06.12.1944	Attacked and sank *U-297* off Cape Wraith with Goodall
01.02.1945	Belfast for repairs
04.1945	Convoy escort for JW66 to Kola Inlet
29.04.1945	Sailed for United Kingdom and sank *U-307*
05.1945	Henry Robb shipyard for refit
06.05.1945	Leith
27.07.1945	Sailed for Rosyth Dockyard
23.08.1945	Sailed for join the East Indies Escort Force
25.10.1945	Colombo
29.11.1945	Sailed for Singapore
12.1945	East Africa
08.03.1946	Trincomalee
05.1946	Devonport and entered reserve
1949	Brigham and Cowan for a refit
07.1950	Re-entered service at Devonport and joined 6th Frigate Flotilla
Late 1950	Londonderry, Gibraltar and Bayonne
01.1951	Home Fleet Exercises
03.1951	Devonport
Autumn 1951	Home Fleet Exercises
01.1952	Devonport for Loch class frigate modernisation programme. *Loch Insh* was the prototype for the programme.
05.1953	Refit commenced
07.1954	Refit completed
06.09.1954	Recommissioned at Devonport
09.1954	Portland and Malta
10.1954	Operated with Destroyer Command Mediterranean
Autumn 1954	Persian Gulf
02.1955	Refit at Colombo
03.1955	Persian Gulf
04.1955	Dubai, Sharjah, Ras-al-Khaima
20.05.1955	Went to aid of Dutch tanker SS *Argea Prim*
25.05.1955	Bahrain
08.1955	Paid off at Devonport ahead of refit
11.10.1955	Recommissioned
Early 1956	Work up at Portland
27.02.1956	Sailed for Middle East
04.1956	Iraq

Handwritten annotations:

(Musketry Course of Deyutlaw)

(Trincomalee Xmas 53.

to Ceylon, Andaman Is, Nicabar Is, Chittagon, Madras, Visgapatm, Colombo, Aden. UK

(Gibraltar) UK

Devonport.

05.1956	Visited Daiyr, Asalu and Lingeh in Iran
Summer 1956	Operated around Aden during Egyptian crisis
07.1956	Persian Gulf
10.10.1956	Salvaged MV *Hang Kong* off Bahrain
04.11.1956	Sitra
11.1956	Red Sea during Operation Musketeer
25.12.1956	Bahrain
28.12.1956	Sailed for United Kingdom via Mombasa, Simonstown and Freetown
08.02.1957	Devonport for a major refit
07.01.1958	Refit completed
02.1958	Work up at Portland and Londonderry
04.1958	Liverpool and Le Havre
05.1958	Sailed for Middle East
Late 1958	Karachi, Cochin and Bombay
03.1959	East African Coast
05.1959	Devonport for refit
07.1959	Returned to service
16.11.1959	Sailed for Aden
24.11.1959	Met cruiser *Gambia* in Red Sea
17.12.1959	Exercise Shop Window at Aden
Early 1960	Persian Gulf
11.02.1960	Umm Said
03.1960	Karachi for short refit
16.04.1960	Exercises with Pakistani warships
Late 04.1960	Exercise Khargex II off Iran
10.05.1960	Abadan
12.05.1960	Khorramshah
02.07.1960	Mombasa
07.07.1960	Tanga
07.1960	Seychelles, Bird, La Digue, Dennis Island and Frigate Island
28.07.1960	Aden
09.08.1960	Mombasa for amphibious exercise with *Bulwark*
25.08.1960	Steering gear failure in Straits of Hormuz
03.09.1960	Sailed for United Kingdom via Muscat
09.09.1960	Amphibious exercise at Muscat
27.09.1960	Malta
05.10.1960	Taken in hand at Rosyth for refit
10.01.1961	Refit completed
02.1961	Trials
18.03.1961	Portland for work up
04.05.1961	Londonderry
26.05.1961	Bournemouth
04.06.1961	Sailed for Middle East with deck cargo for Operation Vantage in Kuwait
15.07.1961	Sailed from Malta with 7 coastal minesweepers for Aden
22.07.1961	Bahrain

02.08.1961	Relieved *Loch Alvie* in Task Force 317
24.08.1961	Went to the aid of Spanish tanker *Mequinenza* at Shah Alum Shoal
04.09.1961	Exercise FOMEX IV off Yas Island
11.09.1961	With frigate *Chichester* patrolled off Kuwait to deter Iraqi invasion
14.09.1961	End of Operation Vantage
13.10.1961	Dhow Patrol
03.11.1961	Sailed to Karachi with 3 minesweepers for Exercise MIDLINK IV
17.11.1961	Start of MIDLINK IV exercises but experienced boiler troubles
27.11.1961	Arrived Karachi for defect repairs
11.1961	Visited Bombay
04.12.1961	Karachi for a docking period
04.01.1962	Bahrain
01.1962	Visited Sharjah, Dubai, Abu Dhabi and Yas Island
01.02.1962	Bahrain
12.04.1962	Annual Inspection
13.04.1962	Start of tour of East African ports
23.04.1962	Gan following civil unrest
23.05.1962	Aden and collected minesweeper *Tarlton*, which was towed to Malta
02.06.1962	Malta
20.06.1962	Devonport
22.06.1962	Formally decommissioned from service
1963	Sold to Malaysia and renamed *Hang Tuah*
1963	Extensively refitted at Portsmouth
17.04.1964	Undocked
11.09.1964	Harbour trials
30.09.1964	Trials completed
12.11.1964	Sailed for Malaysia
1971	Converted to training ship
1977	Withdrawn from service

HMS LOCH KATRINE
(HMNZS ROTOITI FROM 1948)

HMS Loch Katrine *seen at Malta before her transfer to the Royal New Zealand Navy in 1948.*

(Ken Kelly Collection)

Henry Robb Shipyard received the contract for the construction of a Loch class frigate on 25 January 1943. Soon the prefabricated sections of the ship were being assembled next to the slipway in preparation for the first steel plates of the hull to be laid on 31 December the same year. Given the yard number 347 the job of building the frigate was to take another eight months to the launching stage. *Loch Katrine*, as she was named, entered the water for the first time on 21 August named after a loch near the town of Callender. Almost a year since she was laid down on 29 December 1944 *Loch Katrine* was completed and handed over to the Royal Navy under the command of Lieutenant Commander R A Cherry RNR.

1945 started with *Loch Katrine* taking passage to Tobermory to store and then on to escort aircraft carriers in the North West Approaches. After her initial work up period she joined the 20th Escort Group at

Londonderry but only for three days. On 28 January she sailed south to Gibraltar for convoy escort duties. The convoy safely arrived at the Rock on 4 February and *Loch Katrine* joined a UK bound convoy on Valentine's Day.

On her return to Londonderry on 20 February *Loch Katrine* transferred to the 24th Escort Group, (comprised of *Loch Quoich, Loch Tarbert* and two River class ships), and became the senior officer's ship of Commander John Valentine Waterhouse DSO.

Commander Waterhouse was born in Bucklow in Cheshire on 14 February 1911. During his naval career he served onboard the cruiser *Arethusa* and the minelayer *Latona*. Whilst commanding the destroyer *Viscount* he was awarded a DSO when he rammed and sank a German U-boat on 14 October in the Western Approaches.

Waterhouse transferred command to the sloop *Egret* and then became training commander at HMS *Canada*

in Halifax in Nova Scotia. In 1944 he returned to sea with the command of Rochester until he was transferred to the new *Loch Katrine*. Postwar Waterhouse continued to serve in the Royal Navy and following an Antarctic Cruise was awarded an OBE.

After a period on Gibraltar to the United Kingdom convoy defence *Loch Katrine* sailed north for Londonderry. She repeated the journey to Gibraltar on 10 March arriving at The Rock six days later. The next nine days were spent at Gibraltar assembling the ships necessary for another return convoy to the United Kingdom. Once the ships had sailing orders *Loch Katrine* and the other escorts took the convoy under their protection sailing for Liverpool where limited leave was granted to the crew until the frigate sailed on 2 April bound once again for Gibraltar.

Loch Katrine and the other ships of the convoy arrived safely on 7 April. Yet again she was to escort another return convoy to Liverpool once all the merchantmen had been assembled. The convoy sailed on a five day passage on 12 April. During the journey north *Loch Katrine* and the Canadian escort HMCS *Evenlode* collided causing slight damage to both ships.

With the end of the war in Europe in early May attention turned to destroying Germany's surrendering U-boats. Operation Deadlight would see the sinking of dozens of submarines off Northern Ireland. On 6 May *Loch Katrine* waited in the North West Approaches to collect any U-boats flying a black flag as per the surrender instructions issued by the victorious Allies. Upon completion the frigate returned to Liverpool to join in the celebrations that had continued from VE Day in the city.

In June the frigate was taken in hand for a refit period at Londonderry when extra weapons were added on the quarterdeck for service in the Pacific. Following completion of the refit the frigate sailed on 8 July in company with sister ship *Loch Quoich* for the Far East with stops made at Gibraltar, Aden and on 4 August at Colombo.

The following month saw her operating in the Bay of Bengal and the Malacca Straits. On 7 September *Loch Katrine* was one of the Allied ships present at Singapore to witness the signing of the official

Japanese surrender documents. The celebrations lasted only for two days before *Loch Katrine* was ordered to sail initially on patrol in local waters and then on to Bangkok, where on 4 November she landed officers from the British Consular Office to reinstate the embassy in the city.

Upon completion of the official duties she returned to Singapore on 11 November. At Singapore Lieutenant Commander Bidwell RNR took command and on 5 December took the warship to Batavia to act as a guardship there. Her presence was necessary to ensure that law and order was maintained following a period of opposition to the return of Dutch colonial rule. She remained in the region until near the end of the year before taking part in the repatriation of civilian war internees to Singapore from Padang and other locations.

The New Year of 1946 started well for *Loch Katrine* with the ship operating on convoy protection duties in the Malacca Strait. Later in the month she visited Vizgaptan before returning to Singapore on 21 January. At Singapore a change of command ceremony was staged to mark the transfer of command to Lieutenant Commander A C D Leach DSC RN.

The following month the frigate was kept busy conducting air sea rescue operations as well as relieving sister ship *Loch Achray* on 12 February. For the next ten days the ship patrolled the waters assigned to her without any incident and on 23 February returned to Singapore where the crew discovered that they would be heading home the following month and *Loch Katrine* would, upon reaching Portsmouth, be placed in reserve.

On 25 February *Loch Katrine* together with sister ship *Loch Tarbert* sailed for the United Kingdom via the Mediterranean. Just over a month after starting their journey the two frigates arrived at Portsmouth on 29 April and were quickly de-stored and prepared for a lengthy stay in the reserve fleet at the Hampshire Naval Base.

In 1947 the frigate along with others of the class were offered for sale to the New Zealand Navy. The asking price of £234,150 was agreed the following year. Part of the cost included the provision for the ships to be refitted at Portsmouth Dockyard before

being transferred to Kiwi control. A number of names appeared in the frame for the new ship including Tawara but eventually it was decided to name the ships after lakes in New Zealand with *Loch Katrine* being given the name *Rotoiti*.

The ship spent most of the early part of 1949 under refit, before commissioning on 7 May at Portsmouth under the command of Lieutenant Commander A M Seymour DSC RN. Nine days later the ship was formally renamed as HMNZS *Rotoiti* by Mrs W H Jordan, wife of the New Zealand High Commissioner. After some trials in British waters the frigate sailed for her new home in June calling at Gibraltar where the opportunity was taken to work the ship up alongside ships and units of the British Mediterranean Fleet.

Having resumed her journey to New Zealand the frigate made visits to Aden along with sister ship *Tutira* before arriving at Auckland to join the 11th Frigate Squadron. With his duties as delivery captain completed Lieutenant Commander A M Seymour DSC handed over command of the frigate to Lieutenant Commander A C B Bloomfield on 2 September at the start of her career in the Royal New Zealand Navy.

The ship's programme for the autumn saw her operating in the South West Pacific with visits made to amongst others Raou before returning home to New Zealand in November. 1950 started with a continuation of local exercises that lasted into the spring. May saw the start of a two month deployment to the South

HMNZS Rotoiti *on 14 June 1949.*   (Steve Bush Collection)

Sea Islands with port calls made to Suva, Ocean Island and Tawara, whilst the ships destination was Hauraki Gulf for exercises with the rest of the frigate flotilla ahead of a deployment to Korea under the umbrella of the United Nations following an appeal for forces to be sent to the troubled country.

On 18 September Lieutenant Commander E E Turner DSC RNZN took command of *Rotoiti* and took the warship into the warzone after stops at Hong Kong, Darwin and Sasebo in October. Upon her arrival on 5 November the frigate relieved her sister ship *Pukaki* and quickly assumed the role of escort vessel for convoys travelling in Korean coastal waters. Her first convoy took her to Inchon before deploying on patrol in December.

The closing month of the year saw the frigate carrying out humanitarian missions when she rescued refugees trying to reach safety as well as taking representatives of the world's press to the Han River area.

When, in January 1951, Inchon and Chinampo fell to enemy attack the ship was ordered to patrol the approaches to the region in order to intercept any ships that could resupply enemy forces. This tactic allowed the Allied evacuation shipping free passage away from the two communities. The Allies were, however, determined that Inchon would not remain in enemy hands for long and the frigate was fully involved in the re-occupation campaign between February and June.

After a maintenance period in Kure in July she returned to Chinampo harbour on 17 July to attack enemy gun positions at Sogon-Ni Point. During the attack an assault party from the frigate was organised comprising of fourteen men. Under cover of gunfire from their ship the men raided the shore. In the brief confrontation that followed two enemy soldiers were captured and brought back to the frigate under guard as prisoners of war.

Later on 25 August *Rotoiti* carried out another bombardment of enemy positions at Sogon-Ni and an

During her career in New Zealand HMNZS Rotoiti *remained virtually unchanged from her Royal Navy appearance.*
(Steve Bush Collection)

armed party from the frigate was again put ashore that also included a number of Royal Marine Commandos from the cruiser Ceylon. The attackers came under stiff resistance from the determined defenders and sadly Able Seaman Marchioni from the New Zealand Navy was killed in the action.

September saw the frigate resume her usual patrol pattern off Korea's west coastline whilst the following months saw the announcement of a number of awards to the ships company; the captain, Lieutenant Commander B E Turner receiving a Distinguished Service Cross and later the US Legion of Merit.

By 23 October *Rotoiti* was back at Kure and took passage that day for Hong Kong. Two days into the journey the frigate received a distress call from the British steamship SS *Hupeh*, which had been boarded by twenty armed pirates in the Yangtze estuary in position 31.16N 122.54E at 1435 on 25 October. The SS *Hupeh* was a merchantman carrying some cargo as well as women and children.

The pirates immediately altered course and took the ship in a southerly direction. *Rotoiti* intercepted the hijacked vessel at 2200. The pirates then threatened reprisals unless they were given safe conduct to Tung Cho Island. Fearing for the safety of the passengers *Rotoiti*'s captain agreed and escorted the vessel to the island. Once the pirates reached their destination they left the ship and their unwilling hostages unharmed.

Following this drama *Rotoiti* resumed her passage to Hong Kong before proceeding onto North Borneo, Brisbane and finally back home to Auckland.

On 30 November the frigate was paid off and immediately re-commissioned for further service with the 11th Frigate Squadron. The ceremony also saw a change of command with the ships new commanding officer being Lieutenant Commander G O Graham DSC RN. With the warship back in commission it was announced that following trials and work up in January 1952 she would return to continue her work off Korea.

Rotoiti sailed on 7 January calling at Hong Kong, Raoul and Suva en route to the warzone where she remained until relieved on 2 February by *Hawea*.

On the 12 January the warship returned to West Korea coastal operations arriving on station after three days steaming. Her duties included reconnaissance of enemy positions ashore and on 22 January bombarding those positions in the Han River estuary. During her attack the North Koreans mounted quite an effective rate of return fire on the ship from three separate gunnery positions. *Rotoiti* moved off from the Han River to avoid any possible damage and casualties amongst her ships company. The frigate continued to operate off Korea throughout February and March and in April arrived at the Japanese port of Kure for a maintenance period and to allow her crew some leave.

By 3 May *Rotoiti* was back on patrol, this time operating in the region of the Kirin-Do Channel where she fired sixteen rounds at enemy positions ashore. The following month was spent mostly on patrol before taking passage to Hong Kong for another maintenance period away from the front line. It was only a short absence from Korea as the warship returned to operations in July.

After spending the autumn on patrols and convoy escort duties off the West Coast of Korea, the New Zealand warship spent the first few days of October in Kure arriving on 6 October. *Rotoiti* received a prestigious honour when on 11 October she was visited by The First Sea Lord, Admiral Sir Rhoderick MacGriger whilst at Kure. He toured the ship and spoke to the ships company and thanked them for their hard and sterling work in trying circumstances.

After maintenance had been carried out on the ship and the last of the leave periods had been taken the frigate returned to sea and assumed her patrol off Korea in October. The following month she operated with her sister ship *Hawea* before celebrating Christmas at Kure.

1953 started with a return to Sasebo for a rest period, having been relieved by *Hawea*, but the frigate was soon back on patrol on Korea's west coast. February would prove to be the ships last Korean war patrol and would prove to be reasonably uneventful. On 28 February she left Korea bound for home with visits paid en route to Sasebo, Hong Kong and finally Sydney. At the last port she rendezvoused with her sister ship *Kaniere*.

On 19 March the frigate arrived safely back at her home port of Auckland and was de-stored in prepara-

tion of a planned refit that started the following month. The refit was not as extensive as that carried out on Royal Navy sister ships, but did see the installation of the Type 277Q height finding radar. After post refit trials the ship was placed in reserve, where she remained until she was reactivated for service in support of the British nuclear bomb tests at Christmas Island, Operation Grapple.

Once her systems had been tested, the frigate recommissioned in February and soon thereafter sailed to join sister ship *Pukaki* at Christmas Island, where she arrived on 31 March 1957. The two Kiwi ships were used to monitor the effects of the nuclear blasts and this duty continued until 25 June when she sailed back to New Zealand for leave and a maintenance period.

In August the frigate received a new commanding officer in the form of Lieutenant Commander L E Hodge RNZN and he took the frigate back to Christmas Island for more duties associated with the British nuclear weapon tests. The frigate remained in the area until nearly the end of the year. In December she took part in a joint naval exercise with the Australian Navy before spending Christmas back in her home waters.

The start of 1958 saw the frigate based out of Auckland whilst in February she was taken in hand for a planned refit that lasted until April. Upon successful completion of her trials and work up the frigate joined the 3rd Frigate Squadron and took passage to Sydney in Australia to operate with units of the Australian fleet. Upon completion the frigate sailed north to meet up with Royal Navy warships at Singapore and participated in a lengthy series of exercises and visits that included Hong Kong and numerous Japanese ports of call.

It was whilst *Rotoiti* was off Japan that she joined with the US Navy for joint exercises before returning to Singapore for a docking period. Local workmen scraped the frigate's bottom and gave her a fresh coat of paint just ahead of commencing an anti-piracy patrol off the coastline of North Borneo. The autumn months saw further exercises off Singapore and Hong Kong before she spent the festive period at Singapore.

After some time alongside at Singapore the warship sailed in early January 1959 for some sea time before returning to the base for another docking and maintenance period. February, however, saw her sail to assume guardship duties at Tawara and Ellice Islands during that year's Royal visit to the islands. Later in the month *Rotoiti* rendezvoused with the Royal Yacht *Britannia* with HRH the Duke of Edinburgh onboard. The Duke crossed to the frigate by jackstay for a brief tour as both ships made for Hong Kong. *Rotoiti* left the Royal Yacht in April and sailed independently back to Auckland for duties with the 11th Frigate Squadron.

In June 1959 the frigate took part in a series of naval exercises before heading back to the dockyard at Auckland for a planned refit programme. Work on the ship included the modernisation of her electronics, habitation improvements and her armament was updated with the substitution of two 40mm Bofors mountings instead of the wartime vintage 2pdr Pom Pom weapons. The refit lasted until the end of the year. When she re-commissioned in January 1960 the ship was under the command of Lieutenant Commander R L Harding RNZN.

February saw the frigate joining the Commonwealth Strategic Reserve based at Singapore that included Australian and Kiwi exercises off the city of Sydney. The following month was just as busy for the New Zealand warship with a journey to Singapore and participation in Exercise Sealink ahead of a visit to Bangkok. In May *Rotoiti* continued to exercise with US, Japanese and British forces in the region and also visited Hong Kong and Japanese ports including Kobe in June.

In July the frigate returned to Singapore and participated in the Malayan patrols in the region throughout the summer and into the autumn of 1960. During October she paid ports of call to Langdau, Port Swettenham and Pangkor before sailing for Hong Kong at the beginning of November. She took part in a major naval exercise staged in the waters of the British colony and upon completion went on to visit Bangkok.

December was spent at Singapore and Hong Kong whilst January 1961 saw Rotoiti participate with US Navy units again just prior to an official visit to the Japanese capital city of Tokyo.

Rotoiti's globetrotting continued in late January with visits to Singapore, Manila and then to home waters around New Zealand. The warship went onto visit Port Moresby and Noumea before berthing alongside at Auckland naval base in March.

The Loch class frigate resumed her normal operations around the coastline of New Zealand throughout the summer months before being taken in hand for a short refit. Towards the end of this command of the ship was transferred to Lieutenant Commander Q A Lawrence RNZN.

In October the ship returned to operational status within the New Zealand Navy and resumed her planned series of port visits until the end of the year. 1962 proved to be a very busy year for the Kiwi ship with a number of naval exercises as well as visits planned to Raoul Island and Sydney in Australia.

After visiting Suva in May, the frigate returned home to Auckland where she was taken in hand for another refit. The refit gave the frigate all the equipment necessary to take part in Exercise Deep Freeze in Antarctic waters on behalf of the US Navy. The refit was completed in September and on 8 October *Rotoiti* sailed from Auckland to Lyttleton. At the latter port the ships officers and crew were told in a briefing what to expect in the Southern Ocean. Twelve days later on 20 October she arrived on station. Operation Deep Freeze was a scientific led expedition into the world's last great uncharted and mostly unexplored continent. Each ship taking part carried with it equipment to study and record a wide variety of data including weather patterns, oceanography and hydrography.

On 1 November the frigate returned to Dunedin to allow the crew some rest and recuperation before returning to duty on 12 November. Nine days were spent on the operation before she set course for Wellington having successfully completed her role in Operation Deep Freeze. The next time the frigate put to sea was when she ventured no further south than the waters of the west coast of the South Island of New Zealand.

On 12 December, *Rotoiti* spent a day at Omeha Bay painting the ship ahead of her arrival at Auckland. The warship remained at her homeport over the Christmas period before starting 1963 with various flotilla duties off New Zealand.

In March *Rotoiti* undertook a lengthy series of Kiwi exercises before spending much of June on a cruise around South Pacific Islands including Apia, Lifuka, Atufu, Wallis Island and Suva. On completion the frigate headed for Auckland for summer leave to be granted to the crew.

Upon their return onboard, the warship sailed on another cruise of the Pacific Islands making port visits to Apia and Fakofa. When she returned to New Zealand the ship was taken in hand for a docking period at Auckland.

The warships successful participation in the American led Operation Deep Freeze saw her nominated for use in the second series of experiments and patrols in the region which were to start in October and last another two months. The ship, however, was replaced by *Pukaki* for the duties in the Southern Ocean and Rotoiti herself became escort and guardship for the visit by Her Majesty the Queen Mother on her tour of New Zealand.

1964 would prove to be a very busy year for the frigate. In January she was at Auckland and the crew prepared the warship for the Royal Escort duties of the Royal Yacht *Britannia*. The Royal party's tour would take in Fiji and New Zealand from 3 February. Seven days later the Kiwi ship rendezvoused with *Britannia* at Lautoka to escort her back to New Zealand. The British ship would sail again on the 14 February to make port visits to Wellington, Timaru, Bluff and Dunedin and throughout New Zealand the frigate remained a constant companion. Finally on the 28 February *Rotoiti* left *Britannia* after the Queen Mother had left the Royal Yacht to fly to Australia.

News reached the ship in March that her future role in the fleet was to be as a training ship, specifically for New Entry Seaman ratings. She assumed this role almost immediately and together with the cruiser Royalist sailed for the waters around Suva to conduct basic sea training.

The Kiwi warship went onto make further visits throughout the summer on the training cruise calling at Raoul, Lautoka, Rotuma, Funfuti and Lambasa before returning to New Zealand towards the end of July.

Upon her return to Auckland *Rotoiti* spent a period in dockyard hands into the early part of 1965.

January 1965 saw the frigate continuing her training role with a brand new commanding officer in the form of Lieutenant Commander K C H Cadman RNZN. As part of her duties in February whilst off the North Island with the cruiser *Royalist* the frigate carried out a series of trials with rubber dinghies. The spring of 1965 was however when it was announced that after many years of faithful service the Loch class frigate was to be retired from active service and be replaced by a more modern Type 12 or Leander class frigate. In August she made a series of farewell visits around New Zealand before finally paying off into reserve at Auckland. *Rotoiti* would only remain in reserve for a relatively short time and was soon sold to Hong Kong Rolling Mills for scrap. *Rotoiti* left under tow bound for Hong Kong on 28 November 1966 and demolition of the former frigate started the following February.

Chronology

25.01.1943	Ordered from Henry Robb
31.12.1943	Laid down
21.08.1944	Launched
29.12.1944	Completed
Early 1945	Joined 20th Escort Group at Londonderry
28.01.1945	Took passage to Gibraltar
20.02.1945	24th Escort Group at Londonderry
03.1945	Convoy escort duties between Gibraltar and United Kingdom
04.1945	Collided with HMCS *Evenlode*
05.1945	Operation Deadlight
06.1945	Refit at Londonderry
08.07.1945	Sailed for Far East with *Loch Quoich*
09.1945	Bay of Bengal area
07.09.1945	Singapore for official Japanese surrender
04.11.1945	Bangkok
11.11.1945	Singapore
05.12.1945	Batavia guardship
01.01.1946	Malacca Straits
25.02.1946	Sailed for United Kingdom and reserve at Portsmouth
29.04.1946	Arrived Portsmouth
1948	Sold to New Zealand Government
1949	Refit at Portsmouth
07.05.1949	Commissioned into New Zealand Navy as *Rotoiti*
06.1949	Sailed for New Zealand
Late 1949	South West Pacific
Early 1950	Visited Suva, Ocean Island and South Sea Islands
18.09.1950	Sailed for Korean operations with UN forces
05.11.1950	Arrived off Korea
01.1951	Inchon and Chinampo
17.07.1951	Attacked gun position at Sogun-ni Point in Korea
25.08.1951	Bombarded Sognu-ni
09.1951	West Coast patrol off Korea
23.10.1951	Maintenance and leave at Kure
25.10.1951	Went to aid of Hupeh, which had been taken by pirates
30.11.1951	Paid off and re-commissioned at Auckland
07.01.1952	Korean patrol until 02.02.1952
22.01.1952	Bombarded enemy on Han River estuary
03.05.1952	Operations in the Kirin-Do Channel
10.1952	Kure
28.02.1953	Took passage to Auckland from Korean war patrol
19.03.1953	Auckland for refit

04.1953	In reserve
31.03.1957	Brought forward from reserve for Operation Grapple, the British nuclear bomb tests at Christmas Island until 25.06.1957
07.1957	Auckland
08.1957	Christmas Island for Operation Grapple
25.11.1957	Home waters
02.1958	Refit at Auckland until April
05.1958	Operations with Royal Australian Navy
06.1958	Singapore, Hong Kong and Japan
Late 1958	Borneo Patrol
02.1959	Guardship at Tawau and Ellis Island
06.1959	Naval exercises off New Zealand
06.1959	Refit at Auckland
01.1960	Recommissioned
02.1960	Commonwealth Strategic Reserve at Singapore
03.1960	Exercise Sealink with visit to Bangkok
10.1960	Visited Langdau, Port Sweetenham and Pangdor
12.1960	Singapore and Hong Kong
01.1961	Tokyo with US Navy
Summer 1961	Short refit at Auckland
08.10.1962	Sailed for Exercise Deep Freeze in Antarctica
20.10.1962	On station in Antarctica
01.11.1962	Dunedin
03.1963	Local exercises off New Zealand
06.1963	Visited Apia, Lifuka, Atufu, Walk Island and Suva
10.1963	Returned to Antarctica with US Navy
01.1964	Escorted Royal Yacht *Britannia* on tour of Fiji and New Zealand
10.01.1964	Lotoka
01.1964	Royal tour including visits to Wellington, Bluff and Dunedin
03.1964	Became training ship for new recruits
Summer 1964	Training cruise to South Sea Islands
Spring 196	Announcement of planned withdrawal from service
08.1965	Farewell tour of New Zealand
08.1965	Sold to Hong Kong Rolling Mills for scrap
02.1967	Arrived Hong Kong for breaking up

HMS Loch Killin

The classic post war view of a Royal Navy frigate, Loch Killin*'s compact size and powerful armament are seen to good effect.* *(Crown Copyright/MoD)*

The Admiralty placed job No J11854 with Burntisland Shipbuilding on 6 March 1943 for a Loch class frigate. The shipyard gave her the yard number of 283 and laid down the first components on the slipway on 2 June 1943. Construction to the launching stage was speedy being achieved in six months with the ship tasting water for the first time on 29 November 1943. Another five months would pass before the ship was completed on 12 April 1944 and took the name *Loch Killin* named after an inland loch near Inverness.

In April 1944 upon completion of sea trials *Loch Killin* joined the 2nd Escort Group under the command of Lieutenant Commander D Darling, DSC RANVR.

At the end of the month the frigate was in the River Clyde conducting trials with her Squid anti-submarine mortar system. These trials continued into May, when she worked with the Underwater Research Establishment at Fairlie.

On 10 May *Loch Killin* was at Tobermory to complete her work up that ended with a visit to Liverpool on 1 June prior to joining the fleet assembling at Plymouth for the D-Day landings. Her role was to patrol the South West Approaches to prevent U-boats from attacking the invasion fleet.

On 2 July *Loch Killin* sailed into Liverpool and remained there for a fortnight before resuming operations in the English Channel on 18 July. On the last day of the month together with *Starling*, *Loch Killin* were operating South West of the Scilly Isles when they attacked and destroyed the Type VIIC submarine *U-333* under the command of Kaptainleutnant Hans Fiedler who had only assumed command eleven days before.

Both ships searched for survivors but none were

found. *Loch Killin* thus became the first ship to sink a submarine with the new Squid anti-submarine weapon.

In August *Loch Killin* sailed into the Bay of Biscay where on the 6 August she detected and attacked the German Type VIIC submarine *U-736* under the command of Oberleutnant Rheinhard Reff. Men from *Loch Killin* struggled to rescue German sailors from the water, but witnesses reported seeing the last few men on the submarine being swept back into the sinking U-boat to their deaths including the Captain and many of his officers. Those that were saved and were given fresh clothes and medical attention as most had swallowed oil and water. The German's were later transferred to a Canadian destroyer for transportation to Falmouth.

The U-boat was sunk south west of the port of St Nazaire. Nineteen of the boat's crew were recovered from the water. *Loch Killin* herself had sustained some damage to her propeller during the attack. Three days later the frigate was involved in the attack on another U-boat, the Type VIIC *U-608* under the command of Oberleutnant Wolfgang Reisener. The boat was attacked by HMS *Wren*, *Loch Killin* and an RAF Liberator aircraft South West of St Nazaire.

The submarine was damaged and resting on the bottom whilst repairs were undertaken by her crew. *Loch Killin* remained on the lookout for any movement from the submarine below. The damage was too extensive to repair and the German Captain surfaced and surrendered before scuttling his submarine. Reisener's English was impeccable as he had been educated at Cambridge University before the war. The rescued fifty two men were given fresh clothes and a good meal onboard the British frigate.

Two days later *Loch Killin* attacked the Type VIIC submarine *U-385* under the command of Oberleutnant Hans Guido Valentiner, which was later bombed by Sunderland flying boats. The frigate needed repairs to be made to her propellers so made for Liverpool where a dry dock was available. She arrived on 13 August where she also transferred to the 17th Escort Group.

With repairs completed the frigate sailed north on 20 August to Scapa Flow where she joined the other ships in the group on patrols in the North West

Seen in her wartime camoflauge scheme Loch Killin *was involved in the destruction of the German U-boats* U-333, U-736 *and* U-385.
(Crown Copyright/MoD)

Approaches and between the Fareroes and the Norwegian coast.

On 14 September the crew were given leave when the ship arrived back to the River Clyde. She remained there until 27 September when she sailed to Scapa Flow to resume her anti-submarine patrols in the North West Approaches. She remained until 26 October.

After a fortnight *Loch Killin* sailed to resume her duties with the 17th Escort Group out of Scapa Flow.

On 4 December the frigate was once again on the River Clyde for leave and repairs. The remainder of December was spent on detachment in the English Channel searching for U-boats.

1945 started with a drama when on 5 January *Loch Killin* collided with HM Trawler *Quadraille*. The frigate was damaged but still able to attach a tow line to the smaller vessel and take her to Portsmouth where both ships were taken in hand for repairs. Upon completion of these *Loch Killin* sailed on 25 January to patrol the familiar grounds of the North West Approaches. While in the area she put into Belfast and a further visit was made to the Clyde. The following month she operated in the English Channel again before returning to Scapa Flow on 3 March.

The following month the frigate transferred her operating base to Plymouth and on 11 April deployed with Cranston and Burges. Two days into the patrol the force discovered the German Type VIIC/41 submarine *U-1063* under the command of Kapitanleutnant Karl Heinz Stephan off Start Point, Devon. *Loch Killin* attacked the submarine with gunfire and depth charges. As it began to sink the frigate came close to rescue seventeen members of the ill-fated crew, the captain was not amongst them.

In June 1945 *Loch Killin* was nominated to join the Rosyth Escort Group to protect convoys from the United Kingdom to Norway. A number of Norwegian nationals boarded the frigate for the passage, which saw *Loch Killin* visit Stavanger, Bergen and Trondheim.

On 22 June Lieutenant Commander C W Hancock RN took command of the ship and on 1 July *Loch Killin* returned to Rosyth Dockyard. The need for escort vessels had reduced dramatically since the end of the European war and the frigate was declared suitable for reduction to reserve status.

In August she was guardship at Rosyth before sailing south the next month to Devonport where she paid off into reserve. After de-storing the ship entered Category 'B' reserve on 7 November 1945. Later she was used at Dartmouth Sub-Division as a static training vessel

When Dartmouth Sub-Division closed *Loch Killin* was towed around the coast back to Plymouth. The frigate remained there until towed to London in 1949 for a further refit. During the refit the dry dock in which the warship was being worked on flooded in March 1949 causing some damage. Being a relatively new warship the ship was considered for modernisation but in 1951 this plan was abandoned, instead *Loch Killin* was transferred to the Reserve Fleet Ship Division at Penarth where she arrived in June 1956. She would spend another four years in inactivity before finally being released for disposal on 12 April 1960. A few months later the ship was sold to BISCO who contracted out the demolition work to J Cashmore of Newport.

Battle Honours

ATLANTIC 1944   ENGLISH CHANNEL 1945   BISCAY 1944   ENGLISH CHANNEL 1945

Chronology

06.03.1943	Ordered from Burntisland Shipbuilding
02.06.1943	Laid down
29.11.1943	Launched
12.04.1944	Completed
04.1944	2nd Escort Group
10.05.1944	Tobermory
01.06.1944	Liverpool
02.07.1944	Liverpool
31.07.1944	With *Starling* attacked and sank U-333
08.1944	Bay of Biscay patrols
06.08.1944	Attacked and sank *U-736*
09.08.1944	Attacked *U-608* which later surrendered
11.08.1944	Attacked *U-385*
13.08.1944	Liverpool to join 17th Escort Group
20.08.1944	Scapa Flow
14.09.1944	Clyde before returning to Scapa Flow
04.11.1944	Clyde
05.01.1945	Collided with HM Trawler *Quadrille*. Portsmouth for repairs
25.01.1945	Resumed patrols
04.1945	Transferred to Plymouth
11.04.1945	Attacked *U-1063* off Start Point
06.1945	Rosyth Escort Force
08.1945	Guard ship Rosyth
07.11.1945	Category B reserve at Dartmouth/Plymouth
1949	London for refit
03.1949	Damaged in flood whilst in refit. Upon completion to reserve
06.1956	Reserve at Penarth
12.04.1960	Sold for breaking up by J Cashmore of Newport

HMS LOCH KILLISPORT

HMS Loch Killisport *at speed clearly showing her mix of anti-aircraft guns and anti-submarine weapons.*
(Crown Copyright/MoD)

Loch Killisport was built by Harland and Wolff shipyard in Belfast with work starting on 28 December 1943. She was launched on 6 July 1944 and the hull was then towed across the Irish Sea for fitting out at Liverpool, where she was completed on 9 July 1945.

After completing her initial trials she was accepted into the Royal Navy and given over to the command of Lieutenant Commander G Butcher DSC RNVR. After storing at Tobermory the frigate's first journey as a commissioned Royal Navy warship was to the Clyde areas on 9 August where she was fitted with extra equipment and ventilation systems for her forthcoming service in the East Indies Fleet.

By 16 September 1945 Loch Killisport had reached Aden where she collected a brood of 30 Motor Fishing Vessels. The frigate was nominated to act as the escort for this flotilla of vessels during their passage to the Indian port of Cochin. The group arrived safely and the British frigate then continued onto Colombo where she arrived on 5 October.

The autumn of 1945 saw the frigate utilised in a variety of support roles from Singapore to Java and Sumatra but mostly on convoy escort duties to and from Bangkok and Singapore.

On 4 November Loch Killisport was at Batavia and extra space was found onboard for prisoners of war and civilians who were to be transported back to Singapore for repatriation; the frigate arriving at Singapore eight days later.

On 11 January 1946 Loch Killisport sailed to Batavia where six days later she rescued a Dutch family from Grissee, in Indonesia, and returned them to safety. The ship, meanwhile, continued in her support

role with a visit to Padang before returning to Singapore on 30 January.

February was spent in the Indian Ocean at Trincomalee and Kilindini. On 25 February news was received that the warship was to return to the United Kingdom to pay off into reserve. *Loch Killisport* started the first leg of this journey on 4 March when she sailed from Trincomalee under the temporary command of Lieutenant Commander N G Chesterman DSC RNR who took her home to Devonport arriving in April.

In April command of the frigate was transferred to Lieutenant Commander Charles Courtney Anderson RN. Anderson was born in Ireland on 8 November 1916 and eventually joined the Royal Navy as a cadet. His first experience at sea was onboard the cadet training cruiser Frobisher in 1938 and then for another year on the Achilles in the Home Fleet.

When war broke out Anderson was an instructor on Motor Torpedo Boats at HMS *Vernon* in Portsmouth before becoming the commanding officer of *MTB 67* at HMS *Beehive* in Felixstowe. He would later transfer to the Mediterranean and command both *MTB 215* and *MTB 216*.

In June 1944 he was executive officer of the destroyer *Wivern* before assuming command of *Cassandra* on 10 July 1945. His command of this destroyer was to be a brief one as in April 1946 he took command of *Loch Killisport*. Anderson would eventually serve in Naval Intelligence and be a naval attaché to Bonn before being promoted to Rear Admiral on 7 January 1969.

Loch Killisport remained in reserve at Plymouth until 1949. The following year the frigate was in July, towed to Sheerness Dockyard in Kent for a refit to bring her back to life. Upon completion in November 1950 she became part of the 6th Frigate Squadron. Her post refit trials, however, proved to be most unsatisfactory and the ship returned to Sheerness for more work to be undertaken. *Loch Killisport* eventually successfully completed her trials programme in February 1951 and joined the Home Fleet for a series of exercises and port visits.

She stayed with the Home Fleet through until March with visits that included Londonderry and Gibraltar before leave was granted to the ships company at Chatham when she arrived on 16 March. The leave was interrupted on 23 April when *Loch Killisport* was one of a large armada of naval vessels dispatched into the English Channel to search for the ill fated submarine *Affray*. The search continued into June long after any hope of finding any survivors had passed.

HMS *Loch Killisport* rejoined the Home Fleet programme of visits that included most successful visits to Berwick and Whitby. Summer leave was granted when the ship returned to Chatham Dockyard on 25 July. The opportunity was also taken to carry out some repairs whilst she was in dockyard hands.

The ship was returned to her crew in early September and she rejoined her flotilla at Portland and Londonderry. She spent the rest of the summer undertaking flotilla duties before returning to Sheerness for a routine docking period and repairs.

1952 would prove to be a mixed year for the warship with the first quarter spent on fleet exercises and high profile visits that included Malta and Monaco before being selected to enter the reserve fleet in April. She would remain there until April 1953 when she was towed to the Millwall shipyard of Green and Silley Weir for a refit. The refit continued until June 1954. After harbour trials she was commissioned in August 1954 for sea trials only to be paid off upon completion for work to be carried out to give the frigate suitable equipment for service in the Far East. The work was carried out at Chatham Dockyard, who also cocooned much of the upper deck equipment to prevent moisture entering the systems. She remained in this state until selected to replace the sloop *Flamingo* in the Persian Gulf and was commissioned for service in February 1955. Her new commanding officer was Commander E N Forbes DSC RN.

After sea trials in the North Sea and a visit to Portsmouth *Loch Killisport* arrived at Portland for her work up and weapons trials on 16 March. Five days later she sailed south for Gibraltar and Malta where she arrived on 1 April. After some exercises en route with the fleet in the Mediterranean the frigate continued on her journey to the Middle East with stops at Aden, Salahah and Khor Kuwai in Kuwait before arriving at Bahrain on 8 May.

After only five days the frigate was on dhow patrol in the Persian Gulf. The normal operating practice was to inspect any suspicious vessels and also to make courtesy or official ports of call to a number of communities in the region. For *Loch Killisport* amongst her ports of call in the first month of her deployment included Abu Musa, Sharjah and Khor Fakkan in the United Arab Emirates.

On 19 May the frigate, whilst at Muscat, received radio reports of an incident involving two merchant vessels, the Dutch Tabian and an Italian oil tanker MV *Argea Prima*. The two ships had been in collision and the tanker was on fire near to the entrance to the Straits of Hormuz.

Loch Killisport sped to the scene of the accident and arrived there the next morning to find a US Navy replenishment ship USNS *Cossatot* conducting fire fighting operations towards the blazing tanker which had been abandoned by her crew. *Loch Killisport* assisted the American effort and together the blaze was slowly brought under control after two days of firefighting.

The frigate *Loch Insh* and another merchant vessel, the *Esmeralda*, arrived to try and tow the crippled ship

A fine shot of Loch Killisport *leaving the harbour at Malta.*   (Crown Copyright/MoD)

into harbour but the tow later failed. Engineers put onboard the *Argea Prima* eventually got the damaged ship underway and she sailed into Bahrain for repairs. *Loch Killisport*'s Engineering Officer and a Senior Engine Room rating were later awarded the Queen's Commendation for fire fighting during the incident.

After six days at sea *Loch Killisport* followed the tanker into Bahrain on 26 May. The next fortnight was spent alongside before the frigate sailed to Mina-al-Ahmadi in Kuwait on 8 June at the start of a patrol of the Northern Gulf area. Upon completion the ship sailed back to her base port of Bahrain ahead of a planned docking and refit period at Colombo where she arrived on 2 July.

Loch Killisport was refurbished over the course of the next month and sailed from the city on 3 August bound for Trincomalee. The frigate was to take part in

the major naval exercise JET 55 based out of the large natural harbour at Trincomalee. For the best part of the next month the ship was involved in the exercises and practiced manoeuvres against aircraft, surface ships and submarines. Upon completion of JET 55 *Loch Killisport* sailed for Mauritius where she arrived for a two day visit on 17 September. At the island she embarked the Governor for his annual tour of the British dependencies in the Indian Ocean under his control. The frigate visited each in turn making visits to the islands of Agalega, Diego Garcia, Salomon, Peros Banhos and Rodriguez.

On 14 October the frigate returned the Governor and his party to Mauritius at the end of a very successful tour of the islands. The frigate anchored in the harbour and spent the next six days enjoying the hospitality of the tropical island as well as many of the

Seen making a southbound passage of the Suez Canal Loch Killisport *spent a great deal of her career East of Suez.*
(Ken Kelly Collection)

famous watering holes ashore. There was also the opportunity for runs ashore and beach parties.

After a hugely enjoyable time on 20 October *Loch Killisport* sailed for the Seychelles and onwards to Tanga. The ships' itinerary also saw visits paid to Mombasa and Salalah. In November as well as a period spent on fishery patrol off the coast of Oman.

On 22 December just ahead of the planned Christmas celebrations onboard the frigate *Loch Killisport* arrived at Mina-al-Ahmadi in Kuwait. After Christmas the ship moved on to Aden.

On 1 January 1956 the frigate was relieved by her sister ship *Loch Fada* but remained at Aden for a further nine days before resuming her journey back to the United Kingdom. She was routed through Malta and Gibraltar before arriving at Portsmouth on 2 February. The frigate was soon taken in hand for a refit that lasted until 9 April when she was paid off. The next day *Loch Killisport* re-commissioned for service in the Middle East. She was equipped with accommodation onboard for a detachment of Royal Marines and became the first Loch class ship to be so equipped.

Loch Killisport's new commanding officer, Commander G Hathaway took the frigate to Portland where over the next few weeks she was tested and worked up with ever more demanding tasks asked of the frigate and her complement. After further training in Londonderry, *Loch Killisport* was declared operational for service in the Middle East and in August sailed taking the long way round the Cape of Good Hope because of the closure of the Suez Canal. This route allowed the opportunity of visits to be made at Freetown, Capetown and Mombasa.

The frigates busy deployment continued into October with visits paid to Charack, Lingeh in the United Arab Emirates, Henjam in Iran and Qism in Iraq. The following month she added Doha, Yaz and Muscat to the official ports before going to the assistance of the American oil tanker *Olympic Games* which had run aground off Bahrain on 15 December. Incredibly the British frigate the very next day found herself going to the aid of another tanker, the British *Athel Monarch* which had also run aground near Bahrain. The operation to rescue the latter ship was hampered by rising winds, darkness and the proximi-

ty of unmarked coral reefs, eventually the ship being recovered safely.

The festive season was spent at Bahrain whilst the start of 1957 saw visits paid to a number of local ports of call. On completion she had a period of routine maintenance at Karachi that saw her out of service until the end of February. The following month the frigate returned to her station in the Persian Gulf and carried out a patrol in the Southern Gulf.

At the beginning of April *Loch Killisport* arrived at Cochin together with the oiler RFA Wave Protector. After four days in the port she sailed together with the cruiser Newcastle on Monday 8 April for aircraft tracking exercises that also involved a selection of RAF aircraft. The next day the force arrived at Trincomalee. On Monday 15 April the cruiser *Ceylon* arrived in the harbour and *Loch Killisport* fired a seven gun salute upon her arrival.

Three days later the frigate set sail for Bahrain and undertook a series of anti-submarine exercises utilising her squid launcher before securing alongside sister ship *Loch Alvie* at 1740 at F Buoy at Khor Kaliya on Thursday 25 April. After patrols in the Northern Gulf the frigate sailed into the Iraqi port of Basra before sailing down the coast to Iran for some exercises with the Iranian Navy in June at Kharg Island.

Late June marked an important milestone for the frigate as it was the moment in the commission that announcements were made for her return home to the United Kingdom sailing for home the following month.

In August the frigate made the first passage of a Royal Navy ship through the Suez Canal since it had been re-opened after the Suez crisis. She stopped at Gibraltar for fuel and stores and then made for Portsmouth. The customs men searched the ship before it was allowed into port but after a short stop at the Hampshire naval base the frigate returned to Chatham and prepared for a short refit.

The refit was completed after two months on 15 October when she re-commissioned again under the command of Commander T J Davies RN. After sea trials the ship headed to the south coast for work up and weapons training around Portland in November. *Loch Killisport* headed back to Portsmouth at the end of

these trials for some remedial work to be carried out that lasted until the time she left for her passage to the Middle East in February 1958.

After calling at Aden *Loch Killisport* relieved sister ship *Loch Fada* in April at Muscat and immediately started her turn on the Batina coast patrol. Throughout the coming months the frigate continued the usual itinerary of port visits and exercises with, notably, the Iranian Navy in June.

On Monday 1 September *Loch Killisport* was in Dry Dock at Karachi when at 2050 his Excellency the High Commissioner for Pakistan and Naval Advisory Officer arrived onboard the British warship for a discussion about the planned joint exercises between Pakistan and Great Britain. The conversation lasted for three hours when the gentlemen left the ship. *Loch Killisport*, herself, finally left dry dock with the assistance of local tug *Merle Duggan,* early on Tuesday 9 September and had completed her basin trials by the end of the day. Two days later the ship set sail for Muscat in company with the carrier *Bulwark*. On 13

September *Loch Killisport* went to the aid of the French oil tanker *Fernand Gilabert* and the Liberian tanker *Meilka*, which had been in collision during a period of bad weather in the Persian Gulf off Oman. *Loch Killisport* was joined in this operation by the aircraft carrier *Bulwark* and the frigates *Puma*, *St Brides Bay* and *Loch Alvie*. *Loch Killisport* took the French ship under tow towards Karachi where the two vessels arrived on 20 September. Upon completion the frigate resumed her dhow patrols throughout October.

Towards the end of the month the British warship re-entered the waters off Karachi to take part in the annual naval exercise JET 59 that continued until almost the end of the year.

1959 started with the dreaded annual inspection onboard at her base port of Bahrain. Every man onboard spent days cleaning and cleansing every compartment of the ship in order to pass the inspection. Upon completion of the onerous task the frigate sailed to Aden.

After the frigate had then visited Djibouti and

HMS Loch Killisport *served in the Far East on the Malaya Patrol where her relatively small size but powerful armament made her ideal for patrolling close off shore and for intercepting smuggled arms and ammunition.*
(Crown Copyright/MoD)

Massawa the ship set course for a return journey to Portsmouth Dockyard where upon arrival she was once again taken in hand for a three month refit. The work would continue until 12 April when she was officially re-commissioned for further service in the Persian Gulf under the command of Commander R A Rawbone RN.

Late spring and early summer was spent in UK coastal waters perfecting the operation of the warship but in September the frigate set sail for a return to the hot conditions found at Bahrain. The ship was routed through the Mediterranean with stops at Malta and Aden before finally arriving at Bahrain in October. The next month saw her on dhow patrol stopping and inspecting any vessel suspected of carrying illegal arms and ammunition. In December she left the Gulf for Karachi for a docking period and also to take part in the major naval exercise with the Indian Navy and other allied forces, Exercise JET 60. The Royal Navy had provided a strong force of ships including the aircraft carrier *Centaur*.

The forces started to assemble in mid February 1960 which also included the Indian aircraft carrier *Vikrant* and the destroyer *Carysfort*. Upon completion of the exercise *Loch Killisport* made for Karachi where for the next month the ship was in refit. At the beginning of March the frigate was returned to service and was once again back in the Persian Gulf on patrol duties with the usual ports of call in the northern sector - all receiving a visit from the British ship.

In March *Loch Killisport* together with sister ship *Loch Lomond* took part in Exercise Winged Khanga that was centred on a number of Royal Fleet Auxiliaries. The following month saw the frigate back in the Northern Gulf where, once again, she operated with sister ship *Loch Lomond*.

After visiting Mina-al-Ahmadi, the frigate returned to Bahrain and then onto Abadan with *Loch Insh* where the ships companies took part in the Queen's Birthday Parade at Khorramshar.

Loch Killisport received an urgent call from sister ship *Loch Insh* requesting a replacement Boiler Room fan in July to replace a defective one onboard. *Loch Killisport* sent one over to *Loch Insh*, which was headed to East Africa with the Flag Officer Middle East

onboard. *Loch Killisport*, meanwhile, made return visits to Aden and Muscat with only one of her boiler fans operational. This meant that upon arrival at Aden the frigate was delayed for some time whilst a replacement fan was sought out; once fitted the frigate resumed her passage home to the United Kingdom.

In September 1960 after a brief visit to Portsmouth she made for Rosyth where the frigate was paid off into refit. The refit was set to be a lengthy one with the installation of much new equipment including a new fibreglass shield on a new 4-inch gun mounting and new air conditioning units. The refit continued until 12 September 1961 when she re-commissioned for service with the 3rd Frigate Squadron, Far East under the command of Captain M F Fell DSC RN who was also Senior Officer of Squadron.

Sea trials were carried out in the North Sea and Forth areas before sailing in October to Portland to work up and carry out weapons trials. After a brief visit to Portsmouth in November the frigate sailed to relieve *Cardigan Bay* at Singapore the same month. *Loch Killisport* sailed through the Mediterranean and stopped for fuel and supplies at Aden. By January 1962 she had arrived at her new base port of Singapore.

In February the frigate assumed her role of patrolling the Borneo conflict area based at Tawau. In 1961 the British Government wished to withdraw from its colonial responsibilities in South East Asia and proposed a way to combine its three colonies on the island of Borneo into a new Federation of Malaysia.

The plans were not universally accepted especially by the left wing North Kalimantan National Army (TNKU), who on 8 December 1962 staged an insurrection, which later came to known as the Brunei revolt. Their aim was to capture the Sultan of Brunei as well as Brunei's important oil fields. Superior British armed forces quashed the insurrection but it was not until 18 May 1963 that the last elements of the TNKU were captured. Even still the British 'police action' would continue for another three years until 1966.

During breaks in active operations *Loch Killisport* also undertook a number of naval exercises with

friendly local naval forces including the annual JET 62 and Exercise Sea Devil with US Navy warships before visiting Manila and Subic Bay where she was hosted by the US Navy.

By the beginning of July *Loch Killisport* was at Singapore before sailing to Hong Kong on Friday 5 July with the frigate *Plymouth*. The pair carried out gunnery practice en route and also ran into a number of heavy rain squalls before arriving at Hong Kong after six days at sea. Whilst at Hong Kong the weather worsened considerably and on Friday 20 July the ships company was recalled from leave due to the arrival of Typhoon Kate. At 1943 the ship proceeded to sea to ride out the storm in company with British and American warships including USS *Carter Hall*, USS *Black* and USS *Wexford*. By Sunday 22 July the storm had abated enough for the frigate to return to Hong Kong. Four days later *Loch Killisport* sailed to start a Borneo patrol that saw her visiting the island of Labuan around 8 nautical miles off Borneo and the city of Sandakan before returning to Hong Kong on Wednesday 15 August after refuelling at sea from RFA *Gold Ranger*. After a period of maintenance the ship was back at sea in August for another Borneo patrol.

Upon her return some time was spent at HMS *Tamar* before *Loch Killisport* put to sea bound for Sydney. On Tuesday 28 August King Neptune's messengers arrived onboard and informed the crew that they would be crossing the equator at lunchtime the following day. The next day King Neptune duly arrived on the frigate's quarterdeck and the men took part in the good natured tradition of crossing the line.

The last day of August 1962 saw *Loch Killisport* join up with a group of British warships centred on the cruiser *Tiger*. Also in company were the destroyers *Caprice* and *Cassandra*, the tanker *Wave Ruler* and the submarine *Ambush*. The ships were all taking part in the annual naval exercise Tucker Box with the Royal Australian Navy.

Upon completion she sailed further into the Pacific bound for New Zealand where a planned tour of the country was started. Throughout October *Loch Killisport* stopped at a wide variety of ports including

Bluff and Wellington.

En route back to Hong Kong the frigate made official visits to Suva, Gilbert Island and Ellis Islands. Once back at Hong Kong the frigate was taken in hand for a period of maintenance carried out by the crew.

Loch Killisport under the command of Captain M F Fell DSO, DSC, sailed from Hong Kong at 1645 on New Years Day 1963 with instructions to take the destroyer *Barossa* and any other ships under his orders and carry out operations as required. The immediate aim was to intercept and apprehend the rebel leader Azahari, who was reputed to be about to make a break from Manila, possibly for North Borneo or Indonesia. The probable jump off points for Azahari, were thought to be either the Tawi Tawi group of islands or the Turtle Islands and surface and maritime air surveillance was maintained over the area. In the event Azahari did not make his expected journey.

At 0800 on 11 January *Loch Killisport* arrived at Labuan to participate in Operation Parsons Nose, which was planned to be the apprehension of several high ranking rebels as well as the interception of small craft and to enforce the nightly curfew. Parsons Nose was subsequently abandoned because of extensive flooding and the need to provide immediate relief to those civilians most affected.

Loch Killisport relieved the depot ship *Woodbridge Haven* on 11 January as Labuan guardship.

On 22 January the frigate arrived back at Singapore and was six days later paid off prior to a refit at the naval base. On the last day of the month the new ships company joined the ship which had just started its refit. On 1 March the frigate was re-commissioned with Captain W S Simpson CBE, DSC RN as commanding officer and also as Senior Officer of the Squadron. *Loch Killisport* still, however, was not quite ready for service with the refit continuing until June when harbour and sea trials commenced.

It was during these trials that on 1 July the warship was called in to assist in the search for a crashed Sea Vixen aircraft. Two days later after having been released from the search operations *Loch Killisport* was at Kuchin for her standard patrols to begin.

By the 17 July she was on passage to HMS *Tamar*

at Hong Kong for a maintenance period and remained at the colony into early August taking the opportunity to exercise with Army and Air Force personnel stationed at Hong Kong. After almost a month *Loch Killisport* sailed back to Tawau to resume her patrol duties. The passage was most unpleasant with rough seas and a strong wind but eventually the warship arrived after four days of battering on 16 August.

For the next ten days the ship was operating out of Tawau before embarking a contingent of Gurkha soldiers for passage to Semporna Bay on the 26 August. Once there the ship carried out a three day patrol of the North East coastline looking for any suspicious activities.

On the last day of August the British ship was open to visitors at Tawau as the ships-company and locals celebrated Tawau's Independence Day. The frigate welcomed many hundreds of visitors throughout the day, all asking a great many questions of the British men onboard.

With the celebrations over it was time, on 2 September, for the frigate to set sail to Singapore. The four day passage was uneventful. After five days alongside *Loch Killisport* embarked the Band of the Royal Marines and on 11 September set sail to Kuching in Malaysia to attend the formal ending of Colonial rule in the state.

Sadly the frigate's arrival at Kuching was not a success as the frigate grounded on entering the harbour on the 13 September and had to be pulled clear. Once

Flying her paying off pennant Loch Killisport *cuts a dash. Note the modified turret housing for the twin 4-inch mounting.* (Crown Copyright/MoD)

free of the obstruction damage control parties assessed the ships structure before she proceeded to her berth in the harbour where the Captain and senior officers welcomed onboard a number of VIP's from the city.

After two days in port *Loch Killisport* sailed on 15 September having first embarked the Governor of Sarawak and Lady Warren for the formal departure ceremony. *Loch Killisport* carried the pair back to Singapore where the frigate arrived after two days at sea. At Singapore the Governor and Lady Warren were transferred to the aircraft carrier *Ark Royal* before taking part in a series of convoy defence exercises that finished badly on 19 September when *Loch Killisport* was involved in a collision with the Royal Fleet Auxiliary tanker *Tideflow*. Fortunately neither ship was badly damaged in the incident.

The following day *Loch Killisport* was back alongside at Singapore where she remained for six days. By 2 October *Loch Killisport* arrived at Gan where she stayed for the next eight days enjoying the local facilities. She then sailed for Male in the Seychelles before returning to Gan two days later and stayed there until the end of the month. On 31 October *Loch Killisport* sailed to take part in the planned CENTO exercises off Penang and Singapore. Upon completion the frigate arrived at Singapore Naval Base on 14 November. A week later she sailed to take up the Borneo Patrol duties again arriving at Tawau four days later.

By 3 December she was on her way back to the familiar surroundings of Singapore Dockyard where she arrived four days later. The ships company quickly got to the task of de-storing the ship and preparing her for dry docking in the floating dry dock *AFD10*, where she remained until 4 January 1964.

After sea trials locally *Loch Killisport* sailed for Hong Kong on 11 January where she arrived after five days at sea. After spending the remainder of the month at the colony *Loch Killisport* joined other Royal Navy vessels in the region for a number of exercises en route back to Singapore on 29 January. The frigate's new commanding officer, Lieutenant Commander K D Erskine assumed command on 7 February and a week later the ship tied up alongside at Singapore.

The next ten days saw frenetic activity in preparing the ship for her annual Sea Inspection, which was conducted by the Flag Officer 2nd in Command Far East Station. Every compartment was spotless for the inspection, which fortunately *Loch Killisport* passed with flying colours.

Having completed her inspection the frigate sailed the next day to take passage to Tawau for patrol and support duties in the region. The patrols were mostly nondescript and routine but they continued through until 21 March when *Loch Killisport* sailed for Hong Kong.

After a five day passage the frigate arrived at Hong Kong where the ships company were granted leave ashore. Many found the much frequented old haunts, whilst some others explored and sampled the vivid culture of the British colony.

All too soon the ship departed on 6 April to resume the patrols off Borneo. Again the patrols there were mostly routine with just an occasional incident or junk to be investigated and inspected. *Loch Killisport* spent almost three weeks off Tawau before sailing back to Singapore at the end of her commission on 24 April.

On 1 May *Loch Killisport* re-commissioned for further service with the 26th Escort Squadron but with a new commanding officer Commander Sayer RN. The new crew also had as a signal officer Lieutenant A E P Briggs, who was one of the three survivors from the doomed battlecruiser *Hood* sunk by the German battleship *Bismarck* on 24 May 1941.

The 1 May also was a melancholy day for some because it saw the disbandment of the 3rd Frigate Squadron. Three days later *Loch Killisport* was back conducting a shakedown cruise in local waters off Singapore and in the Malacca Straits. The shakedown continued for most of the month only returning to the dockyard on 23 May.

Further exercises were staged at the beginning of June at Tioman before the frigate sailed onto Penang for a three day visit on 12 June. After returning to Singapore *Loch Killisport* embarked a platoon of Gurkha soldiers for transport to Tawau and once at the island carried out a series of patrols in the region until 18 July when she was relieved and dispatched to Hong Kong.

On 6 August the frigate set sail for the Thai Capital city of Bangkok to take part in a series of naval exer-

cises with a variety of international warships including Thai, American and British. Upon completion the ship returned to Bangkok where she was open to visitors alongside *Manxman* and many thousands of locals toured around the British ships.

On 17 August together with the *Manxman, Loch Killisport* sailed to start the second half of the international exercises off Singapore. When these were completed the pair parted company with the frigate making for Singapore, where she arrived on 24 August having battled through very heavy weather and mountainous seas.

September would see the frigate return to patrolling off Tawau where on the 19 September she went to the aid of the Panamanian registered merchantman SS *Chopin* which had run aground. Ships divers from the Royal Navy ship were sent over with pumps to assist the merchant vessels own engineering team. The combined effort allowed the stricken vessel to be pulled free and taken under tow. *Loch Killisport* and SS *Chopin* arrived at Tawau on 22 September.

Two days later the warship resumed her interrupted patrol off Tawau until relieved and made for Singapore for an arrival on 9 October. Towards the end of the month *Loch Killisport* sailed for Hong Kong with exercises en route with the frigate *Brighton* and the destroyer *Cassandra*. All three ships arrived at Hong Kong on 30 October.

In November the frigate sailed from Hong Kong and made for Singapore exercising en route to Malaysia. Upon her arrival at the naval base on the 21st she was taken in hand for a refit. Upon completion, in March 1965, saw *Loch Killisport* undertaking patrols along the coastline of Malaysia looking for insurgents. On 20 March the British frigate reached the port of Tanjong Panchor where the ships company welcomed onboard a contingent of personnel from the British Army. A week later she was back alongside in the welcoming environment of Singapore Naval Base.

After a few days she was back at sea on 1 April for a four day interception patrol. The patrol ended when the ship returned to her base at Singapore. The month

HMS Loch Killisport *spent over a decade in reserve at Portsmouth before being scrapped in March 1970.*
(T. Ferrers-Walker)

would see a number of visits made including those to Port Dickson and a return visit to Tamjong Panchor. Later when at Kuching on the 6th, she embarked men from the 39th Gurkha regiment for passage to Hong Kong. *Loch Killisport* arrived after five days at sea and remained at HMS *Tamar* or within the harbour for a fortnight before sailing for Sattahip, Thailand on 21 April. The purpose of the visit was to attend a formal meeting with the Commander in Chief of the Royal Thai Navy who was one of many local dignitaries welcomed onboard the British frigate. Another reason for the visit was to undertake a series of exercises with ships of the Thai Navy and other units of the Royal Navy including the submarine *Andrew*. The two days of exercises proved to fruitful for both navies and ended with *Loch Killisport* sailing for Singapore.

11 May saw *Loch Killisport* return to the dockyard at Singapore where she stayed for ten days in preparation for another journey to Tawau for one final patrol off the waters of Borneo. This time she was to operate with the coastal minesweepers offering the small vessels welcome respite from the dangers of inshore patrols. By 5 June her task had been completed and *Loch Killisport* sailed for the Philippine capital of

Manila together with the frigate *Whitby* for an official four day visit from 8 June.

From Manila *Loch Killisport* paid a final visit to Hong Kong. The twelve days spent at the colony allowed time for new friends and old associations to be rekindled and addresses exchanged before she sailed for Singapore on 23 June. *Loch Killisport* left Hong Kong with the men manning the sides and as she arrived at Singapore four days later the men again manned the sides of the ship as she flew her paying off pennant ending a long and active career in the Royal Navy.

The frigate's route home to the United Kingdom took her via Gan, Aden, Malta and a final stop at Gibraltar on 29 July where gifts for loved ones back home were purchased. *Loch Killisport* sailed on 1 August arriving at Portsmouth on 4 August to pay off. She secured at Fountain Lake Jetty and within weeks had been de-stored and emptied of life.

Loch Killisport remained in reserve at Portsmouth until 20 February 1970 when sold for breaking up at Hughes Bolcow in Blyth arriving under tow on 18 March 1970.

Chronology

28.12.1943	Laid down at Harland and Wolff
06.07.1944	Launched and fitted out at Liverpool
09.07.1945	Completed
09.08.1945	Clyde area
16.09.1945	Aden
05.10.1945	Colombo
Autumn 1945	Java and Sumatra areas
04.11.1945	Batavia
12.11.1945	Singapore
11.01.1946	Took passage to Batavia
30.01.1946	Singapore
04.03.1946	Sailed from Trincomalee for United Kingdom
04.1946	At Plymouth for refit and reserve
07.1950	Transferred to Sheerness for refit
11.1950	Refit completed and joined the 6th Frigate Flotilla
02.1951	Sea trials completed and joined Home Fleet
06.1951	Visited Berwick and Whitby and Home Fleet exercises
Summer 1951	Refit at Chatham Dockyard
09.1951	Rejoined flotilla at Portland
Early 1952	Mediterranean
04.1952	Reserve at Chatham Dockyard
04.1953	Towed to Millwall Shipyard of Green and Silley Weir for refit
06.1954	Refit completed
07.1954	Further work undertaken at Chatham Dockyard
16.03.195	Portland for work up
01.04.1955	Malta
08.05.1955	Bahrain
19.05.1955	On scene of collision between *Tabian* and MV *Argea Prima*
26.05.1955	Bahrain
02.07.1955	Refit at Colombo
03.08.1955	Took passage to Trincomalee for Exercise JET 55
17.09.1955	Mauritius and Indian Ocean
22.12.1955	Mina al Ahmadi
02.02.1956	Portsmouth for refit
10.04.1956	Commissioned for service in Middle East
Summer 1956	Training at Portland and Londonderry
08.1956	Sailed for Middle East via Cape Horn
10.1956	Visited Charak, Lingeh, Henjam and Qism
15.12.1956	Went to assistance of American tanker *Olympic Games*

16.12.1956	Went to assistance of British tanker *Athel Monarch*
Early 1957	Persian Gulf Patrol
04.1957	Naval exercises with Indian Navy
08.1957	Portsmouth
08.1957	Chatham Dockyard for refit
15.10.1957	Re-commissioned
02.1958	Took passage to Middle East
Early 1958	Persian Gulf Patrol
13.09.1958	Went to assistance of French tanker *Fernard Gilbert* and Liberian tanker *Melika*
20.09.1958	Towed French ship to Karachi
Early 1959	Persian Gulf Patrol before returning to Portsmouth
12.04.1959	Refit completed
Spring 1959	UK waters
Summer 1959	Dhow Patrol in Persian Gulf
01.1960	Exercise JET 60
03.1960	Exercise Winged Khanga
05.1960	Exercise CASPEX 5
09.1960	Portsmouth
09.1960	Rosyth
12.09.1960	Re-commissioned into 3rd Frigate Flotilla
01.1962	Singapore for Borneo Patrol
07.196	Visited Japanese port of Kakodate Ominato
09.1962	Visited Hong Kong and Sydney
09.1962	Exercise Tucker Box and visited New Zealand
Autumn 1962	Maintenance at Hong Kong
01.01.1963	Took passage to Sandakan
22.01.1963	Singapore
28.01.1963	Paid off into refit
01.03.1963	Re-commissioned
03.07.1963	Borneo Patrol
06.09.1963	Singapore
13.09.1963	Grounded at Kuching during independence ceremonies
19.09.1963	Collided with RFA *Tideflow* during exercises
Autumn 1963	Gan, Seychelles and Penang
14.11.1963	Singapore
04.01.1964	Left floating dry dock *AFD10* at end of refit
16.01.1964	Hong Kong
29.01.1964	Took passage for Singapore
Early 1964	Borneo Patrol
26.03.1964	Hong Kong
06.04.1964	Borneo Patrol
24.04.1964	De-commissioned at Singapore
01.05.1964	Re-commissioned into 26th Frigate Squadron
12.06.1964	Penang

06.08.1964	Bangkok for naval exercises
24.08.1964	Hong Kong
19.09.1964	Whilst off Borneo went to assist merchant ship SS *Chopin*
22.09.1964	Arrived at Tawau with SS *Chopin* in tow
09.10.1964	Singapore
10.1964	Exercises off Hong Kong with *Brighton* and *Whitby*
30.10.1964	Hong Kong
21.11.1964	Singapore for refit
03.1965	Refit completed
20.03.1965	Visited Tan Jong Panchor
Spring 1965	Visited Port Dickson, Kuching, Hong Kong and Sattahip
11.05.1965	Singapore
21.05.1965	Borneo Patrol
08.06.1965	Manila with *Whitby*
23.06.1965	Sailed from Hong Kong for Singapore
27.06.1965	Singapore
29.07.1965	Gibraltar
01.08.1965	Took passage for Portsmouth
04.08.1965	Arrived Portsmouth to pay off for final time and entered reserve
20.02.1970	Sold for breaking up by Hughes Bolcow at Blyth
18.03.1970	Arrived under tow for demolition

HMS LOCH LOMOND

The modular construction of the Loch class hull is shown to good effect in this image of Loch Lomond.

(Crown Copyright/MoD)

The first steel plates for the construction of *Loch Lomond* were placed on the slipway at Caledon Shipbuilding in Dundee on 7 December 1943. Just over seven months later, on 19 June 1944, the ship was launched. Final fitting out was completed on 16 November 1944 and the ship was handed over to the Royal Navy under the command of Lieutenant Commander R E H Partington RNR.

After storing at Tobermory in the Western Isles of Scotland, *Loch Lomond* joined the 17th Escort Group at Greenock on 11 December. It was from there that the frigate started her wartime service on convoy escort duties in the Irish Sea and North West Approaches.

1945 saw her head south to the Channel areas as the concentration of shipping to the continent required extra protection from possible German U-boat activi-ty. After two months in the English Channel, *Loch Lomond* sailed north to Scapa Flow and from there to conduct patrol duties in the Irish Sea.

In April 1945 the ship was at Plymouth before returning to Greenock at the beginning of May. With the war in Europe won attention turned to the growing need for escorts in the Far East and *Loch Lomond* was one of the vessels selected for further service against the Japanese. As a consequence of this decision she was taken in hand for a refit, to add extra anti-aircraft weapons, at Pembroke Dock. Other alterations includ-ed the modification of the ships ventilation systems to better cope with the tropical heat in South East Asia.

May, saw the appointment of a new commanding officer in the form of the Australian Lieutenant Commander S Darling DSC RANVR.

On 28 June the frigate started her journey to join the

British Pacific Fleet calling at Aden en route. Having reached Colombo on 23 July *Loch Lomond*'s first task in the region was to provide escort for the amphibious landings codenamed Operation Zipper on the Malayan coastline in August. These operations continued throughout September with the warship being present at the landings at Port Swettenham.

There was another change of command during this period with the ship being transferred to the command of Lieutenant Commander K G Webb RNR. On the 12 September *Loch Lomond* was operating out of Singapore and provided escort cover between Kuching and Labuan to Singapore.

Later in the year with the war in the Far East over *Loch Lomond* served for a while as guardship at Sabang in November before returning to Singapore on Christmas Eve.

The new year of 1946 started with patrol duties out of Singapore, but word soon reached the ships company that she was heading home to be decommissioned into the reserve fleet. There were many mixed feelings onboard but there was still plenty of work to be done before she would return to Portsmouth in April.

The first of these occurred on 2 February when *Loch Lomond* and sister ship *Loch Glendhu* were assigned the task of being guardship at Batavia where ten days later she escorted the surrendered Japanese *U-181* which was to be sunk by gunfire from *Loch Glendhu* and sister ship *Loch Lomond*. The Type IXD2 U-boat was under the command of one of Germany's more decorated submarine Commanders Kapitan zur see Kurt Freiwald. The boat had sailed from Bordeaux in France on 16 March 1944 and arrived at Penang on 8 August. On 31 August she was at Singapore and made another three war patrols sinking the last of the boat's 27 victims, the American *Fort Lee* on 2 November 1944. She was taken over by the Japanese in May 1945 following the end of the war in Europe and officially entered service as *I-501* on 15 July. *I-501* was captured by the Allies when Singapore was recaptured and the decision was taken to scuttle the submarine offshore. Later *Loch Lomond* would also sink the former *U-862*, another Type IXD2 U-boat, which like *U-181* had been acquired by Japan on 6 May 1945 at

Singapore.

Upon completion of this task *Loch Lomond* started her return voyage to the United Kingdom by setting course for Trincomalee where she arrived on 19 February. The journey saw the warship routed via Aden and the Mediterranean before arriving at Portsmouth where the process of de-storing the warship quickly took over.

In July 1946 *Loch Lomond* was laid up at Portsmouth Dockyard where she remained for another three years until she was refitted for further service in 1949. At the end of the work on 22 November 1949 the frigate was returned to the reserve fleet at Portsmouth. Finally in 1950 *Loch Lomond* was brought forward for operational service that saw her receiving a further refit prior to starting sea trials and workup in the autumn of 1950. On Friday 22 September the frigate was commissioned whilst in No 11 Dry Dock at Portsmouth into the 2nd Frigate Flotilla for service in the Mediterranean under the command of Commander H R Moore RN.

The following Monday the ship was moved from No 11 dock to the South Wall of basin 2 to allow the final stages of the work to be completed. On Saturday 14 October *Loch Lomond* was again moved to a berth on Fountain Lake Jetty. Finally on Monday 13 November the frigate sailed for initial sea trials with guns, squid and depth charge throwers all being put through their paces in the English Channel. She returned to Portsmouth after two days at sea and remained there until Friday 17 November when she sailed to Portland to complete her work up. After a week at the Dorset base the frigate sailed north to Londonderry and conducted an anti-submarine exercise en route with the aircraft carrier *Vengeance* and the destroyer *Finisterre*.

At Londonderry the frigate spent the closing days of the month conducting a lengthy series of exercises with *Loch Tralaig* and *Loch Arkaig* as well as the destroyers *Crispin* and *Creole*. Once of an operational standard the frigate was declared to the fleet and on 12 December she sailed from Portsmouth to join the rest of the flotilla operating out of Malta.

With the flotilla up to full strength in January 1951 *Loch Lomond* spent the early part of the month exer-

HMS Loch Lomond *at anchor at Malta.*   *(T. Ferrers-Walker Collection)*

cising in Maltese waters and visited Dragomesti in Greece before returning with the destroyer *Gravelines* and the sloop *Mermaid* to Lazzaretto Creek on Thursday 11 January. She remained there until Saturday 29 January when she headed to sea with sister ship *Loch Dunvegan*. In February *Loch Lomond* replaced sister ship *Loch Scavaig* at Aqaba before returning to Malta the following month. The next few months were spent on routine patrols out of Malta with occasional visits including an enjoyable trip to Marmarice in Turkey in July. The following month saw Exercise Beehive where the frigate operated with the massive American aircraft carrier USS *Coral Sea*. Whilst later in October the ship visited the French Riviera. 1951 finished much as it had started with the frigate operating out of Malta.

In January 1952 *Loch Lomond* was taken in hand for a brief refit at Malta before sailing into the Red Sea in March where she would remain throughout April. On 10 April *Loch Lomond* located and escorted a number of Motor Minesweepers of the 120th Motor Minesweeper Flotilla until relieved on this duty by sister ship *Loch Quoich*. *Loch Lomond* instead made for Aqaba where she assmed the area guardship role. On 12 May she was ordered to take part in a night landing exercise and land a platoon to attack the seaward defences on Elephant Island peninsula in Aden.

Loch Lomond approached Aden from the eastwards passing close to Sinaila Point before slipping the motor cutter and whaler at 1905 in a position two and a half cables from Round Island. The ship then proceeded astern for half a mile keeping bows on to Elephants Back before turning to the southwards.

At 1920 searchlights from Elephants Back illuminated *Loch Lomond* and the boats which were then about half way to their assigned beach. This had been expected as there was a bright half moon and good visibility. *Loch Lomond* retreated to the southwards zigzagging and engaging the searchlight with simulated close range weapons.

A number of unlit dhows and merchant vessels at anchor made navigation more difficult but the starshell firing position was reached by 2015 as arranged. Two starshells were fired to burst off Conquest Bay until the red very's light terminated the exercise. The exercise was observed as *Loch Lomond* approached Elephants Back illuminating and engaging the defences with simulated gunfire.

The landing party was re-embarked from Gold Mohur beach at approximately 2115. They were extremely wet externally, largely from perspiration and suitably refreshed internally by the kindness of the defending forces.

With the exercise completed the frigate made for Malta after transiting the Suez Canal. *Loch Lomond* entered Valetta Harbour on 19 May where leave was granted.

The following month and into July saw her taking part in fleet wide exercises that culminated with the frigate being employed as guardship at Port Said in August. In the first week of September 1952 *Loch Lomond* took part in the Mediterranean Fleet's Summer Cruise, together with the aircraft carrier *Glory*, the cruiser *Cleopatra*, destroyers *Daring, Armada, Chequers, Chieftain, Chivalrous, Gravelines, Vigo* and *Saintes*, the frigates *Loch Dunvegan, Meon, Mermaid* and the despatch vessel *Surprise, Manxman* and the submarines *Sanguine, Sentinel* and *Sturdy*. The exercises started in the Western Mediterranean when the force operated with the French Navy off the naval base at Toulon.

On 31 October *Loch Lomond* sailed for the United Kingdom arriving back at Portsmouth where she was laid up pending the start of her modernisation refit at Charles Hill Shipyard in Bristol. During the refit a case of malicious damage to some electric cables was discovered onboard the ship, which caused the planned completion date to be postponed. With repairs and the refit completed in November *Loch Lomond* started her post refit trials programme, which continued into the early part of 1955. She arrived at Chatham Dockyard to be fitted with air conditioning units for service in the Persian Gulf - the work not being completed until 19 April when she commissioned for service. Her new commanding officer was

Commander B M D L'Anson RN.

After taking passage to Malta to work up in May *Loch Lomond* spent the next two months preparing the ship and crew for the extended deployment ahead. At the end of July together with sister ship Loch Alvie, she sailed to Bahrain.

On 26 July *Loch Lomond*'s engineers went to the assistance of the Royal Fleet Auxiliary tanker RFA *Wave King*, which had experienced some technical difficulties with her feed pumps. Their efforts were much appreciated but a more permanent solution to the problem onboard the tanker was found at Mina-al-Ahmadi. *Loch Lomond*, meanwhile, continued on to Bahrain.

For the next few months the ship patrolled the Persian Gulf on dhow patrol with occasional port visits. At the end of September the ship left for the cooler, if rainy climes of Ceylon. While at Colombo the ship underwent a self refit, with the ships company living in accommodation ashore. Both watches also went up country for a short period of leave combined with the annual musketry course amongst the mountains of Diyatalana. Once back at sea the cruise was thoroughly enjoyable for everyone onboard with visits paid to Port Blair, Rangoon, Chittagong and Madras. The ships visit to Rangoon coincided with that of the First Secretary of the Soviet Union Nikita Kruschev.

Christmas was spent at Trincomalee with *Loch Alvie* and the cruiser *Gambia*, flagship of Admiral Sir Charles Norris, Commander in Chief East Indies.

The start of 1956 saw the warship back in the Persian Gulf. During her second spell in the Gulf *Loch Lomond*'s ships company were called upon to help quell civil unrest in Bahrain. The populace had risen up against despotic rule by the sheik and it resulted in calling in the Army. *Loch Lomond* herself was positioned at Sitra on BAP Co's fuelling jetty to guard the European community in the event of danger to them and their property. Fortunately the platoons were never landed and the situation was quickly restored. *Loch Lomond* remained in the Gulf until sailing back to the United Kingdom via Aden, Malta and Gibraltar for a refit at Chatham Dockyard arriving on 26 April.

After four months in dockyard hands *Loch Lomond*

emerged to recommission under the command of Commander D G Roome MVO RN. Also joining the ship were a detachment of Royal Marines who it was decided would be useful in boarding operations on dhows in the Persian Gulf.

The ship worked up around Portland throughout the autumn before taking part in an exercise Cut Loose held in September and October.

Before heading back to the Persian Gulf a series of port visits had been organised to European towns and cities including Flushing and a most enjoyable seven

days spent in the French seaside town of Dieppe.

Finally on 14 November *Loch Lomond* left Chatham Dockyard for the Middle East taking the long African route to get there due to the closure of the Suez Canal. The frigate made refuelling stops at Gibraltar, Freetown and Simonstown before entering the Indian Ocean. After a further port of call to Mombasa, *Loch Lomond* finally arrived at Bahrain in December where she relieved sister ship Loch Fyne as the duty frigate.

The new year of 1957 started with more dhow patrols before making for Karachi in February for an

While passing through the Straits of Hormuz, in April 1960, Loch Lomond *received a distress call from the Shell tanker* Volvatella. *A seaboat is seen approaching the tanker to transfer the Medical Officer. (Ken Kelly Collection)*

interim docking period. She remained in port for around four weeks receiving maintenance before returning to the Persian Gulf to resume her patrols in the region and in particular in the Northern Gulf where she made a number of port visits including one to Mina-al-Ahmadi.

Late spring and early summer saw the frigate continue the interception and inspection of dhows but also saw visits paid to Aden, Djibouti and Kameran Island. Tension in the region increased in the summer months and *Loch Lomond* was drawn away from her planned programme to head for Ceylon where civil unrest was rampant as indeed was the sea en route, the frigate having to battle some treacherous waves and strong winds.

Upon her eventual arrival men were put ashore to assist the local authorities in restoring law and order. Once the situation was calmed the ship remained on call at Trincomalee until relieved by sister ship *Loch Alvie*.

For *Loch Lomond* it must have appeared that it was out of the frying pan and into the fire when on her return to the Persian Gulf she was called upon to assist in quelling more civil unrest this time in Oman, where Royal Marines from the British frigate were again put ashore to help local law enforcement officers bring the civil unrest under control. The Royal Marines were eventually relieved by men from the Kings Shropshire Light Infantry brought up from Kenya.

On 10 August the frigate sailed from Bahrain to render aid to the Italian merchant ship SS *Aragonoese*, which had anchored off the island of Jazirah Qais in Saudi Arabia. The Italian vessel had mechanical troubles and after a thorough investigation by men from *Loch Lomond* it was decided to take the stricken ship in tow. The tow began the next day and the British ship took the other to Sitra in Bahrain, where they both arrived safely on the 12 August. After a brief period alongside, *Loch Lomond* sailed the next day to resume her patrols in the Persian Gulf.

On 20 September the frigate returned to Bahrain from her latest patrol but only spent four days alongside before heading back out to sea for further patrols in the Northern Gulf. On 8 October at the end of this patrol she once again tied up alongside in Bahrain and

started preparations for her return to the United Kingdom. *Loch Lomond* was routed through the Suez Canal with stops at Aden, Kamaran Island and Gibraltar.

Before arriving at Chatham on 12 November to pay off *Loch Lomond* suffered a near disaster onboard when a major fire broke out in No 2 Boiler Room. The blaze was so severe that the oil supply had to be shut off by Stoker Petty Officer Robert Barlow, who received the British Empire Medal (Military Division) for his quick thinking in shutting off the supply. The blaze was then brought under control by fire fighting damage control parties on the frigate.

The frigate eventually arrived safely at Chatham and was soon taken in hand by dockyard workers for the planned refit at nearby Sheerness Dockyard some ten miles downstream from Chatham. The refit of *Loch Lomond* would be the last undertaken by Sheerness Dockyard before it closed in May 1960. The refit was completed in September 1959 after extensive work was done to fit air conditioning units in the forward superstructure of the frigate.

On 1 September at 1500 the frigate was recommissioned alongside the West Wall of the Great Basin at Sheerness Dockyard, the service being conducted by the Reverend P M Dodwell, Chaplin of the Royal Dockyard. *Loch Lomond*'s new commanding officer was Commander C B Armstrong RN. A Royal Marines detachment were also embarked.

Loch Lomond conducted basin trials at Sheerness throughout the autumn months and after further machinery defects were ironed out she sailed for Portland on 22 November for her work up. This was interrupted in December by bad weather in the English Channel and as a consequence the frigate returned to Chatham for Christmas leave on 12 December with the intention of re-starting the work up in the New Year.

January 1960 was spent finishing the work of the previous year in and around Portsmouth and finally on 3 February *Loch Lomond* set sail again for Bahrain.

The early part of the year saw the frigate patrolling off Somaliland before entering into a maintenance period at Bahrain on 6 March. After eleven days of work on the ship *Loch Lomond* sailed to resume her

patrols. In addition to port visits the frigate took part in Exercise Winged Warrior with the aircraft carrier *Centaur* and the destroyer *Lagos*. At its conclusion and back in Bahrain *Loch Lomond* welcomed onboard the Minister of Defence Harold Wilkinson MP.

The beginning of April saw her operating in the Gulf of Oman when on 5 April the *Loch Lomond*'s doctor and First Lieutentant went to the aid of a man, from the tanker *Volvatella*, who had been taken ill. Three days later the British ship made a port visit to Doha. The following month was a busy time for the ships complement with a major naval exercise - Khargex II - with the Iranian Navy and sister ship *Loch Insh*. Amongst the other ships taking part in this exercise were Pelang, Keyura, Mehran, Mahan, Tinan, Larak and Hormuz. Upon completion the ships were thrown into another series of exercises with CASPEX V with *Loch Killisport* and *Loch Insh*.

The exercises were a complete success and having been released from them *Loch Lomond* made for Karachi for a routine docking in the port. The ships bottom was scrapped and repainted and some work was carried out to topside fittings and fixtures too. Extra time in dock was necessary, however, to complete work on the ships sonar dome.

In June at the end of the maintenance period the frigate returned to the Gulf, with visits throughout the summer months paid to Banda Abbas, Qeshm and Lingeh in Iran. In July the dhow patrols proved their worth when with *Loch Fada*, *Loch Lomond* stopped a vessel and found quantities of arms onboard. The crew were arrested and the weapons seized.

The ancient walled city of Muscat was next on the agenda for *Loch Lomond* where an official visit was made. This was followed by another official port of call in August to Doha before returning to Bahrain. On

Loch Lomond *at anchor off Aden in January 1961 towards the end of her 12 month commission on the Persian Gulf Station.* *(Ken Kelly Collection)*

Loch Lomond at anchor off Little Quoin Island at the eastern end of the Persian Gulf. A fault had developed in the lighthouse but the light was soon back in working order thanks to a party of officers and senior ratings from the ship who investigated and rectified the defect. (Ken Kelly Collection)

Monday 22 August the British frigate sailed to Bombay and exchanged identities with the American Gearing class destroyer USS *Forest Royal* en route. Five days later *Loch Killisport* arrived at Bombay Harbour and fired a 13 gun salute to the flag of Flag Officer at Bombay, Rear Admiral S G Karmarkar who also later visited the ship. On Tuesday 30 August the ships complement organised a childrens party for hundreds of local Indian children, who all had a wonderful time onboard the British frigate.

It was soon, however, back to the business of more exercises and these continued into early September and proved to be very successful for both navies. *Loch Lomond* sailed back to Bahrain on Friday 2 September where she later put to sea with a film crew onboard. The cameramen were onboard to shoot a recruitment film that was entitled 'First Left Past Aden'.

Later, in September, the frigate visited Mina-al-Admadi in Kuwait and Qatar before being visited by the First Lord of the Admiralty Lord Carrington in October. After a maintenance period the ship put to sea to take part in Exercises HALLMARK and MIDLINK III, which also included sister ship Loch Fada and units of the US Navy including submarines and guided missile cruisers. Exercise MIDLINK III ended with the ships returning to Bahrain to undertake their annual inspections. Frantic work onboard all three Loch class ships was undertaken in preparation of the inspections, cleaning and scrubbing and insuring all equipment functioned correctly. *Loch Fada* and *Loch Ruthven* acted as consort for *Loch Lomond* during her inspection period, which was successful.

Upon completion the frigate patrolled off the Trucial coast and went on to visit Doha, Abu Dhabi and Dubai before spending Christmas at Mina-al-Ahmadi for the festive season. It was also time to bid the film crew farewell as they left the ship.

On 27 December *Loch Lomond* started her return journey to the United Kingdom where she arrived at Chatham on 26 January 1961 to pay off into refit at the dockyard. Dockyard workers completed the list of works in July and returned the refurbished warship back to the Royal Navy under the command of Commander D T Smith RN.

Loch Lomond and her ships company were worked up at Portland throughout the spring and summer and only in October did she sail for the Persian Gulf. En route the frigate called at Malta and Tripoli before assuming her patrol duties in the Gulf in November. The following month saw a major naval exercise in the region which culminated in the Christmas celebrations which were staged at Mina-al-Ahmadi.

In January 1962 the ship started another patrol of the Persian Gulf with visits paid to the usual regional ports including Doha, but in February *Loch Lomond* sailed out of the Persian Gulf and into the Indian Ocean for planned visits to Cochin and Bombay in India. At the latter port the frigate was docked for an inspection before sailing back to her home port of Bahrain in April.

The following month saw *Loch Lomond* join Royal Navy and Iranian vessels in Exercise Khargex off Kharg Island before returning to Bahrain in June. The flexibility of the Loch class frigate design was shown to full effect when in July *Loch Lomond* carried out a hydrographical survey along the Omani coastline but particularly around Bandar Khairan.

After arriving at Aden in August, *Loch Lomond* was dispatched to nearby Djibouti. The warships mission was to assist in the salvage operation that had begun on the merchant ship SS *Medina Princess*. The ship had suffered extensive damage from flooding whilst alongside in the main port in the country. The flooding, it was alleged, had been undertaken deliberately by a number of disatisfied crew members. The British warship's emergency party tried to stem the flooding, but the attempt resulted in a complete failure.

The *Medina Princess* was later towed to a safe anchorage in the harbour. After being thanked for their efforts *Loch Lomond* set sail back to Aden and a brief tour of East African ports.

In the autumn of 1962 the frigate's commander received news from the Ministry that his ship would not return to the United Kingdom for her planned refit and would instead be refitted locally at Singapore to save time and money with the cost of relocating the warship half way around the world. The same did not, however, apply to the crew who were to be returned to the United Kingdom by air and a replacement crew sent to Singapore in a similar fashion.

HMS Loch Lomond *about to replenish at sea. Note the rocket launcher rails on the sides of the 4-inch gun forward.*
(Crown Copyright/MoD)

Before any refit, however, the frigate needed to complete her planned programme which included visits to Mombasa, Tanga, Dar-es-Salaam and Gan before arriving at Singapore ahead of the refit. The ship was swiftly de-stored and the crew sent home to the United Kingdom as local workmen restored and enhanced the ships equipment, accommodation and

weaponry. Finally on 18 October, with great ceremony, *Loch Lomond* was re-commissioned for further service with the Far East Fleet under the command of Commander P D Nichol RN.

The final months of 1963 were spent undertaking trials and work up in local waters around Singapore before sailing for Hong Kong where the frigate arrived on 7 March. After almost a fortnight at the colony the ship continued her journey onto Indonesia where she relieved the Type 61 frigate *Llandaff* on patrol duties during the Konfrontasi operations. After nine hard days on patrol the destroyer *Caesar* arrived on 30 March to relieve her and upon signalling to the destroyer left to return to Singapore.

The following month saw the Loch class frigate off Gan as guardship whilst on 14 May she sailed for Singapore. It was a far from trouble free return passage with the gunnery officer injured during a diving accident and on the 22 May the ships port propeller shaft broke causing a considerable loss of speed. Fortunately *Loch Lomond* was only one day away from the dockyard facilities at Singapore at the time and using her one surviving propeller shaft secured alongside.

The damage was immediately investigated as the frigate was docked down in a dry dock at the base and the ships company put up in shore accommodation.

After spending the whole of June in dry dock *Loch Lomond* was once again afloat on 29 June. There were still, however, problems with the frigate as her basin trials were reported to be unsatisifactory and even after a month's work on the ship she still required more.

Loch Lomond's itinerary was starting to look to be on shaky ground and her planned Borneo patrol was delayed by her ongoing mechanical problems. Finally, on 10 July, the ship sailed from Singapore at the start of her latest patrol from Labuan where a local group of police officers joined the ship.

The remainder of the month saw the ship patrolling the waters around Labuan and Tawau before sailing for Hong Kong on 2 August for a period of leave for the crew. After four days alongside *Loch Lomond* was once again back at sea.

After stopping off at Singapore the frigate returned to Gan in early September. Gan was also the location for the unpleasant task, on 10 September, when the ships company gathered for the burial at sea of Able Seaman Dallas who had died whilst the ship was at Gan. Later in the month the ship took part in a lengthy series of naval exercises that culminated in *Loch Lomond*'s arrival at the Seychelles on 4 October.

After only three days at the paradise island location the British warship was once again at sea and bound for Gan and then onto Singapore with more exercises with sister ship *Loch Killisport* en route. October finished with a quick visit to Kuching and November around Tawau. The crew busied themselves intercepting local small craft (Kumpits) that carried illegal arms and ammunition throughout the month *Loch Lomond* was on station. At the end of her patrol cycle the frigate arrived at Hong Kong on the last day of November.

December saw *Loch Lomond* taking part in a series of exercises whilst on 16 December the ships latest commanding officer Commander B L Spark RN took command. Further fleet exercises in the waters off Singapore followed before the crew enjoyed Christmas at the naval base. With the festive celebrations over *Loch Lomond* sailed for Penang on 29 December.

Loch Lomond's last operational year started on 2 January 1964 when the frigate sailed from Penang and headed out to sea together with the Royal Marines Band, who were taking passage to the island of Gan. After five fairly uneventful days at 1030 on 8 January the frigate crossed the equator and welcomed onboard King Neptune and his court for the famous Crossing the Line Ceremony. Later in the day she rendezvoused with the tanker RFA *Wave Sovereign* and refuelled before arriving at Gan the following day where she met *Alert*.

At 0855 on Saturday 11 January the frigate sailed setting course for Colombo. After two days steaming she arrived and was there for the official visit by Commander in Chief Far East.

During her stay at Colombo *Loch Lomond* was opened to local people who toured the ship with great interest. Another visitor to the British warship was the Captain of the Royal Malaysian patrol vessel KD Sri Pahang. The men of *Loch Lomond*, meanwhile, took time to assist with the Cemetery Restoration Project ashore.

On Friday 17 January *Loch Lomond* manoeuvred with half sister ship Alert before the former sailed for Singapore.

The frigate arrived at Singapore through the Eastern

Entrance and secured at 0700. The frigate *Lincoln* secured on her the next day and the two ships were later joined by the auxiliaries *Eddyrock*, *Plumleaf* and *Gold Ranger*.

Loch Lomond sailed for Labuan on Tuesday 4 February and arrived at Tawau after two days steaming. There she embarked two Malay policemen and started her sea patrols in the region with the Malaysian patrol boat KD *Sri Perak* and replenished her fuel from RFA *Tideflow*.

She completed her patrols on Saturday 29 February and made for Hong Kong where she secured on the North Wall on Wednesday 4 March. The frigate only spent four days in the colony before returning to Singapore where she was taken in hand for a refit and maintenance period. The men were accommodated in HMS *Terror* whilst the work was carried out on their ship. On Saturday 11 April the men staged the *Loch Lomond* Swimming Gala which started at 0930 in the morning and lasted for most of the day.

Three days later their ship was released from the dock and was later secured on the destroyer *Cambrian*. On Tuesday 16 April an incident that could have been much worse occurred on the quarterdeck. According to the ships log, 'At 1315 CO_2 bottles exploded on the Quarterdeck. No one hurt remainder sprayed with cold water!'

The ships refit and trials programme was completed on 24 April and *Loch Lomond* sailed from Singapore to Gan where she assumed the role of guardship of the island. The following month she relieved *Cambrian* as guardship of the Seychelles where she stayed for just under a week. On the Monday of the visit the Governor of the islands arrived onboard and told the Captain of news of an overdue fishing boat and requested that the frigate commence a search for the vessel. The ship put to sea but soon received news from Port Victoria that the vessel had arrived home safely. On the return journey to Gan *Loch Lomond* embarked the British Foreign Office representative. On Thursday 4 June a demolition party from the frigate left the ship to scuttle an RAF gash barge. The frigate would shuttle between Gan, the Seychelles and Singapore until near the middle of June. On Friday 26 June *Loch Lomond* arrived at Singapore where maintenance was carried out on the ship for a fortnight before she sailed for Hong Kong on 3 July.

Loch Lomond was scheduled to take part in a lengthy series of naval exercises in the region, but upon her arrival at HMS *Tamar* a faulty engine caused her to need more repairs. Suitably repaired *Loch Lomond* sailed for Manila and then onto Borneo for the Borneo Patrol based for the next few weeks out of Tawau. Her tour of duty there lasted until 21 August when a relieved crew tied up alongside the wall at Singapore Naval Dockyard.

After a period of leave the ship was next at sea on 9 September for a series of fleet exercises that ended when *Loch Lomond* carried out a Malaysian coastal patrol where she met up with sister ship *Loch Fada*. The opportunity was also taken to visit Tumpat, Dungan and Kuantan in Malaysia before returning once more to Singapore.

Loch Lomond's troublesome port engine caused further problems for the engineers when on 10 October it required seven hours of work to repair it whilst off the Malayan west coast. Permanent repairs were made to the engine upon the frigates arrival in Hong Kong a week later.

After spending her last visit to Hong Kong *Loch Lomond* sailed for Singapore where on 4 November she sailed flying her paying off pennant. The frigate was routed back to the United Kingdom via Gan, Aden, Port Said and Gibraltar. She sailed from the Rock on Wednesday 9 December and arrived off Portsmouth four days later. She anchored south of Spit Sand Fort overnight before sailing into port the following morning. On Thursday 17 December the Captain left the ship for the last time and the following day *Loch Lomond* was cold moved to 7 Berth in the Tidal Basin, where she was formally decommissioned.

The following February *Loch Lomond* was declared for the disposal list. A buyer took two years to find and after all useful parts and equipment had been stripped out of the former frigate at Chatham Dockyard in 1967 she was sold to BISCO. The demolition work on the frigate was carried out by Metal Industries at Faslane where *Loch Lomond* arrived on 7 October 1967.

Chronology

07.12.1943	Laid down at Caledon Shipbuilding, Dundee
19.06.1944	Launched
16.11.1944	Completed
11.12.1944	Joined 17th Escort Group at Greenock
Early 1945	English Channel
03.1945	Scapa Flow
05.1945	Refit at Pembroke Dock. Extra AA guns fitted
28.06.1945	Sailed for Far East
23.07.1945	Colombo for Operation Zipper in Malaya
12.09.1945	Singapore area
11.1945	Guardship at Sabang
24.12.1945	Singapore
19.02.1946	Trincomalee
03.1946	Portsmouth
07.1946	Reserve fleet at Portsmouth
22.09.1950	Recommissioned into 2nd Frigate Flotilla
13.11.1950	Sea Trials commenced
17.11.1950	Work up at Portland
11.1950	Exercises off Londonderry with *Vengeance* and *Finisterre*
12.12.1950	Sailed to Malta to join flotilla
02.1951	Aqaba
03.1951	Malta
Summer 1951	Exercise Beehive
01.1952	Short refit at Malta
04.1952	Red Sea area
12.05.1952	Amphibious exercise on Elephant Bank peninsula in Aden
19.05.1952	Malta
31.10.1952	Sailed for Portsmouth to await refit and reserve
1954	Refitted at Charles Hill Shipyard, Bristol
11.1954	Refit completed
Early 1955	Fitted with air conditioning at Chatham Dockyard
19.04.1955	Works completed
05.1955	Sailed for Malta
Late 07.1955	Sailed for Bahrain with *Loch Alvie*
26.07.1955	Went to assistance of RFA *Wave King*
Summer 1955	Dhow Patrol
04.1956	Refit at Chatham Dockyard

08.1956	Returned to service
09.1956	Exercise Cut Loose
14.11.1956	Sailed for Middle East from Chatham via South Africa
Early 1957	Dhow Patrol
Summer 1957	Civil unrest in Ceylon and Oman
10.08.1957	Went to assistance of merchantman SS *Aragonoese*
12.11.1957	Arrived at Chatham Dockyard to pay off
11.1957	Reserve at Sheerness Dockyard
11.1957	Refit at Sheerness Dockyard
09.1959	Refit completed. Last refit carried out at Sheerness before dockyard closed in 1960
22.11.1959	Sailed for sea trials at Portland
12.12.1959	Chatham Dockyard
03.02.1960	Sailed for the Middle East
03.1960	Exercise Winged Chariot with *Centaur* and *Lagos*
05.04.1960	Gave medical aid to tanker *Volvatella*
05.1960	Exercise Khargex II with *Loch Insh*
05.1960	Exercise Caspex V
06.1960	Visited Banba Abbas, Qeshm, Lingeh and Qai
27.08.1960	Bombay for exercises with Royal Indian Navy
09.1960	Exercises Hallmark and Midlink III
27.12.1960	Sailed for United Kingdom
26.01.1961	Arrived Chatham Dockyard to pay off for refit
07.1961	Returned to service
10.1961	Sailed to Middle East
01.1962	Persian Gulf
02.1962	Indian Ocean
03.1962	Exercise Khargex off Kharg Island, Iran
07.1962	Hydrographical survey off Oman
08.1962	Salvage operation on SS *Medina Princess*
Summer 1962	Refit at Singapore
18.10.1962	Recommissioned
07.03.1963	Hong Kong
03.1963	Indonesian conflict Konfrontasi operations
30.03.1963	Relieved by destroyer *Caesar*
04.1963	Gan guardship
14.05.1963	Singapore
22.05.1963	Propeller shaft broke *(Down No.1 Ben Rm)*
23.05.1963	Singapore for repairs
29.06.1963	Refloated from dock but more work necessary
10.07.1963	Sailed from Hong Kong for Labuan
02.08.1963	Hong Kong
04.10.1963	Seychelles
10.1963	Gan and Kuching
11.1963	Patrols off Tawau

30.11.1963	✓	Hong Kong · *left BISNS 'NEVASA' arrived UK 23 Dec 1963.*
16.12.1963		Recommissioned at Singapore
29.12.1963		Sailed for Penang
02.01.1964		Sailed from Penang
01.1964		Gan, Colombo and Singapore
04.02.1964		Sailed for Tawau
04.03.1964		Hong Kong for a four day stay
03.1964		Refit at Singapore
24.04.1964		Refit and trials completed
04.1964		Gan guardship
26.06.1964		Singapore
03.07.1964		Sailed for Hong Kong
07.1964		Manila and Borneo Patrol
09.1964		Visited Tumpat, Dungun and Kuantan
10.10.1964		Port engine failed at sea required 7 hours of work by engineers to restore power
04.11.1964		Sailed from Singapore wearing paying off pennant
13.12.1964		Arrived Portsmouth for the last time
18.12.1964		Decommissioned
02.1965		Disposal list at Chatham Dockyard
1967		Sold to BISCO
07.10.1967		Arrived Faslane for breaking up by Metal Industries

HMS LOCH MORE

HMS Loch More *one of three ships involved in the destruction of the German U-boat* U-1024 *on 12 April 1945*
(Crown Copyright/MoD)

Loch More was ordered from the Dundee ship-yard of Caledon Shipbuilding on 2 February 1943. Construction commenced on 6 March the following year. The building process was swift with the hull entering the water for the first time on 3 October 1944. Five months would, however, elapse before *Loch More* was completed on 24 February, much of this time having been spent fitting improved weaponry such as Squid anti-submarine mortars and the much more capable Type 277 sonar set.

After shipbuilders sea trials were completed the frigate was commissioned and subsequently joined the 8th Escort Group under the command of Lieutenant Commander R A D Cambridge DSC RNR. After storing at Tobermory on the Isle of Mull, *Loch More* carried out her work up in Scottish waters before finally joining the other vessels of the group at Greenock in early April.

She was soon in action on the 12 April when,

together with *Loch Glendhu* and *Loch Achray,* she attacked the German Type V11C/41 submarine *U-1024* under the command of Kapitanleutnant Hans Joachim Gutteck with depth charges. The U-boat surfaced and was raked with gunfire from the Royal Navy ships. Thirty seven of the U-boat's crew survived the attack after abandoning the stricken boat. Men from *Loch More,* including Midshipman J R Watson, ERA 3rd Class C A Baker rowed over to the empty submarine and boarded her to establish a tow line but when the weather conditions worsened the tow failed and the submarine eventually sank but not before a great deal of valuable information and documents had been recovered for later analysis. The two men would later receive an MBE and a BEM respectively.

Loch More resumed her patrols in the Irish Sea before sailing south mid month to the South West Approaches based out of the Welsh port of Milford

Haven. In May the frigate was declared suitable for service in the East Indies and was taken in hand for a refit after brief visits to Belfast and Scapa Flow for participation in Operation Deadlight - the scuttling of captured German submarines off Northern Ireland. On 6 June she commenced a refit on the Clyde when new ventilation and anti-aircraft armaments were added to the ship. In early July *Loch More* carried out her post refit trials before starting her passage to Alexandria on 17 July.

Eleven days later she arrived at Port Said at the start of her southerly transit of the Suez Canal and onward journey into the Indian Ocean. *Loch More* arrived at Colombo on 12 August where she was detailed to participate in Operation Zipper at Trincomalee. Zipper was the escort of convoys ahead of the planned invasion of the Malaysian peninsula. Throughout late

August and September the frigate supported forces in the region before returning to Singapore on 12 September. At Singapore *Loch More*'s duties consisted of escorting transport vessel's from the Dutch East Indies carrying former prisoners of war back from captivity. On 3 October she sailed to Saigon to collect civilians who had been caught up in the conflict and escorted them back to safety. On the return passage she was joined by sister ship *Loch Scavaig* and the damaged landing ship *Queen Emma*, all the ships arriving safely at Singapore on 12 October.

The following month saw the frigate serve as guardship at Sourabaya before returning to Singapore on the last day of the month.

In January 1946 the frigate loaded with stores and sailed from Singapore to Vizagapatam in the Bay of Bengal where they were urgently needed and then

Seen late in her career Loch More, *like many of the Loch class, spent years patrolling the Persian Gulf and Indian Ocean.* *(Crown Copyright/MoD)*

promptly returned to base at Singapore. She carried out a similar supply run on 10 January only this time the destination was Bangkok. She remained in the Gulf of Siam for air sea rescue duties before returning to Singapore on 4 February. After three days alongside she took passage to Trincomalee where on the 17 February her new commanding officer, Lieutenant Commander J Raban Williams took command.

Under his command *Loch More* sailed for Bombay where she was to conduct special duties following the failed Royal Indian Navy mutiny there. Upon her arrival at the port she conducted operations with the cruiser *Glasgow* until the end of the month.

On 2 March 1946 she sailed to Karachi before sailing on to Singapore where she was needed in support of ongoing military operations in the region. The following month was spent in the waters around Sumatra and Java whilst May saw *Loch More* operating out of Bangkok. June saw the announcement to the crew that the ship would be returning home to the United Kingdom but the news also said that she would reduce to reserve upon her arrival at Sheerness Dockyard.

Loch More made her way home via Rangoon and Trincomalee before arriving at Sheerness where she paid off into reserve. Between August and December 1946 the frigate was laid up at Sheerness awaiting a return for return service. She was in reserve, however, for four years until 1950 when she was brought forward to join the 5th Frigate Flotilla. The work to refurbish the frigate took until November to complete and with a new ships company it was necessary to complete a full work up period in Londonderry waters before she deployed with the flotilla to the Mediterranean. *Loch More* finally arrived at Malta in March 1951 at the start of the deployment.

Later that year she was deployed as guardship at Aqaba and Port Said. She took part in the Fleet Exercise and Visits Programme with ships of the flotilla including the NATO exercise Symphonie Deux in October. The two week exercise was plagued by bad weather but saw serious contributions from the Canadian aircraft carrier HMCS *Magnificent* and HMCS *Micmac*, French cruiser *George Leygues*, HMS *Mermaid* and the cruiser HMS *Liverpool*.

She was refitted at Gibraltar early in 1952 and rejoined the Flotilla in June to take part in the Fleet Summer Cruise Visits and Exercise Programme including Exercise Longstop.

Loch More was, in February 1953, returned to the Reserve fleet but hopes were high that she would be modernised for further service, sadly this never materialised and instead the frigate was sent to Hartlepool where her systems were preserved. The aim of this enterprise was probably to interest the Government of Ceylon into buying the ship, but they turned down the offer and *Loch More* was sold to BISCO for scrap. The frigate arrived at the scrapyard of T W Ward at Inverkeithing in August 1963.

Battle Honours

ATLANTIC 1944

Chronology

02.02.1943	Ordered from Caledon Shipbuilding
06.03.1943	Laid down
03.10.1944	Launched
12.04.1945	Attacked *U-1024* with *Loch Glendhu* and *Loch Achray*
05.1945	Operation Deadlight
06.06.1945	Refit on River Clyde
17.07.1945	Sailed to Alexandria
12.07.1945	Colombo before Operation Zipper in Malaya
09.1945	Escort of PoW transports
01.1946	Visited Vizgapatam and Bangkok
04.02.1946	Singapore
02.1946	Bombay following failed Royal Indian mutiny
08.1946	Decommissioned at Sheerness and laid up in reserve
1951	Mediterranean Service
Early 1952	Refitted at Gibraltar
02.1953	Reserve including period at Hartlepool
1956	Refitted with aim of selling ship to Ceylon. Sale fell through
08.1963	Arrived for breaking up at TW Ward at Inverkeithing

HMS LOCH MORLICH
(HMNZS TUTIRA FROM 1949)

HMS Loch Morlich *would see service with the Royal Canadian Navy during the Second World War and from 1949 as* HMNZS Tutira *with the Royal New Zealand Navy.*   *(Crown Copyright/MoD)*

On 13 February 1943 Swan Hunters shipyard at Wallsend received eight ship contracts for Loch class frigates. One of these was for the construction of *Loch Morlich*. She was named after a loch near Inverness. Construction started on 15 July 1943 and by 20 January 1944 the ship was named and launched. Seven months later on 2 August the ship was completed and transferred to the Royal Canadian Navy which provided the crew under an Inter Government Agreement in exchange for Algerine Class minesweepers built in Canada also manned by the Royal Canadian Navy. After her initial sea trials *Loch Morlich* commissioned on 17 July 1944 for service with the 8th Canadian Escort Group under the command of Lieutenant Commander L L Foxall RCNVR.

The start of her career was marred when on completion of her harbour trials the frigate struck a buoy and suffered some damage. Her work up commenced in the waters around Tobermory before sailing to Londonderry on 28 July to join the rest of the Escort Group.

Between August and September the frigate operated in the Western Approaches area on the lookout for U-boats. Bad weather in the area caused damage to the ship and she was withdrawn and made for London for repairs to be made.

In the autumn of 1944 *Loch Morlich* deployed in support of anti-submarine operations and convoy escort duties which were routed through the English Channel due to the reduced enemy air threat.

The New Year saw the frigate transfer to the waters off the Canadian Eastern Seaboard with the rest of the 8th Canadian Escort Group. The group patrolled the Canadian waters until returning to the United Kingdom in May. On 8 May she transferred back to

Royal Navy control and paid off in June at Sheerness where she was reduced to reserve.

Loch Morlich remained laid up until sold to the New Zealand Government with five sister ships. She was initially given the name *Waiarapa* and given a new pennant number of F517.

Between January and March 1949 *Wairarapa* was under refit at Sheerness Dockyard. In early April she sailed the short distance up the River Medway to Chatham Dockyard where she was formally accepted into service. She had also changed her name again time this to *Tutira* and was named as such by Lady More, wife of the Commander in Chief Nore on 11 April. Eight days later *Tutira* was commissioned into the Royal New Zealand Navy under the command of

Lieutenant Commander F J Rand RN.

Each of the six Loch class frigates transferred to New Zealand was named after lakes in the country. Lake Tutira can be found in the Hawke Bay area of North Island. She sailed from Chatham Dockyard with sister ship *Rotoiti* (ex *Loch Katrine*) and headed for the Mediterranean to work up based at Malta before sailing on to New Zealand with Lieutenant Commander W H Brereton in command. The former British frigate arrived at her new home of Auckland in August and soon started a series of deployments in the South Pacific region.

In October *Tutira* operated off Australia with ports of call paid to Jervis Bay and Sydney, Melbourne and Hobart before returning home to Auckland at the end

In RNZN service Tutira *remained virtually unaltered from the basic Loch class design.* (Steve Bush Collection)

of November. The final month of 1949 saw the frigate visiting Campbell Island and MacQuarrie Island before spending Christmas alongside at Auckland.

1950 started normally with flotilla operations dominating the frigates planned programme but on 12 May a new Commanding Officer, Lieutenant Commander P J Hoare RN assumed command and it was only a matter of weeks before the frigate was on a war footing. On 29 June New Zealand provided men, ships and equipment to the United Nations campaign in Korea. *Tutira* was one of the ships nominated to prevent an invasion of South Korea by the Communist North.

On 3 July the ship slipped out to sea bound for Japan where the UN naval force was being assembled in company with *Pukaki*. First stop was to refuel her tanks at Port Moresby before arriving at Hong Kong on 19 July. Some remedial work was necessary onboard the frigate and this was completed by a shipyard at the British colony. Upon completion the frigate sailed for escort duties to protect UN ships travelling between Pusan and Japan.

The famous amphibious landing at Inchon on Korea's west coast took place on 15 September and *Tutira* had been a significant part of the escort force of the convoy. With the marines ashore the frigate continued patrolling the waters off the beachead to protect the men ashore from a sea borne attack.

Tutira's next actions were under the command of the US Navy Task Group and saw the frigate used off the proposed Wosan landings site on 16 October. Upon her arrival off Wosan the landings were delayed due to a large mine field laid by the North Korean forces.

The frigate maintained a series of patrols with her sister ships until November when she returned to Sasebo.

1951 saw *Tutira* patrolling coastal waters on the lookout for enemy action and generally to defeat any attempt to penetrate the United Nations lines. January also saw the withdrawal of forces from Inchon and Chinampo areas and where possible Tutira assisted with the evacuation. The ebb and flow of the conflict saw Inchon back in UN hands in February and it was from here that Tutira patrolled - sometimes in company with minesweepers from the South Korean Navy.

April found *Tutira* at Kure where repair work was carried out on the frigate. Upon completion she was relieved by *Hawea* on 26 April. *Tutira* returned home to New Zealand via Hong Kong and Brisbane before arriving at Auckland on the last day of May.

July saw the frigates final operational exercises when she took passage to Australia. Upon her return to New Zealand the frigate was reduced to reserve and laid up at Auckland in September 1951 where she remained laid up until December 1961. She was sold for demolition in Hong Kong and the following year was towed away for scrapping.

Battle Honours

KOREA 1950-1951

Chronology

13.12.1943	Ordered from Swan Hunters
15.07.1943	Laid down
20.01.1944	Launched
17.07.1944	Commissioned into 8th Canadian Escort Group
02.08.1944	Completed
Autumn 1944	Anti Submarine Operations
Early 1945	Canadian Eastern Seaboard
08.05.1945	Returned to Royal Navy. Paid off into reserve at Sheerness
Jan-Mar 1949	Under refit at Chatham following sale to New Zealand. Renamed *Wairarapa*.
11.04.1949	Renamed *Tutira*
10.1949	Australian waters
11.1949	Auckland
12.1949	Campbell Island and MacQuarrie Island
29.06.1950	Deployed with United Nations to Korea
15.09.1950	Amphibious landings at Inchon
16.10.1950	Amphibious landings at Wonsan
01.1951	Withdrawal of UN forces from Inchon and Chinampo
04.1951	Repairs at Kure
09.1951	Laid up at Auckland
12.1961	Sold for breaking up in Hong Kong

HMS LOCH QUOICH

HMS Loch Quoich *seen early in her Royal Navy career.* (Crown Copyright/MoD)

Named after an inland Loch near Inverness in the Scottish Highlands *Loch Quoich* was ordered on 25 January 1943 from Blyth Shipbuilding Company. Given the yard number 298 construction commenced on 3 December and progressed smoothly with the hull entering the water on 2 September 1944. She was then towed to Bolcow's shipyard in Sunderland where she was berthed alongside Battleship Wharf to be fitted out. Final work finished on 11 January 1945 and she was commissioned under the command of Lieutenant Commander G McClelland DSC. Her acceptance had been delayed due to a number of defects discovered on the first round of trials. Some old sea dogs even blamed the presence of some Wrens onboard for jinxing the trials.

After working up around Tobermory she began her operational service with the 24th Escort Group based at Londonderry on the last day of January. February

was her first full month in commission and proved to be an eventful one with operations in the Irish Sea occupying her time. She also collided with the frigate *Dart* whilst at Greenock and watched as a Barracuda aircraft fatally crashed into the sea near the ship. Tragically one of the aircrew had a brother onboard *Loch Quoich* serving as the ships Navigating Officer.

On 16 February the frigate sailed to join the convoys bound for Gibraltar as part of the 37th Escort Group. The first convoy was KMF41 which sailed from the Clyde on 10 March and comprised of eleven ships and eight escorts. The return journey was to escort MKF41 back to Liverpool leaving Gibraltar on 25 March and arriving at Liverpool five days later with sister ship *Loch Katrine*. On 31 March she left the Clyde and escorted the troop convoy KMF42 comprising of nineteen ships with five escorts including *Pioneer, Pursuer, Dart, Ulster Queen, Loch Katrine*

and *Loch Quoich*. Onboard the merchantmen were 21,526 troops.

The following month she repeated the route escorting KMF43 to Gibraltar with seventeen ships and seven escorts including *Queen Emma, Loch Katrine, Ness, Icarus* and *Princess Beatrix*. The convoy arrived at Gibraltar on 23 April and the returning MKF43 left for Liverpool on 29 April 1945 and arrived at the mouth of the River Mersey on 5 May having safely protected the seventeen merchantmen to the United Kingdom.

With the end of hostilities in Europe came the surrender of numerous German warships and particularly operational U-boats. On 7 May *Loch Quoich* met three U-boats which were flying black flags indicating their surrender and running on the surface and escorted them to Loch Foyle.

The success in the Europe was in contrast to the situation in the Far East and Loch Quoich was nominated for service in the Pacific. To facilitate this, the frigate was refitted in Londonderry. Six extra 20mm Oerlikon guns were fitted. When the work was completed the ship sailed for Colombo in June under the command of Lieutenant Commander J E B Healey RNVR.

After her arrival the frigate was one of many British ships involved in convoy escort duties for the ships being assembled for Operation Zipper, the assault on Port Sweetenham. These operations lasted until September when *Loch Quoich* was sent to Singapore.

The need to repatriate prisoners of war across the whole of South East Asia occupied a great deal of time and saw the frigate making a number of journeys to collect and relocate personnel from many different nations. Later in October the warship took officials from the British Embassy back into the former Japanese territory of Bangkok so that they could re-establish the British Embassy in the Thai capital city.

In November *Loch Quoich* continued her important mission by escorting the landing ship *Persimmon* to Sumatra. Onboard the *Persimmon* were troops of the Lincolnshire Regiment who would be present to accept the official Japanese surrender.

After further repatriation missions and duty as guardship at Sabang the frigate carried out patrols of Indonesian waters to prevent the transportation of illegal weapons by rebels who were actively protesting against the return of Dutch colonial rule. With many casualties on both sides of the conflict the situation was quickly spiralling towards chaos.

Upon completion of this mission *Loch Quoich* returned to the tropical idyll of Trincomalee where she joined the East Indies Fleet. The closing months of the year saw her operating in the Indian Ocean and in December she arrived at HM Dockyard in Bombay for a routine docking period where her bottom was scraped and machinery and equipment was updated and repaired.

1946 started with a transfer to Karachi ahead of a flight of VIP personnel across the Indian Ocean. *Loch Quoich* together with the destroyer *Petard* and frigate *Taff* were stationed off Gwadar to provide rescue should anything untoward happen to the aeroplane and its passengers. In the event the flight was uneventful.

Something that was far from uneventful, however, occurred on 21 February in Karachi when the Royal Indian Navy suffered its first and most damaging mutiny. The Loch class frigate sailed from Karachi at high speed to provide a Royal Navy presence on 27 February.

Loch Quoich remained in the city until 10 March having been relieved by sister ship *Loch More* and was only released for other duties once the mutiny had been quelled by local forces in the area. *Loch Quoich* returned initially to Karachi before commencing a patrol that saw visits paid to Bombay, Colombo and Trincomalee. At the latter the ships commanding officer handed over command to his successor, Commander J E Fentor RN, who also assumed the role of Senior Officer (Frigates), East Indies.

In early April *Loch Quoich* became involved in a sort of farce, when she towed the yacht *White Bear*, which had been requisitioned in 1939 for war service back from Colombo to its former owner who was in Kilindini. The nine day tow ended with the owner refusing to accept the vessel owing to her poor material state. The result being that the *White Bear* was towed all the way back to Colombo for another nine days behind *Loch Quoich*.

A similar circumstance occurred on 8 May when the frigate started out escorting the tug *Crocodile* from Colombo to Cochin. Two days into the journey the tug's machinery failed and *Loch Quoich,* once again, took the vessel in tow. Fortunately Trincomalee was only a day away and the Crocodile's engines were soon under repair.

Repairs were the order of the day for the frigate as well, having left Trincomalee she took passage to Colombo where on 24 May she entered into a refit that lasted until July.

Following successful sea trials the frigate resumed her duties this time as the Senior Officers vessel in the Persian Gulf until the end of the year.

At the start of 1947 *Loch Quoich* operated out of Trincomalee as part of the East Indies Squadron but in February she returned to Singapore for a much needed refit and to meet her new commanding officer, Commander S S Stamwich RN. Stamwich was also Senior Officer (Frigates).

The refit was completed in March and after sea trials in local waters the frigate sailed to Penang and then onto Trincomalee at the start of a deployment in the Persian Gulf.

The autumn months were spent visiting ports of call around the Gulf and inspecting dhows. In September she visited Colombo before sailing back to Singapore in October where she was taken in hand for another refit that lasted until the end of the year.

In January 1948 *Loch Quoich* was designated to patrol in the Indian Ocean before diverting to Mogadishu for security duties in Somalia where a series of civil disturbances had broken out. The frigate put armed men ashore to try to control the situation. Upon release she resumed her interrupted Indian Ocean patrol with a variety of interesting ports visited including Lamu, Mombasa, Zanzibar, Dar es Salaam and the Seychelles.

In April combined Royal Navy and Royal Indian Navy exercises off Ceylon were the order of the day. Whilst in May the frigate's Ships Company welcomed onboard the ships latest commanding officer, Commander G F M Best RN whilst on duty in the Persian Gulf.

The next few months saw the frigate visit as many ports across the region as possible on both official and unofficial business. Many contacts were established and friendships made with local sheiks, chieftains and local businessmen.

1949 started with the ship still operating in the Persian Gulf but after a series of ports of call she sailed (in March) for Trincomalee and then onto Singapore where she was taken in hand for a lengthy refit that would ultimately last until October. Upon completion of the work on the frigate a new commanding officer and Senior Officer for the Flotilla joined the ship in the form of Commander E T L Dunsterville RN. Any intention he may have had to quickly take the ship out of refit for trials was cast asunder when after a survey of the work carried out it was deemed necessary to rectify a number of problems. This delayed completion of work until December. Eventually the Commander completed the post refit trials and set sail in December for Trincomalee at the start of a patrol in the Indian Ocean.

1950 would prove to be a busy year for the frigate with a variety of civil functions to attend, including in April the official ceremonies for the return to Italian administration in Mogadishu. Following this successful occasion the frigate sailed to Colombo where she spent some time undertaking a self refit with dockyard assistance. During this time another change of command took place with Commander E F S Black DSC RN appointed to command the ship as well as becoming Senior Officer of the flotilla.

Following her return to sea *Loch Quoich* deployed in the Indian Ocean undertaking numerous patrols as well as taking part in a joint Royal Navy and Indian Navy exercise off Cochin in October. The autumn months saw further visits paid to Galle and Cocos Islands before arriving at Singapore in late November.

In December 1950 *Loch Quoich* entered into refit at Singapore in the floating dock *AFD10.* Once completed the frigate took passage in February 1951 to Penang, Nicobar, Calcutta, Vizgapatam and finally anchored in the wide natural harbour at Trincomalee.

At the end of August the warship arrived at Colombo on the 25th at the end of a quiet period of patrolling the Bay of Bengal.

After further visits to the Maldives, Seychelles, Mombasa, Tonga, Mauritius and Rodriguez Loch Quoich returned once again to Trincomalee in June. After a few days there the frigate took passage to Colombo where she was taken in hand for a period of self refit that lasted until August. After trials the warship resumed her duties in the Indian Ocean based once more at Trincomalee.

By September *Loch Quoich* had been re-deployed to the Persian Gulf. Official visits were paid to numerous ports across the region including Bahrain, Mina al Ahmeda and the ancient city of Muscat. She remained in the Gulf protecting British interests until November when she visited Karachi en route to Colombo ahead of a major Royal Navy, Royal Indian Navy exercise off Cochin in India.

January 1952 started with a patrol of the Bay of Bengal followed by brief visits to Chittagong and Port Cornwallis late in the month. February, however, saw *Loch Quoich* return of Singapore for a refit in the Naval Dockyard that lasted until April.

Upon completion of the work at Singapore *Loch Quoich* returned to sea and took passage to Trincomalee. Upon her arrival the frigate was assigned the task of escorting motor minesweepers from the 110th Minesweeping Flotilla, bound for Aden, assuming the task from sister ship *Loch Lomond*. Once the small MCM's had been delivered safely the frigate returned to her usual tasks of patrolling the Indian Ocean. Even here, however, the usual routine was broken in June when the Mau Mau rebellion broke out in Mombasa. Between 1952 and 1960 an anti colonial movement grew in British East Africa (now Kenya). It was led by the most populace Kikuyu ethnic group which dominated the Mau Mau movement and led directly to independence for Kenya. In 1952, however, men from *Loch Quoich* were landed into the city of Mombasa to aid in the swift return of civilian control. This task saw the frigate remaining near Mombasa throughout June and into July.

Upon being relieved she returned to her usual routine. Visits were made to Lindi, Mirawas, Reunion Island, Mauritius and Cochin into August.

In September the ship carried out a period of dock-ing at Colombo before continuing her deployment in the Persian Gulf throughout October. The following month saw a number of interesting ports of call made to Mombasa, Lamu, Malindi and Dar es Salaam. The closing stages of the year saw a return to patrolling the Indian Ocean with a brief spell at Mombasa in support of the British Army ashore as they fought the Mau Mau Rebellion before the frigate returned to Trincomalee. It was at this last destination that the ships latest commanding officer Commander J A Harper DSC took command of the frigate.

In January 1953 the frigate took passage to Singapore from where she carried out a patrol of the Bay of Bengal. During the patrol *Loch Quoich* visited numerous ports to make friendly associations at Vizgapatam, Chittagong, Rangoon and Penang. Upon her return to the Dockyard at Singapore she entered a dry dock and soon had hundreds of workers scuttling about her during a planned four month refit in the dockyard.

At the end of May the frigate carried out a series of post refit trials before resuming her operational tasking in July with a period of detached service in the Persian Gulf calling at Bahrain, Doha and Basra in Iraq.

In September 1953 *Loch Quoich* visited Karachi for a very successful visit that included many social functions ashore and plenty of sightseeing for the crew. After this visit the frigate continued her operational tasking in the Indian Ocean. One of the highlights of which was the embarkation of the Governor of Mauritius on 10 October for a tour of the dependencies of Agalega, St Brandon and the island of Rodriques, where the ship carried out a period of self maintenance awaiting the arrival of her sister ship *Loch Insh* to relieve her on station. The latter's refit was, however, over running so *Loch Quoich* remained on station.

The frigate spent December around Trincomalee. January 1954 saw the ship deploy to India and the west coast of Burma and with visits to Calcutta, Chittagong, Port Blair and the Nicobar Islands before setting course back to Trincomalee in April. The following month *Loch Quoich* sailed to the Maldives en route back to the United Kingdom. After sailing

through the Mediterranean and stopping at Gibraltar the ship arrived at Portsmouth for the last time in June 1954 flying her paying off pennant.

The frigate did not stay in reserve for long, after being placed on the disposal list in 1957 she was sold for scrap to BISCO for recycling by Clayton Davies. She was towed away to Dunston on the River Tyne arriving on 13 November for demolition to commence.

Battle Honours

ATLANTIC 1945

Chronology

25.01.1943	Ordered from Blyth Shipbuilding Company
03.12.1943	Laid down
02.09.1944	Launched and then completed by Bolcow's Shipyard, Sunderland
11.01.1945	Completed and joined 24th Escort Group at Londonderry
02.1945	Collided with frigate *Dart* at Greenock
16.02.1945	Sailed for Gibraltar on convoy escort duties
05.1945	Operation Deadlight
05.1945	Refitted for service in Far East at Londonderry
08.1945	Operation Zipper in Malaya
11.1945	Escorted landing ship *Persmisson* to Sumatra
11.1945	Sabang and Indonesian patrols
12.1945	Indian Ocean with East Indies Fleet
21.02.1946	Karachi during Royal Indian Navy mutiny
24.05.1946	Refit at Colombo
07.1946	To Persian Gulf
02.1947	Refit at Singapore
03.1947	Penang, Trincomalee and Persian Gulf
01.1948	Civil disturbances at Mogadishu
01.1948	Lamu, Mombasa, Zanzibar, Dar es Salaam and Seychelles
04.1948	Combined exercises with Royal Indian Navy
01.1949	Persian Gulf
03.1949	Refit at Singapore
12.1949	Refit completed
05.1950	Mogadishu
1950	Indian Ocean
02.1951	Penang, Nicobar, Calcutta and Vizagaptam
24.04.1951	Colombo
09.1951	Persian Gulf
01.1952	Bay of Bengal patrol plus visits to Chittagong and Port Cornwallis
04.1952	Escorted vessels of 110th Motor Minesweeper squadron to Aden
09.1951	Persian Gulf
Autumn 1952	Indian Ocean
10.10.1953	Tour of UK dependencies in Indian Ocean
01.1954	Indian Ocean
05.1954	Sailed for the United Kingdom

06.1954	Reserve at Portsmouth
1957	Disposal list
1957	Sold to BISCO for demolition by Clayton Davies at Dunston
13.11.1957	Arrived River Tyne for breaking up

HMS LOCH RUTHEN

A post-war image of Loch Ruthven *underway.*   *(Crown Copyright/MoD)*

On 25 January 1943 the Bristol based shipyard of Charles Hill received the contract for the construction of a Loch class frigate. The yard gave the ship the yard number 298 and work started on the project on 4 January 1944. Construction of the hull was swift and on 3 June 1944 she was launched and named *Loch Ruthven* after an inland loch near Inverness by the Duchess of Beaufort. Final fitting out, continued until 6 October 1944 when she was handed over to the Royal Navy.

In October 1944 the frigate carried out sea trials in the Bristol Channel under the command of Lieutenant Commander R T Horam from the Royal Naval Reserve before joining the 2nd Escort Group at Liverpool on 27 October. *Loch Ruthven* had been designated as Senior Officer's ship within the group with Commander D E G

Wemys DSO, DSC as Senior Officer. He had been appointed following the death of the famous Captain F J Walker. Walker had throughout the Second World War developed anti-submarine warfare to a fine art with the use of sonar and depth charges against the German U-boat threat.

Together with other members of the group *Loch Ruthven* sailed on 4 November to carry out an anti-submarine patrol in the North West Approaches. These operations continued into 1945 before the group was sent to the English Channel for convoy duties based out of Plymouth.

In February the group was assigned to protect convoy BTC 81 that sailed from Milford Haven to Scotland on 26 February. The convoy consisted of four merchantmen and four escorts. During the passage the escorts attacked

and sank the German Type VIIC/41 submarine *U-327* under the command of Kapitanleutnant Hans Lemcke and and the Type VIIC/41 submarine *U-1018* under the command of Kapitanleutnant Walter Burmeister. The following month whilst operating off Lands End with the sloop *Wild Goose* a German U-boat was detected. It was attacked and sunk with the loss of all 49 hands. Later investigations discovered the U-boat to be the Type VIIC submarine *U-683* under the command of Gunter Keller.

In April *Loch Ruthven* was sent to patrol the Irish Sea and North West Approaches, whilst plans were being formalised to send her to the Far East. On 5 May she returned to Charles Hill shipyard at Bristol for a refit to prepare her for service in the Pacific. Work was carried out to add extra 20mm weapons to try and fend off determined Japanese aerial attacks. Finally on 30 June *Loch Ruthven* sailed to join the British Pacific Fleet. The frigate was routed through the Mediterranean with calls paid at Gibraltar and Aden before finally arriving at Colombo on 23 July for a briefing prior to the start of Operation Zipper, the proposed landings in Malaya. The planning for the operation had wanted the landings to take place in early August, but was delayed several times at the insistence of the United States.

On 25 August *Loch Ruthven* was at Bombay and in early September sailed in support of Operation Zipper escorting the landing ships involved in the operation.

After the troops had been successfully landed, *Loch Ruthven* was ordered to Singapore where she was put in charge of shipping control duties at the colony on 11 September.

In October *Loch Ruthven* was dispatched to the area around Java and Sumatra to escort the transport vessels taking Prisoners of War back to Singapore. During this time the frigate visited Batavia, Bangkok and Semarang. By December 1945 most of the POW escorts had been completed and in February the crew of *Loch Ruthven* heard the welcome news that they and the ship would be returning to the United Kingdom.

They also discovered their ship was to reduce to reserve upon her arrival at Portsmouth. On 13 February 1946 *Loch Ruthven* sailed from Singapore bound for home. During the passage the frigate went to the aid of the minesweeper *MMS19*, which had suffered a mechanical breakdown and towed the ship to Port Blair in the Andamans.

Four days after leaving Singapore *Loch Ruthven* arrived at the large harbour at Trincomalee, where she spent the next five days before continuing her journey. After a day spent at Amherst the frigate resumed her voyage home but with a new Commanding Officer Lieutenant Commander M J S Phillips. *Loch Ruthven* was routed through the Red Sea and Mediterranean with a brief stop at Gibraltar. Finally after many months away from home the frigate arrived at Portsmouth to de-store and prepare for reduction to the Reserve Fleet.

Loch Ruthven would remain in the Reserve Fleet until 1952 when she was brought forward for a refit at Plymouth. The intention had been to return the ship to active service sooner but more pressing modernisation programmes, of the aircraft carrier *Victorious* and the battleship Vanguard had taken precedent. *Loch Ruthven*'s refit continued until March 1953 when she started her trials programme.

Finally on 24 April *Loch Ruthven* was re-commissioned under the command of Lieutenant Commander R A W Pool. The next couple of months proved to be busy ones for the frigate, with May spent conducting a shakedown and June seeing her in the Solent with the rest of the Fleet for Queen Elizabeth II's Coronation Review representing the 3rd Training Flotilla.

On 18 July she sailed to assume her duties with the training squadron around Londonderry. The rest of the year was spent undertaking operational training but November did see her pay a visit to Cairn Ryan in Scotland.

Her duties as a training ship kept *Loch Ruthven* out of the public eye for the most part but she did visit Rothesay in January 1954 before refitting at Rosyth from September for two months.

1955 also proved to be an eventful year with the ship starting the year undertaking training off Londonderry with the frigates *Loch Veyatie* and *Tumult* and the submarine *Subtle*. On 27 January *Loch Ruthven* visited Carrick Fergus Bay and following an early morning arrival the next day secured alongside Belfast's Airport Jetty. Later that day the warship was visited by the Lord Mayor of the City as well as many hundreds of local residents.

On her departure from Belfast on Tuesday 1 February

Loch Ruthven carried out a series of anti-submarine exercises with *Loch Veyatie* en route back to Lisahally. On Monday 7 February when manoeuvring to head to sea, the ship's stern touched the jetty by Queen's Pier but no damage was inflicted on the warship. Once at sea with *Loch Veyatie* she carried out anti-submarine exercises also with the frigate *Relentless*. These exercises continued until the end of March when *Loch Ruthven* sailed south to Portsmouth for that years' Navy Days held over the first weekend of April.

Early on 4 April the frigate slipped to sea and proceeded up the Irish Sea and River Mersey for a visit to Ellesmere Port. By 1155 the ship was being secured in the Eastman Lock of the Manchester Ship Canal. Four days later the Mayor of Ellesmere Port called on the Captain along with a number of civic dignitaries and their guests who wished the captain and the ship bon voyage. At 1505 the ship sailed from alongside and proceeded. Twenty five minutes later *Loch Ruthven* gently collided with the SS *Hecla* by Bowaters Cut, after wrong helm had been applied by the warship. Damage was fortunately slight to both vessels. Half an hour later *Loch Ruthven* entered Eastern Lock and Admiralty Pilot Mr Collins was embarked for the journey along the River Mersey to the sea.

On entering the Irish Sea *Loch Ruthven* headed north to Rothesay for further anti-submarine training with the submarines *Aurochs, Scotsman, Tally-Ho, Thermopylae* and the frigate *Urchin*. For the next four days the frigate operated with these submarines until she returned to Londonderry's No 18 berth on 13 May.

Six days later four American warships, USS *The Sullivans*, USS *McGowan*, USS *Lewis Hancock* and USS *McNair* entered Londonderry harbour ahead of Exercise Play Fish that was held in waters off Iceland. Also involved in the exercise were the frigates *Undine, Urania, Virago* and the depot ship *Maidstone* as well as the Australian HMAS *Queensborough* and the American submarine USS *Gavana*. The first phase of the exercises involved a visit to Hvalfjord as well as Keflavik. It was at the latter that *Loch Ruthven* remained for a period at the end of the May whilst engine problems were repaired. On Monday 30 May with the engines repaired *Loch Ruthven* returned to the exercises with RFA *Wave Sovereign* and upon completion returned to Londonderry

at the end of the exercises.

On Saturday 4 June *Loch Ruthven* put to sea and set course for Exmouth in Devon where upon her arrival the next day she was boarded by a large number of local VIP's who toured the ship and spoke with the Captain. After four hugely successful days at Exmouth, *Loch Ruthven* crossed the English Channel to repeat the success with a visit to the French port of Bayonne in company with *Wizard, Tumult* and *Loch Veyatie*. The ships sailed up the Adour River after having first embarked a local pilot to navigate the river.

By 0830 in the morning *Loch Ruthven* had secured alongside her sister ship and throughout the course of the five day visit welcomed onboard no fewer than 1219 visitors. On the last day of the visit the four ships slipped and proceeded back to Londonderry.

The beginning of July saw a change of scenery when *Loch Ruthven* was at Rosyth for a much needed refit docking down within the Dockyard's No 1 Dry Dock. She remained there until returning to Londonderry on Monday 25 July. The following month seasonal leave was granted to the ships company and on their return in early September *Loch Ruthven* undertook further training and exercises particularly with the Norwegian warships *Stavanger, Oslo* and the submarine *Kya*.

In early October *Loch Ruthven* returned to the River Mersey with a visit to Trafalgar Branch Dock in Liverpool. She sailed from the city on Monday 10 October and crossed the Irish Sea back to Londonderry.

In November the frigate visited Douglas on the Isle of Man where on Thursday 10 November she secured on Victoria Pier. Later the same day the Mayor and Chairman of the Harbour Board were received onboard by the Commanding Officer. After three days *Loch Ruthven* returned to Londonderry for more exercises with *Tumult* and the submarine *Scorcher* and later in the month with the American warships USS *Johnstone*, USS *Perry* and USS *Kennedy* and the destroyer *Aisne*. The exercises ended with all the ships visiting Greenock for the weekend from Friday 25 November. After two days the ships companies took their ships back to sea and continued the exercise with the addition of *Pelican* and the submarines *Tiptoe, Aurochs, Sturdy, Artful* and *Tireless*.

The early days of December were once again spent off Londonderry, whilst on Wednesday 14 December *Loch*

During the course of their careers many Loch class frigates were extensively modernised with the addition of new radar sets. Loch Ruthven *is seen here in the Persian Gulf with the Type 277Q radar on her mainmast.*
(Crown Copyright/MoD)

Ruthven arrived at Portsmouth and secured at No 11 berth where the ships company were granted seasonal leave.

In January 1956 she was taken to Gibraltar to await a refit and placed on standby for further service. After the refit was completed in February *Loch Ruthven* sailed on 6 March 1957. After further trials and assessments the frigate was finally commissioned for a General Service Commission in the Gulf replacing sister ship *Loch Insh* on 16 April under the command of Commander W B Smith RN.

She spent the next three months working up in and around Portland before sailing from Portsmouth for the Middle East in August.

In autumn 1957 the frigate patrolled the Persian Gulf operating out of Bahrain. When a cyclone hit Dubai, *Loch Ruthven* loaded medical supplies and sailed at top speed to render aid to those left injured and homeless. In December the British frigate sailed to the North of the Gulf and amongst other ports visited Bushire before spending the festive period at Mina-al-Amadi.

1958 started with more patrols in the Gulf but was also marked with sadness when in April Corporal Francis Hedges, of the Royal Marines, was killed during detached duty in Oman in action against rebels. The patrols in the Gulf proved their value with *Loch Ruthven* conducting over 200 inspections of local craft. Large quantities of weapons and ammunition were seized in the process.

In June the frigate sailed to visit numerous East African ports with Mombasa being a favourite amongst the crew. After a brief tour of East Africa, *Loch Ruthven* prepared for her return to the United Kingdom through the Red Sea, Suez Canal and Mediterranean. After serving briefly as Aquaba Guardship, *Loch Ruthven* continued her passage to Portsmouth where she arrived in August and was paid off for a refit that lasted until 21 October. At her recommissioning, under the command of Commander R L Evelegh DSC, the new Commanding Officer spoke of her planned return to the Gulf. Before her departure, however, *Loch Ruthven* spent the winter months working up at Portland. Christmas, unlike the previous year, was spent at Portsmouth.

Trials and workup's resumed in the New Year before

sailing to the Gulf in February 1959. Her initial tasking in the Persian Gulf was very similar to her last, stopping and searching dhows for smuggled arms and flag showing at ports of call across the region. In July maintenance on the frigate was carried out at Karachi. Upon completion *Loch Ruthven* resumed her patrols based out of Bahrain. The routine was changed in October when she joined sister ship *Loch Fyne* and other warships for the multi-national naval exercise CENTO in the Indian Ocean.

Loch Ruthven remained active in the Persian Gulf until her planned journey back to the United Kingdom in January 1960. Her arrival back at Devonport on 2 February also saw her pay off for another three month refit. On 28 April the warship was re-commissioned under the command of Captain D P Law MBE, DSC RN. Work up and sea trials took the next few months to complete in the waters around Portland and Plymouth. Finally on 18 August *Loch Ruthven* set sail for another tour of duty in the Persian Gulf.

The frigate arrived six days later at Gibraltar for a brief stop before resuming her voyage to the Middle East.

On 18 September the ship returned to her home base in the region, Bahrain and spent some time alongside for maintenance before once again resuming her patrols in the Southern Gulf. During these patrols on 21 October she joined the survey ship *Dalrymple* and landing ship *Bastion* in the salvage operation of MV *Polyana*. The tanker had suffered a serious fire that had claimed the lives of 15 of her crew. The fires burnt until 29 October. Soon after arriving the frigate took the stricken ship under tow but was later relieved by the *Dalrymple*, which took the MV *Polyana* to Bahrain.

During her resumed patrols off the Batina coast *Loch Ruthven* was visited by Lord Carrington in November. Whilst *Loch Ruthven*'s embarked Royal Marines took part in Exercise Mudlark with soldiers from the Sultan of Oman Regiment. Later in the month the frigate crossed to Iran to take part in Exercise Khargex with units of the Iranian fleet off Kharg Island.

December saw more patrols interspersed with port visits including one to Bushehr before spending Christmas at Mina.

The New Year of 1961 saw the frigate take passage with sister ships *Loch Fada* and *Loch Fyne* to Karachi where she was dry docked for inspections to be carried out on her hull. The three ships were in Karachi to co-incide with a visit to the city by Her Majesty Queen Elizabeth II.

Loch Ruthven remained at Karachi until the middle of February when she returned to Bahrain after exercises with the Pakistani Navy. She arrived on 25 February.

The following month she sailed for the Northern Gulf area before returning to the South to patrol that area at the end of the month. On 8 April the ship received a distress call from the British Indian Steam Navigation Company passenger vessel MV *Dara*. Onboard the vessel was 189 passengers plus 142 crewmembers. A bomb (believed to have been planted by an Omani rebel group or individual insurgents) had exploded outside the vishiwala galley onboard the MV *Dara* and the explosion blew through the engine room bulkhead and up through 2 decks in to the passenger and main lounge areas. Fires immediately broke out onboard. In the confusion following the explosion many people died of burns or drowning after jumping into the ocean from the ship. In total 238 people died onboard the vessel the others were rescued by an armada of British, German, Japanese and Norwegian vessels in the area. Rescue efforts were hampered by strong gale force winds, which also fanned the flames on MV *Dara* into an inferno.

When *Loch Ruthven* arrived the merchantman was on fire around 20 miles off Jazira Tumb off the United Arab Emirates. Together with *Loch Fyne* and *Loch Alvie* the three British warships carried out fire fighting duties. Once the fires were extinguished the ship stayed with the stricken vessel until the *Sea Salvor*, a salvage vessel, arrived to take the badly damaged merchntman in tow. The damage was, however, too extensive and the ship finally succumbed, turned turtle and sank at 0920 on 10 April. The loss of the MV *Dara* was the second worst maritime disaster after the *Titanic* at the time.

In May the ship embarked the Flag Officr Middle East for his annual tour of the region with visits paid to Mombasa, Dar-es-Salaam, Zanzibar and a return visit to Mombasa on 27 June where the Flag Officer took his leave of the ship.

Soon after, the ship received orders to sail with all dispatch to Aden where her presence was required to bolster British forces in the colony due to an Iraqi threat to the

sovereignty of neighbouring Kuwait. The ship would stay at Aden for the remainder of the month as part of Operation Vantage. Upon arrival of sister ship *Loch Insh*, the frigate sailed for the United Kingdom on 3 July.

On 4 August 1961 the frigate arrived at Gibraltar for a brief stop before resuming her onward journey to Devonport where she arrived four days later. Another short stay at Devonport was followed by a fast passage to Rosyth where the ship was taken in hand for a short refit. On 21 September she was re-commissioned under the command of Captain P S Beale RN who also served as Senior Officer 9th Frigate Squadron in the Persian Gulf.

Work continued on the ship until December when *Loch Ruthven* started her work up at Portland. Christmas leave was spent at Portsmouth but in January 1962 the frigate was back at Portland working hard to achieve operational standards.

Throughout the month of March the frigate was prepared for service in the Middle East only sailing for foreign duties in early April. Once on station later in the month she resumed her normal routine of regular port visits and exercises particularly with the Iranian Navy. In July she was at Karachi undergoing routine maintenance in the dry dock facilities at the city.

In August during one of her 'routine' dhow patrols explosives and ammunition were discovered onboard a vessel, which was immediately arrested and the men onboard were later imprisoned.

After visits to Abu Dhabi and Dubai, *Loch Ruthven* exercised with the carrier *Bulwark* during exercise Duffel off the coast of Sharjah. These exercises continued into October. Whilst in November the frigate continued her training program with the CENTO Exercise MIDLINK 5 off Karachi. This particular exercise saw the Royal Navy warship work with Indian forces in the region early in December. Upon completion *Loch Ruthven* made for Mombasa and a planned series of port visits in East Africa including Zanzibar and Pemba.

Christmas was celebrated when the frigate returned to Mombasa.

1963 started with the ship still at Mombasa but two days later she sailed for Aden where the frigate arrived without incident six days later. After a few days storing and cleaning the ship, the crew welcomed onboard Flag Officer Middle East (FOME) for a Flag visit to Djibouti, French Somaliland on 11 February. *Loch Ruthven* sailed the same day and the next morning arrived at Djibouti for a formal two day visit. On her return to Aden the next port of call for the Flag Officer was Massawa, where the ship arrived on 19 January. Massawa was the main port of the Ethiopian Navy and during the visit the FOME attended the Naval Academy, whilst the frigate welcomed onboard the Emperor of Abyssinia. The formal visit ended on 22 January with the ship sailing with men lining the deck and an official gunfire salute to their Ethiopian hosts.

Loch Ruthven arrived back at Aden the next day and FOME disembarked. The ship herself was quickly turned around for another planned visit to Berbera, arriving the next morning. Berbera was, apart from a return visit to Aden, the last official foreign port of call in the Gulf for *Loch Ruthven* before heading for home and being reduced to reserve status. The frigate arrived back at Aden on the last day of the month. The Ascension Day ceremonies were honoured at Aden before *Loch Ruthven*'s ships company stored ship in preparation for the long journey back to Great Britain, which started on 8 February with the ships departure bound for Port Sudan. From there *Loch Ruthven* visited Malta from 22 February. Her next port also proved to be her last, arriving at Devonport Dockyard on 12 March wearing her paying off pennant. Soon she was placed on the disposals list and in May 1963 she was declared surplus for scrapping. Stripped of all useful pieces of equipment the former frigate was sold in November 1966 to BISCO and broken up by Davies and Cann in Plymouth.

Battle Honours

ENGLISH CHANNEL 1945 - ATLANTIC 1945

Motto

Persto et praest : 'I preserve and I excel'

Chronology

25.01.1943	Ordered from Charles Hill, Bristol
04.01.1944	Laid down
03.06.1944	Launched
06.10.1944	Completed
27.10.1944	Joined 2nd Escort Group at Liverpool
04.11.1944	North West Approaches
02.1945	Sank *U-327* and *U-1018*
03.1945	Sank *U-683*
05.05.1945	Refitted at Charles Hill Shipyard
30.06.1945	Sailed for Far East
25.08.1945	Bombay
09.1945	Operation Zipper in Malaya
11.09.1945	Singapore
10.1945	Java, Sumatra, Batavia, Bangkok and Semerang
13.02.1946	Sailed from Singapore to United Kingdom and reserve fleet
24.04.1952	Re-commissioned at Plymouth
18.07.1952	Training duties at Londonderry with 3rd Training Flotilla
Late 1955	Placed in reserve awaiting refit at Gibraltar
Autumn 1957	Persian Gulf
June 1958	East Africa
06.1958	Paid off at Portsmouth for refit
21.10.1958	Refit completed
02.1959	Returned to Middle East
28.04.1959	Re-commissioned at Portsmouth
18.08.1960	Returned to Middle East
21.10.1960	Assisted firefighting on tanker MV *Polyana*
08.04.1961	Assisted firefighting on tanker MV *Dara*
05.1961	East Africa
06.1961	At Aden during Kuwaiti crisis
08.08.1961	Devonport

08.1961	Rosyth for refit
21.09.1961	Re-commissioned for service in Persian Gulf
1962	Middle East Service
01.1963	Mombasa and Aden
19.01.1963	Ethiopian Navy Days at Massawa
12.03.1963	Devonport to pay off into reserve
05.1963	Disposal List
11.1966	Sold for breaking up by Davies and Cann in Plymouth

HMS LOCH SCAVAIG

Seen early in her career Loch Scavaig *was launched by the Queen Mother, Her Majesty Queen Mary, on 9 September 1944.*
(Crown Copyright/MoD)

Loch Scavaig had the honour of a Royal launch performed on 9 September 1944 by the Queen Mother Her Majesty Queen Mary. The story of the frigate, however, went back to 26 January 1943 when she was ordered from the shipyard of Charles Hill in Bristol. The first prefabricated components of the frigate were laid down on the slipway on 31 March 1943. After the royal launching, construction workers at the shipyard completed the Loch class frigate three days before Christmas 1944. Under the command of Lieutenant Commander C W Hancock the trials program for the latest addition to the Royal Navy started within Bristol harbour before progressing in January 1945 to the Bristol Channel area. After the shipbuilder and Admiralty were satisfied with her trials the frigate joined the 23rd Escort Group and joined the rest of the flotilla at Tobermory in Scotland.

On 4 February the work up were completed and training was undertaken in all aspects of anti-submarine warfare off the coastline of Northern Ireland. Indeed it was during one trial exercise that an enemy submarine was detected and immediately the exercise turned deadly real when the captain ordered an attack with the Squid anti-submarine weapon system. Two nearby warships, the *Papua* and *Nyasaland* quickly joined in the search for the U-boat. The following day sister ship *Loch Shin* found a large amount of debris on the surface and it was announced that German Type VIIC/41 *U-1014* under the command of Oberleutnant zur see Wolgang Glaser had been sunk by the combined efforts of the four ships. Lieutenant Commander Hancock was awarded the DSC for his role in the attack and his Asdic operator likewise was rewarded with a DSM.

February proved to be an extremely busy month for the frigate. On the 6th she took passage with *Papua*

and *Nyasaland* to join Force 38 on convoy escort duties. Two days later the frigate sailed south for the Mediterranean. These plans were altered after the ship sustained some damage which required repair work to be undertaken at Milford Haven. On entering the harbour on 16 February the ship's fuel tank was damaged in a collision with a navigational buoy. The resulting extra damage required a docking period in Liverpool, which was reached the following day.

The work was extended to include extra hull stiffening, but upon completion of the repairs *Loch Scavaig* returned to service in mid March with a period spent on patrol in the North West Approaches and around Scapa Flow.

With the end of the war in Europe, the Admiralty decided that *Loch Scavaig* would be a useful addition to the forces ranged against the Japanese in the Pacific and plans for her deployment were drawn up. The need to clear up the results of the European conflict would, however, occupy the frigates time in the early summer of 1945.

After a period at Rosyth, *Loch Scavaig* took part in Operation Doomsday, which was the reoccupation of Norway. On 18 May she together with *Loch Gorm, Papua, Monsarrat* and the minesweeper *Maenad* sailed to Norway. The Norwegian *Trodday* also sailed with the Royal Navy ships that went on to visit Stavanger, Bergen and Oslo to take control of the cities after German occupation. After two days at the capital Oslo *Loch Scavaig* sailed on 22 May to Moss and Horten.

On her return journey to the United Kingdom on 27 May *Loch Scavaig* and *Bahamas* escorted the surrendered German U-boats *U-874, U-975, U-170* and *U-1108* to Scapa Flow as part of Operation Deadlight. Having successfully delivered the first group of submarines *Loch Scavaig* returned to Bergen to collect another batch of enemy warships returning to Scapa Flow on the 4 June with fourteen Type-XXIII U-boats.

Her escorting duties were not quite complete as the frigate was detailed with ensuring the safe arrival of these submarines to Loch Ryan in company with *Loch Achray, Loch More* and *Grindall* as further escorts.

With her European war over *Loch Scavaig* was required for deployment to the Far East and after a leave period in Londonderry the frigate was refitted with extra anti-aircraft guns on her quarterdeck. These four 20mm Oerlikons were, it was hoped, sufficient to deal with the threat posed by Japanese aircraft. On the 9 June the frigates new commanding officer Lieutenant Commander C W Leadbetter RNR took command.

In early July with the ships company back from leave the ship carried out training in Londonderry waters before sailing with the monitor *Roberts* to Gibraltar on 29 July. The ships arrived at Gibraltar on 1 August and after two days at the colony continued their voyage to Alexandria, which was reached after eight days steaming. The two warships remained together until the pair entered the Red Sea when *Roberts* detached.

Loch Scavaig reached Colombo on 27 August and was almost immediately allocated to Operation Zipper - the planned invasion of Malaya. With numerous delays the ship was occupied with escort duties to a number of LCT's heading to Port Sweetenham together with the frigate *Evenlode*.

On 5 September *Loch Scavaig* was at Port Sweetenham and participated in the landings of Indian troops as part of Operation Zipper. After five days she slipped to sea for the passage to Singapore where the formal surrender ceremony was witnessed.

The frigate continued her escort duties in the Bay of Bengal and Straits of Malacca until the end of the month when she revisited Port Sweetenham on the 30th September. The following month she sailed to Saigon where she, together with *Loch More*, would take under tow the mine damaged Landing Ship Infantry *Queen Emma* back to Singapore. The ships all arrived safely on 10 October. After eight days spent in the dockyard the ship returned to sea and spent the remainder of the month off Bangkok on guardship, patrol and interception duties.

After returning to Singapore in early November, *Loch Scavaig* required a period in dry dock for the repair of stern tube linings which had been damaged by a depth charge explosion onboard. The strain of towing *Queen Emma* also contributed to a severe deterioration in the linings. The work continued in the commercial shipyard until 16 December. After trials

of the new equipment *Loch Scavaig* operated in the Bay of Bengal on air and sea rescue duties on the occasion of a visit by His Majesty King George VI to the XIV Army in Burma. The King was flown in by RAF aircraft over the sea and *Loch Scavaig* was in place should any unforeseen situation arise.

When the King's aircraft landed safely *Loch Scavaig* was released to continue her normal operations which saw her arriving at Trincomalee on 29 December.

Operations for 1946 started on 12 January when the Loch class frigate was ordered to assume the role of guardship in the Dutch East Indies. She sailed from Trincomalee and took passage to Singapore. The situation in Sourabaya was rapidly deteriorating as rebels fought for independence and coastal craft were being used to smuggle in weapons and ammunition. *Loch Scavaig* arrived at Sourabaya on 28 January and then arrived at the regions capital Bali. Her first patrol started the very next day.

Throughout early February the ship patrolled the waters off Sourabaya and Semerang before returning to Singapore on the 12th. From Singapore, *Loch Scavaig* sailed on 4 March to Bangkok to embark a party of Italian VIP's. These included the Italian Ambassador and his diplomatic staff. *Loch Scavaig* carried them back to Singapore but not before some officers onboard the frigate had to offer up their cabins to accommodate the Italian dignitaries. *Loch Scavaig* arrived back at Singapore on 21st and disembarked her passengers.

Only three days were spent in port before the frigate was once again at sea bound for Batavia. Her duties were to carry diplomatic staff and civilian passengers from the Dutch Government from Macassar to Kei where the Dutch nationals were landed on 8 April.

The frigate then reversed course and headed back to Macassar where on the 16 April she embarked two Japanese prisoners of war. Interestingly the prisoners were kept on the quarterdeck for the duration of the passage before being taken off the ship upon her arrival at Singapore on 20 April.

Loch Scavaig, meanwhile, was required to relieve the two destroyers *Cavalier* and *Cavendish* at Morotai she sailed after only two days in port. Upon arrival

Loch Scavaig assumed guardship duties over the area that included a number of Liberty Ships used to house Japanese Prisoners of War under Australian Army guards. The frigate remained at Morotai throughout the month of May.

On 1 June the warship sailed for Singapore arriving six days later. Her stay was to be a brief one with time allowed to prepare for the passage back to the United Kingdom. *Loch Scavaig* sailed on 10 June and called at Trincomalee and then Aden on 29 June. Almost a week later she made a northerly passage of the Suez Canal before calling at Gibraltar. Finally on 20 July *Loch Scavaig* arrived at Devonport flying her paying off pennant and was soon reduced to reserve at the naval base. Periodic maintenance of the ship was carried out including work to check the shaft alignment on 24 August when she entered a dry dock at Devonport where she remained until 10 September.

Loch Scavaig remained in reserve until October 1949 when she was refitted by Green and Silley Weir in East India Docks in London. The refit lasted until 16 February 1950. *Loch Scavaig* was one of nine Loch class ships refurbished for further active service in the Mediterranean during this period. On 3 April Commander A H Williams took command on 8 May he presided over the re-commissioning ceremony held at Chatham Dockyard. Work still had to be completed on some aspects of the ships refit and she remained at Chatham until early June when she sailed the short distance down the River Medway to Sheerness Dockyard. There she loaded with supplies and then made the journey to Portsmouth on 5 June. After spending the best part of June alongside at Portsmouth she finally sailed on 23 June for Gibraltar. The passage was eventful following a collision with the tanker RFA *Prestol* en route and upon her arrival at Gibraltar, the frigate was docked to assess the extent of the damage inflicted.

On 5 July *Loch Scavaig* started her five day passage to Malta. The remainder of the month was spent undertaking flotilla manoeuvres before visiting nearby Messina on the last day of the month.

After returning to Malta three days later the frigate remained at the island until 23 August when she commenced the 2nd Summer Cruise in the Aegean with

HMS Loch Scavaig *seen at anchor at Malta with awnings over most of her upper decks.*

(T. Ferrers-Walker Collection)

numerous visits paid to a number of Greek Islands including Crete.

In early September the warship was allocated the task of being Aqaba guardship but before this she paid a four day visit to the Turkish town of Izmir. After a most enjoyable few days enjoying the local hospitality the ship sailed on 12 September to assume her duty at Aqaba, passing through Port Said and the Suez Canal arriving at her destination on 17 September. *Loch Scavaig* remained as guardship for the next twelve days before being relieved and returning to the Mediterranean.

On 4 October the ship, whilst at Athens, embarked

Sir Clifford Norton, British Ambassador to Greece and his wife plus the musical conductor Sir Malcolm Sargent for passage to Malta. The voyage was a most pleasant one for the passengers as the frigate paid visits to the islands of Patros, Kos, Scarpanto, Leros and Amogos before finally arriving at Malta on 12 October. With the passengers safely disembarked *Loch Scavaig* resumed her flotilla duties with the remainder of her squadron.

The flotilla's next agenda item was a planned visit to the Libyan Capital Tripoli in early November. Upon her return the ship was transferred to the 5th Frigate Flotilla together with sister ships *Loch More* and *Loch*

Craggie and remained in and around the waters of Malta until the end of the year.

The ships company of *Loch Scavaig* saw in the New Year of 1951 at Malta and it was here that the frigate was in collision with the destroyer *Chivalrous*. Little damage was sustained by either ship and the pair was soon repaired. On 9 January *Loch Scavaig* left Malta bound for Aqaba where after five days she arrived to assume the role of guardship again. For the next six days the ship was stationed offshore to intercept any suspicious traffic. Finally on 20 January she was relieved and sailed back to Malta via a port visit to Port Sudan.

Early February was spent preparing for the imminent Mediterranean Spring Cruise, which got underway on the 10th of the month. The fleet would go onto visit Aranci Bay, Gibraltar, Cannes, Taranto and Augusta before returning to Malta on the final day of March.

For April and May the familiar surroundings of Malta remained in almost constant view as the frigate remained deployed in the area. June, however, saw another change in tempo of operations with the Fleet 1st Summer Cruise and port visits were made in the Eastern half of the Mediterranean. *Loch Scavaig* and the rest of the force sailed on 4 June and would eventually visit Izmir, Khlos, Milos and Marmarice in Turkey for the Fleet Regatta. The start of July saw a series of exercises before the frigate arrived at Malta on 12 July where she remained until the middle of September.

On 14 September *Loch Scavaig* sailed from Malta and set course for Athens for a three day visit. The ships company had a brief amount of time to explore the historic city, whilst the Captain went ashore and conducted a number of official appointments before sailing on to Crete.

Three days were spent at Crete before *Loch Scavaig* once again visiting Athens. This time only two days were spent in port and leave was rare as the ships company were mostly kept busy preparing the ship for a visit to Istanbul from 24 September.

Loch Scavaig along with sister ship Loch More and the despatch vessel Surprise, was in the Turkish Capital City at the start of a major NATO exercise entitled Symphonie Duex, which involved dozens of warships from a dozen NATO countries. Over the course of the next week the warships practiced attacks on submarines and aircraft with ports of call made on Juan Lea Pins in the French Riviera, the French Naval base at Toulon, Golfe Juan, Nice and Menton for the exercise wash up on 12 October.

After three days *Loch Scavaig* returned to sea for the passage back to Malta, where she remained until 6 December. She then took passage to Port Said to act as guardship at the entrance to the Suez Canal. The British Government had decided it was a prudent move to position a warship at Port Said due to a sustained amount of political unrest in the Middle East region at the time.

1952 started with the ship still at Port Said but after a week the frigate took passage back to Malta, where she rejoined the rest of the flotilla. She remained at Malta until 1 April when she sailed for three days of exercises in the Mediterranean. After a brief three day break at Messina the frigate returned to Malta. The highlight of the month undoubtedly was a visit to Venice in company with the frigates *Cygnet, Peacock* and sister ship *Loch More*. The four British warships were greeted warmly by the residents as the ships companies toured the canals and alleyways of this ancient and beautiful city throughout their seven day stay in Venice.

On the 1 May the ship sailed in company with the rest of her flotilla bound for a three day visit to the beautiful town of Messina and then onwards back the short distance to her base at Malta on 7 May. At Malta there was a change of command ceremony held onboard the frigate when *Loch Scavaig*'s latest commanding officer, Commander A C Mackworth RN joined.

The following month saw the frigate join a large force of British ships on their 1st Summer Cruise, Fleet Exercise and made a series of port visits that included Berletta and Lautaki before a Fleet Regatta was staged at Navarino in southern Greece.

In July news reached the ship that upon her return from deployment to Chatham Dockyard the ship would enter the reserve fleet and that the ships company would be dispersed among other operational

warships in the fleet. The frigates passage home started in September when at Malta she took four motor launches and HM Landing Craft (HQ) *236* under tow. Due to the tow speed was very slow and progress was accordingly laboured across the Mediterranean. Upon arrival at Gibraltar the ship and her brood hugged the coastline of Spain and Portugal with visits made to Lisbon and Santander before finally arriving at Chatham Dockyard in Kent on 15 September.

The frigate was quickly de-stored and placed in reserve where she was laid up with her future yet to be decided. In May 1953 the decision was taken to refurbish and modernise the frigate and accordingly she was towed to Henderson's shiprepair yard at Liverpool where preservation work was carried out. Upon completion *Loch Scavaig* was towed to Gibraltar and joined the Reserve Fleet Sub Division there.

Any plans to modernise the frigate soon disappeared and in 1958 *Loch Scavaig* was placed on the disposal list and sold to an Italian shipbreaker based at Genoa where she arrived on 5 September 1959 for demolition.

Battle Honours

ATLANTIC 1945

Chronology

26.01.1943	Ordered from Charles Hill Shipyard, Bristol
31.03.1943	Laid down
09.09.1944	Launched by Queen Mother Her Majesty Queen Mary
22.12.1944	Completed
01.1945	Bristol Channel and joined 23rd Escort Group
04.02.1945	Attacked and sank *U-1011* with *Papua, Nyasaland* and *Loch Shin*
08.02.1945	Sailed for Mediterranean
02.1945	Sustained damage en route and diverted to Milford Haven
16.02.1945	Struck navigation buoy at Milford Haven sustained more damage
02.1945	Damage required docking at Liverpool
17.02.1945	Liverpool, work extended to add hull stiffening
Mid 03.1945	Returned to service and operated in North West Approaches
18.05.1945	Operation Doomsday - reoccupation of Norway and visited Stavanger, Bergen, Oslo, Moss and Horten
27.05.1945	Escorted *U-874, U-975, U-170* and *U-1108* to United Kingdom
06.1945	Returned to Norway and escorted back a further 14 Type XXIII U-boats back to the United Kingdom
06.1945	Refitted with four extra 20mm anti aircraft guns
07.1945	Training off Londonderry
29.07.1945	Sailed for Gibraltar in company with monitor *Roberts*
01.08.1945	Gibraltar
03.08.1945	Sailed for Alexandria
11.08.1945	Alexandria
27.08.1945	Colombo for Operation Zipper
05.09.1945	Port Sweetenham
10.09.1945	Singapore
30.09.1945	Port Sweetenham
10.1945	Saigon with *Loch More* to escort landing ship infantry *Queen Emma*
10.10.1945	Singapore
18.10.1945	Sailed to assume guardship duties at Bangkok
11.1945	Singapore for refit
16.12.1945	Refit completed
29.12.1945	Trincomalee
12.01.1946	Guardship in Dutch East Indies
28.01.1946	Sourabaya

12.02.1946	Singapore
04.03.1946	To Bangkok to embark Italian VIP's including Ambassador
21.03.1946	Singapore
24.03.1946	Sailed to Batavia
16.04.1946	Macassar to embark Japanese PoW's for passage to Singapore
20.04.1946	Singapore
22.04.1946	Sailed to Morotai to relieve *Cavendish* and *Cavalier*
01.06.1946	Sailed for Singapore
10.06.1946	Sailed for United Kingdom
20.07.1946	Devonport and reserve
10.1949	Refitted by Green and Silley Weir, East Indies Dock, London
16.02.1950	Refit completed
08.05.1950	Recommissioned at Chatham Dockyard
05.06.1950	Sailed from Sheerness to Portsmouth
23.06.1950	Took passage to Gibraltar, collided with RFA *Prestol* en route
28.06.1950	Docked at Gibraltar for repairs
05.07.1950	Took passage to Malta
10.07.1950	Malta
31.07.1950	Messina
Summer 1950	Summer cruise in Aegean, visited Crete, Izmir and Aqaba
04.10.1950	Athens
10.1950	Patros, Kos, Scarpento, Leros and Amogos
12.10.1950	Malta
01.1951	Collided with *Chivalrous* at Malta
14.01.1951	Guardship at Aqaba
10.02.1951	Mediterranean Fleet Spring Cruise
Spring 1951	Malta
04.06.1951	Summer cruise to Izmir, Khlos, Milos and Marmarice
12.07.1951	Malta
14.09.1951	Took passage to Athens for three day visit
24.09.1951	Istanbul for NATO exercise Symphonie Duex
09.1951	Visits to Juan Le Pins, Toulon, Golfe Juan, Nice and Menton
15.10.1951	Sailed back to Malta and stayed there until 6.12.1951
12.1951	Guardship at Port Said
Early 01.1952	Returned to Malta where she stayed until 01.04.1952
Spring 1952	Messina, Malta, Venice, Berletta, Lautaki and Dogamsti
09.1952	Towed four motor launches and HM Landing Craft HQ *236* to Chatham
15.09.1952	Chatham Dockyard and reserve fleet
05.1953	Refit announced and towed to Henderson's shiprepair yard at Liverpool for preservation work to be undertaken
Summer 1953	Towed to Gibraltar and joined Reserve Fleet Sub Division
1958	Disposal List
05.09.1959	Broken up at shipbreakers in Italian port of Genoa

HMS LOCH SHIN
(HMNZS TAUPO FROM 1948)

With awnings over the quarterdeck and towards the forecastle Loch Shin *sails into Malta.* (Steve Bush Collection)

Loch Shin is an inland loch in the county of Sutherland near to Lairg and its namesake ship was ordered from Swan Hunter at Wallsend on 15 February 1943. Job Number 4808 was laid down on 6 September and launched into the River Tyne on 23 February 1944. Fitting out was completed on 10 October.

Upon successful completion of her trials and acceptance on 10 October Loch Shin sailed for Tobermory under the command of Lieutenant Commander A L Turner RNR.

On 10 November the frigate joined the 18th Escort Group at Greenock and proceeded to the North West Approaches. The following month she transferred to Portsmouth for duty on convoy protection duties.

In January 1945 Loch Shin sailed north to the Clyde area as Senior Officers Ship under the command of Commander C A de W Kitcat DSO RN. She deployed

as one of the escorts for the escort aircraft carrier Khedive before heading to the Clyde for repairs to be undertaken, upon completion she sailed on 1 February to join the 19th Escort Group at sea.

On the same day Cotton, Goodall and Loch Insh rendezvoused with the Sector Officer in Loch Insh in an area between the Clyde Light Vessel and 54' 00'N. At 1550 Loch Insh was detached to attend to a problematic Asdic dome and the remainder of the group took over supporting convoy HX333 from New York to Liverpool with 60 merchantmen and other escorts from the 22nd Escort Group. On February 4 Loch Shin participated in the destruction of the German U-boat U-1014 under the command of Oberleutnant sur zee Wolfgang Glaser before arriving at Loch Foyle in the early hours of 5 February.

Upon her arrival at Liverpool on the 25th of the month the frigate was taken in hand for some routine

maintenance. A few days later on the 6 March the ship was transferred to the command of Lieutenant Commander P F Broadhead RNR. The next day she started a patrol in the Irish Sea.

Together with sister ship *Loch Insh*, *Loch Shin* and three other warships joined the Russian convoy JW66 bound for Murmansk on 16 April from the Clyde. The convoy comprised of 27 merchantmen and 25 escorts including *Loch Insh, Loch Shin, Lotus, Offa, Zealous, Zephyr, Zest* and *Zodiac*. Two days later the force was bolstered by the addition of eight destroyers and the cruiser *Bellona*. Just prior to the convoys arrival at the mouth of the Murmansk river *Loch Shin* joined the force protecting the minelayer *Apollo* from possible submarine attack as the *Apollo* laid a series of mines during Operation Trammell off the Kola Inlet.

Intelligence reports had told the force that the German's had no fewer than 120 operational U-boats in the area of the Kola Inlet and as a precaution *Loch Shin* and a number of the other dedicated anti-submarine warships carried out a series of anti-submarine sweeps off the Kola inlet prior to the departure of the United Kingdom bound convoy RA66 on 29 April. The convoy comprised of 27 merchantmen and 23 escorts. With so many possible targets it was not long before *Loch Shin* together with *Anguilla* and *Cotton* co-ordinated an attack on *U-286* under the command of Oberleutnant Willi Dietrich, which resulted in the submarines destruction, there were no survivors.

The convoy arrived safely with the only loss being that of HMS *Goodall* sunk by the *U-286* on 29 April. The return convoy to the United Kingdom arrived on the Clyde on 5 May and *Loch Shin* continued on to Liverpool where she had her boiler cleaned before joining the Rosyth Escort Force in mid May. She operated in the English Channel throughout the next few weeks, but was declared appropriate for use during the occupation of Germany following the collapse of the Nazi regime.

After a brief stopover at Rosyth, *Loch Shin* continued on to Wilhelmshaven, where she arrived on 23 June. The frigate escorted some captured German U-boats back to Stranraer during Operation Deadlight. *Loch Shin* returned to Germany again at the end of July, this time visiting Bremerhaven on the 22nd

before returning to Rosyth six days later.

The following month saw the frigate operating in and around Loch Ryan before spending much of the summer months as part of the Rosyth Escort Force.

On 20 September the frigate arrived at Hamburg and saw the shattered ruins of the port city. The crew were there on occupation duties and also brought supplies for the occupation forces. Loch Shin sailed soon after returning to Rosyth on 22nd of the month. The following month saw the frigate operating in the icy waters off Iceland and also paid a visit to the capital city of Reykjavik. After seven days in Iceland the ship returned home to Rosyth.

Loch Shin arrived at Rosyth on 3 November and eighteen days later Lieutenant Commander S H Lampard assumed command.

The last few months of 1945 were spent around Northern Ireland for Operation Deadlight, the sinking of captured German U-boats. Over the course of the next few months Loch Shin sank *U-2328, U-294, U-1010, U-901* and finally on 10 February 1946 *U-9754*.

On 11 February as *Loch Shin* was participating in Operation Deadlight she received an emergency call from *Empire Mombasa*. The merchant vessel was in difficulties in the North West Approaches and the frigate went to assist as required. Once the emergency was over *Loch Shin* visited Whitehaven on 18 February and Rosyth four days later.

As part of the Allied force that followed the fall of Nazi Germany, *Loch Shin* made a number of visits to Wilhelmshaven before returning to Rosyth where she entered refit in March. The refit continued throughout the spring and summer and only in August was the work completed. After trials in September the frigate operated in and around Rosyth until the end of the year. On 13 November Lieutenant Commander I N Mayfield was appointed to command the ship, which operated out of Rosyth in continuation throughout the first six months of 1947.

In June 1947 she was allocated to the reserve fleet and in July paid off at Harwich. After a few months at the Suffolk base she was transferred to Sheerness in January 1948. She was kept in good condition and was in mid 1948 sold to the New Zealand Government for

£228,350 including the cost of a refit at Chatham Dockyard.

Upon completion of the refit the frigate was given the name *Taupo*, named after the largest lake in New Zealand and also given a new pennant number of F421. On 18 August Commander L P Burke DSC RNZN was appointed to command the latest addition to the Kiwi fleet as Senior Officer's ship of the 11th Frigate Flotilla. The frigate carried out trials and on 3 September was officially renamed by Lady Burrough wife of the Commander in Chief Nore Command, Admiral Sir Harold Burrough.

In September 1948 Taupo visited Portsmouth before a shakedown period at Portland. A Work up was carried out at Malta with two other New Zealand navy vessels *Pukaki* and *Kaniere*.

Upon completion of the work the three ships sailed for New Zealand with ports of call made at Aden, Trincomalee and Singapore in December. She arrived at Auckland for the first time on 5 January 1949.

The following month saw the frigate in the South Pacific, where on 14 February her new commanding officer Lieutenant Commander W H Brereton took command. The frigate remained in the South Pacific throughout the summer months only returning home to Auckland in September. At Auckland on 5 September another change of command took place with the appointment of Commander A B Gilfillan VRD RNR to the ship.

Taupo spent the closing months of the year operating with Australian warships during joint training exercises. The New Year of 1950 saw a dramatic change in scenery for *Taupo* and her crew when it was decided to exchange the ship with the British *Veryan Bay* in the Mediterranean along with *Taupo*'s sister ship *Hawea*. In April the frigates sailed to the Mediterranean via Singapore, Trincomalee and Aden. Eventually in June *Taupo* joined the 2nd Frigate Squadron on the Mediterranean Summer Cruise.

The frigate remained with the Mediterranean Fleet until October when the period of detached duty with the Royal Navy came to an end and Taupo sailed for home in New Zealand. En route the frigate visited Singapore, Darwin and Cairns before finally rejoining the 11th Frigate Flotilla at Auckland in December.

On 23 January 1951 Captain L P Bourke OBE DSC took command of the frigate for operations in home waters before sailing to Australia the following month for a series of joint exercises with the Australian fleet. The Taupo was part of a large New Zealand force assembled for the exercises that also included the cruiser *Bellona*.

After spending the spring months in Australian waters it was good for the sailors to be home again in April, but it was not to be for long as the growing conflict in Korea was drawing more and more naval assets in. *Taupo* was declared as a replacement for sister ship *Rotoiti* and in August she sailed for operations off the Korean coast. On 13 August Lieutenant Commander Kenneth Alston Craddock-Hartopp MBE, DSC RN relieved Captain Bourke in command of the frigate.

Craddock-Hartopp was born on 26 February 1918 and had joined the Royal Navy in 1936. As a midshipman he served onboard the battleship *Rodney* for a month before transferring in June 1937 to the cruiser *Sussex* in the Mediterranean.

Then he specialised in small vessels firstly in the minesweeper *Selkirk*, then MTB's at HMS *Hornet* in Gosport later commanding *MTB49* and *MTB277*. On 23 February he took command of the destroyer *Onslow* before going to the naval staff, RN College, Eaton in Chester. After the war Craddock-Hartopp took command of the *Taupo*.

The next few weeks were spent working the ship up to operational standard and this was carried out en route to Sydney. On 13 September *Taupo* sailed from Australia and headed towards Singapore where she remained for a few weeks refining her operational capabilities before sailing onto Hong Kong on 2 October. Five days later she sailed to Sasebo in Japan where the United Nations fleet of warships from many participating nations was assembled and tasks allocated. On 10 October *Taupo* rendezvoused with sister ship *Rotoiti* and relieved her allowing the latter ship to return home to Auckland.

Taupo meanwhile soon joined Task Unit 95.13 and assumed a patrol pattern off the west coast of Korea. One of her first tasks in the conflict was to assess the suitability of the Han River as an anchorage for Allied

shipping during bombardment missions. To achieve this tasking she carried out a surveying mission whilst under occasional small arms fire from ashore.

After a brief maintenance period at Sasebo towards the end of October *Taupo* returned to Korea the following month and continued to play an active and vital role on the west coast interdicting any suspect merchant vessels and junks. On 11 November *Taupo* came under US Navy control for a period of time on the east coast where she operated in the Haeju area as part of Task Unit 95.22.

On the first day of December *Taupo* targeted and attacked railway targets ashore along with sister ship *Hawea*. These targets were successfully destroyed by accurate and deadly gunfire. The next eleven days passed without incident before *Taupo* sailed for the Japanese port of Kure where she was taken in hand for a refit and to have her bottom scraped on 12 December.

The frigate was out of service for only nine days before she resumed her station on the West Coast patrol once again part of Task Unit 95.12. 1952 started as 1951 had finished with *Taupo* on the West Coast carrying out occasional bombardments of targets of opportunity and alternating with leave periods at Sasebo and maintenance at Kure.

On 6 February *Taupo* ventured to the East Coast of Korea again under US Navy control where she was used to attack railway installations, but it was a fortnight later that the ship found herself in the heat of the action. North Korean forces had massed around Yang Do Island and *Taupo* along with other United Nations and American warships assembled at the island to defend it. *Taupo* with the USS *Endicott* and USS *Sheldon* discovered a number of sampans heading towards the island and the trio sank ten of them. The North Koreans on the mainland saw the action and fired at *Taupo* scoring a number of hits but causing only slight damage onboard.

The next day medical parties from all the warships were landed onto Yang Do Island to treat any casualties, many of which were later transported to the American big gun cruiser USS *St Paul*. Lieutenant Commander K A Craddock-Hartopp's actions during the incident were noted and he was awarded a DSC from the British and a US Legion of Merit from the US Navy.

On 27 March *Taupo* sailed for Hong Kong where Anzac Day on 25 April was commemorated with the ships company providing a guard during the ceremonies held at the colony. With the ceremony completed *Taupo* sailed back to Sasebo on 1 May to continue her role in the Korean conflict.

On 15 May the frigate returned to Sasebo and it was here that the crew heard the news that upon her return to New Zealand the warship would be reduced to reserve status. However, her current role required her to continue the bombardment of the West Coast with regular calls for gunfire support and also the control of shipping movements in her locality. The frigate continued in this role until 9 September when she sailed from Sasebo on her last operational patrol. When she arrived off the West Coast she relieved *Rotoiti* on station and continued on the patrol until 17 September having expended a large number of shells on bombardment duties.

At the end of her wartime duties off Korea, *Taupo* arrived at Sasebo on 17 September, soon after she sailed for Hong Kong and finally arrived at Auckland on 21 October where the crew began the process of de-storing and paying the warship off.

Taupo remained in reserve until she was placed on the disposal list in 1961 and sold on 15 December that year. The following year tugs towed her to Hong Kong where the process of scrapping the warship commenced.

Battle Honours

NORWAY 1940 * ATLANTIC 1945   ARCTIC 1945

As *HMZNS Taupo*   KOREA 1950-52

* Awarded to the first *Loch Shin*

Chronology

15.02.1943	Ordered from Swan Hunters Shipbuilders Wallsend
06.09.1943	Laid down
23.02.1944	Launched
10.10.1944	Completed
10.1944	Tobermory
10.11.1944	Joined 18th Escort Group at Greenock
12.1944	Portsmouth with CTG 125.2
16.03.1945	Russian convoy JW66 to Murmansk
29.04.1945	Return convoy RA66
04.1945	Sank *U-286* with *Anguilla* and *Cotton*
05.05.1945	Clyde
23.06.1945	Wilhelmshaven
06.1945	Operation Deadlight. Destruction of German U-boats
22.07.1945	Bremerhaven for further Operation Deadlight duties
28.07.1945	Rosyth
20.09.1945	Hamburg
10.1945	Reykjavik Iceland
03.11.1945	Rosyth
12.1945	Sank *U-2328*, *U-294*, *U-1010*, *U-901* and *U-9754* off Londonderry
02.1946	Wilhelmshaven
03.1946	Refit at Rosyth
06.1947	Reserve fleet
07.1947	Paid off at Harwich
01.1948	Towed to Sheerness
1948	Sold to the Government of New Zealand
1948	Refitted at Chatham Dockyard
03.09.1948	Renamed *Taupo*
05.01.1949	Arrived Auckland
1950	Mediterranean service with Royal Navy's 2nd Frigate Squadron

12.1950	Rejoined 11th Frigate Flotilla in New Zealand
08.1951	Korean War Service
01.12.1951	Bombarded railway targets
20.02.1952	Yang Do Island and sank ten enemy sampans
20.02.1952	Hit by enemy shellfire
15.05.1952	Sasebo
21.10.1952	Auckland to pay off into reserve
1961	Disposal list
15.12.1961	Sold for scrapping in Hong Kong

HMS LOCH TARBERT

The classic wartime escort hull shape of the Castle and Black Swan corvettes and frigates is seen to advantage in this view of Loch Tarbert.
(Crown Copyright/MoD)

The Troon based shipyard of Ailsa Shipbuilding Company received confirmation of the order, on 24 January 1943, for the construction of a Loch class frigate. Construction commenced almost immediately on the long lead items needed for the ships build. By 30 November 1943 the parts started to come together on the slipway and by 19 October the hull was sufficiently complete to be ready for launching and named after a sea loch on the Isle of Jura. The build of *Loch Tarbert* was slow in comparison with other shipyards undertaking similar work and the ship was not completed until 22 February 1945. The frigate was commissioned under the command of Lieutenant Commander B W Walker DSC RNVR and soon thereafter joined the 12th Escort Group.

In March after some Royal Navy trials a number of defects were discovered that required *Loch Tarbert* to return to her builder's yard for rectification work. Upon completion the ship, sailed for Tobermory to store and resume her duties with the Escort Group. Lieutenant Commander Harris, meanwhile, was taken ill and for a while the First Lieutenant D G Matthews took command of the ship.

On 16 April the ship arrived at Liverpool at the end of her work up period and soon after deployed to cover the anti-submarine patrols between Gibraltar and Great Britain. With the end of the war *Loch Tarbert* became involved in Operation Deadlight, the assembling and sinking by gunfire of surrendered German U-boats in deep water off Northern Ireland. Her involvement started on 7 May when she had been at Liverpool, her patrol area was in the North West Approaches. German submarines had been ordered to fly a black flag and run on the surface. *Loch Tarbert*

only discovered one U-boat, the *U-244* under the command of Oberleutnant zur see Hans Peter Mackeprang which had surrendered at Loch Eribol on 14 May and escorted it into Lisahally; First Lieutenant D G Matthews leading the boarding party onto the enemy vessel.

After spending time in dockyard hands in Liverpool in preparation for service in the Far East *Loch Tarbert* sailed in July escorting the 15-inch gun monitor *Roberts* together with sister Loch class frigate *Loch Scavaig*. Lieutenant Commander W S Thompson took command of the ship on 23 July. The frigate and monitor sailed in company to Gibraltar on 27 July minus *Loch Scavaig*, which was delayed due to a defect that needed repair alongside. *Loch Scavaig* caught up with *Loch Tarbert* and *Roberts* before the three ships arrived at Gibraltar on 1 August.

The three ships separated at Gibraltar with *Loch Tarbert* sailing to Ceylon routed through Malta, Port Said and Aden where she arrived on the 21st. The frigate only stayed long enough to fuel and supply the ship sailing the next morning for Ceylon.

On 27 August the ship arrived at Colombo and it was here that the ships company paid farewell to Lieutenant Commander W S Thompson, who returned to Britain to join Civvy Street. In his absence the First Lieutenant D G Matthews was granted the rank of Acting Lieutenant Commander.

In September the ship operated in and around Colombo in preparation for planned attacks against Malaya as part of Operation Zipper. These operations were subsequently delayed and ultimately cancelled following the capitulation of the Japanese armed forces to the Allies. *Loch Tarbert* was one of the Royal Navy ships then allocated to the East Indies Fleet and sailed for Port Sweetenham on 10 September in company with a number of motor fishing vessels, the tug *Eminent* and three boom defence vessels. After a nine day passage the ships arrived, the passage being a difficult and trying affair with many of the ships suffering mechanical breakdowns that required periods of time under tow.

Once the task had been completed *Loch Tarbert* rendezvoused with sister ship *Loch Glendhu* and sailed to Singapore for a brief visit before returning to Port Sweetenham on 21 September. The frigate remained in this area for most of the next month before returning once again to Singapore on 10 October where she was docked for routine maintenance in the King George V dry dock.

After having a boiler clean and general maintenance the frigate was once again cleared for operational deployment and sailed from Singapore on 27 October. Four days later the frigate welcomed onboard Major General Mansergh and staff officers of the 7th Indian Division for passage to Batavia to command operations against insurgents. *Loch Tarbert* was part of a large naval force comprising of the cruiser *Sussex* and destroyers *Caesar, Carron* and *Cavalier* plus landing craft.

The force arrived at Batavia on 2 November and the General and his staff disembarked from the frigate which in turn set course for Sourabaya and upon arrival assumed the role of guardship. The troubles at Sourabaya saw the ship involved in providing naval gunfire support to troops ashore and through this work *Loch Tarbert* received a commendation.

The troubles continued when on 7 November the landing ship *LST199* hit a mine and the resulting explosion caused damage to her steering gear. *Loch Tarbert* went alongside to assist and recovered the landing craft from the general area. After being relieved of guardship duties eight days later, the frigate returned to base at Singapore. En route to Singapore *Loch Tarbert* escorted no fewer than nine Tank Landing Craft of the 74th LCT Flotilla on the five day passage.

Two days later the frigate sailed with the River class frigate *Taff* for Colombo and Sabang. Upon her arrival at Colombo air sea rescue operations dominated the frigates programme, which later were extended to cover a large area of the Indian Ocean in early December. Towards the end of the year *Loch Tarbert* visited the Cocos Islands where the ships company celebrated Christmas. On Boxing Day the ship sailed for Trincomalee.

1946 started with the ship arriving at Trincomalee, where maintenance was performed on the ship whilst the ship's company enjoyed the local facilities. Many of them also came to the end of their hostilities only

engagements and left the ship to return to civilian life. *Loch Tarbert* meanwhile, was ordered to Singapore for a period of support duties.

On 23 January the ship set sail for Cochin in India. After two days steaming the frigate arrived at the Indian city port where she was to escort a flotilla of fourteen Motor Fishing Vessels back to Singapore. Many of these vessels were in a poor state and indeed on the voyage to Singapore, one *MFV1512* sank with the crew having to be rescued by Loch Tarbert. Another consideration of the escort role to these MFV's was that their top speed was very slow and as a consequence the flotilla only reached Penang on 12 February. At Penang five days were spent making repairs to numerous faults on all fourteen boats before resuming course for Singapore.

Eventually *Loch Tarbert* and her motley collection of fishing vessels arrived at Singapore on 21 February. The Motor Fishing Vessels were then taken into dockyard control releasing the frigate to take up duties as guardship at Palembang.

On 8 March news reached the ship that *Loch Tarbert* was soon to be heading home to Great Britain. The news was tempered with the announcement that the frigate would, upon her arrival at Portsmouth be placed in the Reserve Fleet. Later that day she set sail to Singapore, where she arrived after two days steaming. A further two days were spent at Singapore preparing the ship for the passage across the Indian Ocean to Trincomalee, with a courtesy visit to Penang. The crossing was mostly uneventful and the wide harbour at Trincomalee was sighted on St Patrick's Day. Five days were spent there enjoying the facilities before *Loch Tarbert* resumed her lengthy journey through the Red Sea, Suez Canal and Mediterranean. One final stop at Gibraltar on 25 March was made before the frigate made her final entrance into Portsmouth harbour where on 12 May 1946 she paid off and entered the reserve fleet.

Loch Tarbert would remain there until 1949 when she was refitted in preparation of a tow to Gibraltar in 1951. She was fitted with dehumidifiers during the refit. The move was probably to try and tempt the Portuguese Navy to buy her, but they eventually turned down the offer to purchase her. Finally in 1958 the ship was put up for disposal and sold to Italian shipbreakers who operated out of Genoa. Breaking up the former *Loch Tarbert* started on 18 September 1959.

Chronology

24.01.1943	Ordered from Ailsa Shipbuilding Company in Troon
30.11.1943	Laid down
19.10.1944	Launched
22.02.1945	Completed and joined the 12th Escort Group
03.1945	Defects rectified at builders
16.04.1945	Liverpool
Summer 1945	Operation Deadlight escorting *U-244* to Lisahally
07.1945	Escorted Monitor *Roberts* with *Loch Scavaig*
21.08.1945	Aden
27.08.1945	Ceylon
09.1945	Operation Zipper in Malaya
21.09.1945	Port Sweetenham
27.10.1945	Ordered to Batavia with 7th Indian Division
02.11.1945	Arrived Batavia to deal with insurgents
07.11.1945	Rescued *LST199* after it had struck a mine
01.01.1946	Trincomalee
25.01.1946	At Cochin to escort 14 Motor fishing vessels to Singapore
12.02.1946	Flotilla arrived at Penang
21.02.1946	Flotilla arrived at Singapore
17.03.1946	Trimcomalee
22.03.1946	Took passage to the United Kingdom
12.05.1946	Portsmouth for reserve fleet
1949	Refitted at Portsmouth
1951	Towed to Gibraltar with aim of sale to Portugal. Offer rejected by the Portuguese Navy
1958	Sold to Italian Shipbreaker in Genoa
18.09.1959	Breaking up commenced

HMS LOCH TRALAIG

The strong gun armament of the Loch class is evident in this view of Loch Tralaig *with the 4-inch gun forward and various smaller calibres positioned in the bridge wings and towards the stern.* (Crown Copyright/MoD)

On 2 February 1943 the Dundee based shipyard of Caledon Shipbuilding received the order for the construction of what would become *Loch Tralaig*. Construction of long lead items started immediately, whilst the first keel plates were laid down on the slipway on 26 April 1944. Work continued at a pace and the frigate was readied for her launch date of 12 February 1945 as the first Royal Navy vessel to be named Loch Tralaig. Within four months the final work was completed and the ship was commissioned on 4 July 1945 under the command of Lieutenant Commander M S Wiork DSC RNR.

As was normal practice the Loch class frigate conducted their trials program in the North West Approaches before storing ship at Tobermory. *Loch Tralaig* was in August 1945 fitted with special noise monitors for trials on radiated noise generated by the ships propellers. These trials continued into September.

Having entered operational service a fraction too late to see active wartime service *Loch Tralaig*'s first major role was to have been providing an escort for the surrendered German U-boats from Londonderry to Loch Ryan in Scotland as part of Operation Deadlight as well as merchant ships carrying loads of ammunition that would be subsequently scuttled. In the event damage to the frigate's boilers prevented her from sailing with the German vessels and instead she was taken in hand to affect repairs.

In December 1945 *Loch Tralaig* joined the Training Flotilla in Londonderry and started taking onboard raw recruits and undertook the necessary training for these seamen to learn the art of anti-submarine warfare.

In March 1946 the ship was taken in hand for a refit at Devonport, which continued until May that year. Upon completion the frigate sailed to Londonderry to carry out a training role. There in July Lieutenant Commander V C F Clark DSC too command but his record was marred somewhat by an incident the following month. *Loch Tralaig* grounded off Skipness Point in the Sound of Bute requiring repairs to be undertaken at Devonport. She was still under repair in January when the frigate's latest commanding officer, Lieutenant Commander A D Piper DSC assumed command on 2 January 1947.

Once again *Loch Tralaig* sailed to Londonderry for training duties before attending the Review of the Home Fleet by King George VI, Queen Elizabeth the Queen Mother and Princess Margaret in the River Clyde on Tuesday and Wednesday 22 and 23 July 1947. In August she returned across the Irish Sea to continue her role of training cadets and midshipmen. Later in the year *Loch Tralaig*'s fourth commanding officer in two years assumed command, Commander N J Wagstaff took command of the ship and continued the training role in Northern Irish waters.

Commander Wagstaff was born in 1909 and joined the Royal Navy as a cadet on 1 May 1927 and served onboard the battlecruiser *Repulse* in the Atlantic Fleet. Wagstaff's early speciality was in wireless communications and this capacity in the interwar years he went onto serve onboard the cruisers *Emerald* in the East Indies, *Centaur* in the Atlantic Fleet and *Cairo* in the Home Fleet.

On 27 May 1935 Wagstaff was posted as Signals Officer on the flotilla leader *Faulknor* before being appointed Port Wireless Telegraphy Officer HMS *St Angelo* on Malta. His early war service was served at shore bases at HMS *Victory*, HMS *Cochrane* and HMS *Lanka* in Ceylon before transferring on 3 May 1943 to the battleship *Warspite*. Post War he was appointed to command the frigate *Loch Tralaig* and then went onto command *Osiris* and *Apollo* before becoming a Naval ADC to the Queen.

The following year saw the ship taking part in a number of exercises with the Home Fleet before entering Rosyth Dockyard for a refit in July. The work on the ship was primarily to enhance her anti-submarine capabilities and the installation of a more advanced Operations Room. The refit was completed towards the end of 1948 and after trials in the North Sea *Loch Tralaig* commissioned under the command of Commander R S Blacker RN.

In February the ship struck the Aberfolye Light Beacon whilst sailing in Lough Foyle. The damage to the propeller shaft was substantial requiring immediate attention however all available Royal Navy dry docks were full with work in hand so the frigate was sent to a commercial shipyard on the River Clyde for immediate repair work to be undertaken. The decision had been taken to defer any major work until the ships next scheduled docking period. The Clyde shipyard repaired the warship sufficiently for her to continue in her training role off Londonderry in the immediate future.

The early part of 1950 saw *Loch Tralaig* undertaking a training role at Londonderry again as well as a series of port visits as part of the Home Fleet. The year ended on a sour note, however, when in October the frigate was grounded off Garrison Point at Sheerness. The damage to a log impeller was extensive and required time in dry dock at Chatham Dockyard to repair.

Once back in service the frigate resumed her training role under the command of her latest commanding officer, Commander R G Jenkins, OBE, DSC RN.

The closing stages of *Loch Tralaig*'s service were spent in home waters in the training role with official visits made across Europe and Scandinavia. The frigates final commanding officer, Commander C K Hoyle RN took command and oversaw the frigate's de-commissioning into the reserve fleet at Portsmouth in 1953.

Loch Tralaig would, the following year, be towed to Hartlepool where she was stored in the Reserve Fleet serving as a headquarters and accommodation ship, a role she would maintain until 1961. In 1961 the former Loch class frigate was sold for scrap to BISCO who processed the ships demolition through P & W MacLelland at Bo'ness. *Loch Tralaig* arrived under tow in August 1964 on her final journey.

Chronology

02.02.1943	Ordered from Caledon Shipbuilding in Dundee
26.04.1944	Laid down
12.02.1945	Launched
04.07.1945	Completed
08.1945	Special noise trials in North West Approaches
08.1945	Operation Deadlight
12.1945	3rd Training Flotilla at Londonderry
03.1945	Refit at Devonport
08.1946	Grounded off Skipness Point
18-27.07.1947	Royal Home Fleet Review in the Clyde
07.1948	Refit at Rosyth to improve ASW capabilities
02.1949	Struck Aberfoyle Light Beacon in Loch Foyle
1950	Training flotilla in Londonderry
10.1950	Grounded off Garrison Point at Sheerness
1953	To reserve at Portsmouth
1954	Towed to Hartlepool as HQ and accommodation ship
1961	Sold for scrap to BISCO
08.1964	Arrived P & W MacLelland, Bo'ness for breaking up.

HMS LOCH VEYATIE

The large clear quarterdeck is seen in this photograph of Loch Veyatie. *During World War Two the area was full of anti-submarine weapons.*

(Crown Copyright/MoD)

On 25 January 1945 the shipyard of Ailsa Shipbuilders received the contract from the Admiralty for the construction of two frigates that would eventually be named *Loch Veyatie* and *Loch Tarbert*. The former was laid down on the slipway on 30 March 1944 and launched on 8 October 1945, too late to see active wartime service during the Second World War. The pace of construction accordingly slowed considerably with *Loch Veyatie* being handed over as the last Loch class ship to be built on 13 July 1946.

The ship carried out her sea trials under the command of Lieutenant Commander G W McGuinness RNR in May and June 1946 before commissioning into service with the 4th Escort Flotilla. The frigate's first assignment was to sail to Londonderry with the flotilla and join the Joint Anti-Submarine Training School.

In August there was a change of command as Lieutenant Commander M R S Smithwick assumed command of the frigate, which continued in the training role around the Londonderry coastline with sister ships *Loch Dunvegan, Loch Fada, Loch Tralaig* and *Loch Arkaig*.

The training programme continued into 1947 with occasional port visits made to such places as Barrow in Furness late in the year. After almost three years of continuous service *Loch Veyatie* was in need of a refit and this had been organised for the early part of 1948. The work was to be carried out at Rosyth Dockyard, where the frigate arrived in January 1948. After two months in dockyard hands the ship returned to her flotilla in Londonderry and resumed her regular if uneventful role of training ship for midshipmen and cadets.

In July command of the frigate was handed over to

Lieutenant Commander K A Cradock-Hartopp MBE, DSC RN who like his predecessors continued the important role of training future officers and men in anti-submarine warfare. Numerous port visits were made as part of this training throughout the summer and autumn of 1948.

Loch Veyatie was, in January 1949, in need of another refit to bring the ship up to modern standards. Part of the work package included the installation of the new Type 277P radar. She entered Rosyth Dockyard was soon docked down to complete the work which took until August to complete. When the frigate sailed out of Rosyth to undertake her trials of her new equipment given the codename of the Cannibal trials, she was under the command of Lieutenant Commander I D S Forbes DSC. The Commander had been with the ship since March overseeing the closing stages of the refit. By August with the ship afloat once again he took her back to sea.

Once all the trials had been completed successfully the frigate sailed back to Londonderry to continue her training role. Lieutenant Commander Forbes remained in command until the end of September when Lieutenant Commander P B de B Jeayes RN took over.

The frigate continued her training duties until May 1950 when she returned to Rosyth for a docking period of just over a month. In the summer she took part in the Annual Summer War conducted in the Irish Sea and North West Approaches with numerous submarines ranged against the surface units. This was followed by another major exercise given the codename of Exercise SWX5 again organised by the Silent Service branch of the Royal Navy. With the excitement of these exercises completed by the end of September, normal training duties around Londonderry resumed for the remainder of the year.

In 1951 the Royal Navy faced one of its worst periods in peacetime with a shortage of fuel and men, who had been released from war service to civvy street. Accordingly many ships were laid up and other had a reduced complement. This led to many men receiving much shorter breaks at home and a rising level of malcontent onboard. *Loch Veyatie* suffered from cases of malicious damage to ships systems with many of the

culprits sent to jail for lengthy terms of imprisonment. On 30 January *Loch Veyatie* left Portland for a series of anti-submarine exercises together with the submarines *Aurochs, Sidon* and *Totem* and surface ships comprising T*intagel Castle, Flint Castle, Leeds Castle, Zest, Zephyr* and *MTB 5031*.

In February *Loch Veyatie* operated out of Portland harbour before returning to Rosyth once again for a further period in refit in March. As the refit drew to a close men onboard looked forward to a foreign visit to the Norwegian city of Bergen, but this was cancelled when news reached the ship of the tragic loss of the submarine *Affray* in the English Channel *Loch Veyatie* was one of a fleet of escort vessels sent out to search for the missing submarine. On 6 April *Loch Veyatie* sailed from Rosyth to Plymouth to assist in the search. When all hope was lost the frigate continued around the coast of Devon and Cornwall and on to Londonderry. Her arrival at Lisahally, however, was not a good one. On 2 May as she came alongside she struck the jetty with some force, but fortunately the frigate suffered no significant damage. Sadly this was to be but the first collision of the commission, on the 17 June the frigate also struck the submarine depot ship *Montclare* during a visit to the Clyde.

The longed for foreign visit that had been cancelled earlier in the year was re-instated on the ships itinerary, but instead of Norway the frigate set sail in August for trials out of Portland on new equipment that had been installed on the frigate. The special equipment trials were given the name Candial. The trials continued en route to Denmark, where on the 4 September the frigate entered the port of Vejle. Eight days later together with sister ship *Loch Fada*, *Loch Veyatie* finally visited the Norwegian port of Horten in Oslofjord before going on to visit Kiel in Germany.

Another case of malicious damage was discovered onboard on 29 September when components of the steering gear had been damaged by a loose bolt. Repairs were made to the gear and other systems onboard when the frigate called at Devonport Dockyard throughout October. Upon completion the ship resumed her duties as a training ship.

In December *Loch Veyatie* confirmed her reputation for being accident prone when on 19th she hit No 2

jetty at Devonport Dockyard. The incident caused no significant damage to the frigate.

A new commanding officer was appointed to the ship in the form of Lieutenant Commander Loftus Edward Peyton Jones DSO, DSC, MBE RN. Jones was born on 7 October 1918 and spent his midshipman training onboard the cadet cruiser *Frobisher*. Following successfully completing the course he would spend the pre war years onboard the battleships *Resolution* and *Royal Sovereign* in the Mediterranean until 1938.

Jones had one of the most exciting war records of any commander of a Loch class frigate. The first part of the war was spent onboard the cruiser *Penelope* during the Norwegian campaign and then on to the destroyers Brocklesby and the *Achates* during the Russian convoys receiving a DSC for his work during convoy JW51B on the last day of December 1942 and a DSC for work with convoy PQ16.

On 24 April 1943, he was onboard the submarine *Sahib* which was captured by Italian forces north of Sicily. He was interned as a Prisoner of War at Padula near Salerno. Jones would ultimately spend the next year as a POW but when they moved him by train to Bologna, he took his chance and escaped. His first attempt was unsuccessful and he was recaptured. His second, however from Bologna, was a success. He walked 300 miles to the coast at Anzio in April 1944 and put to sea in a small boat. There he was rescued by an American DUKW. For his enterprise in escaping

A very clean looking Loch Veyatie *seen in the Persian Gulf.*

(Crown Copyright/MoD)

from captivity Jones was awarded the MBE.

The war was still on and in July 1944 Jones was rewarded with a command of his own that of the destroyer *Easton* in the Adriatic and Aegean. After the war Jones served on the aircraft carrier *Theseus* and *President* and was for a time a staff officer (Plans) on the staff of the Flag Officer Western Europe (Fontainebleau). After leaving the Royal Navy he founded and headed the newly created Trinidad and Tobago coastguard service.

Once given permission to proceed to sea *Loch Veyatie* made her way back to Londonderry, where on 8 January 1952 she assisted in the salvage of an Irish drifter called *Maeve*. The fishing vessel had grounded at Inishtrahull, but had damaged her engine and was without power. The crew of the drifter had managed to get the boat afloat once again but required the assistance of the Royal Navy frigate until a local tug arrived to help.

During another refit in June command of the frigate was transferred to Lieutenant Commander T P Ballie Groham on 15 July. Following sea trials the frigate visited Harwich and Copenhagen in August before being involved in yet another collision, this time on 27 August, with a barge. The vessel was under tow off Ymuiden in Denmark and *Loch Veyatie* received some minor damage aft.

September saw one of the greatest naval exercises staged in the post war period, the NATO Exercise Mainbrace. Mainbrace saw hundreds of ships from across the North Atlantic Treaty Organisation assemble in Northern waters to test and evaluate the Alliance's response to possible Soviet attacks. *Loch Veyatie* was one of the ships the Royal Navy sent to take part in the manoeuvres. Upon completion she stayed in the training role until May 1953 when she took passage to Portland in Dorset. At the end of the month she sailed north to visit the Scottish port of Stranraer before sailing back down the Irish Sea and returning to Portland on 4 June. At Portland the ship was scrubbed and painted in preparation for the Coronation Review to honour the new monarch, Her Majesty Queen Elizabeth II. By the 15 June *Loch Veyatie* had taken her position in the Solent and the order had been given to dress the ship overall.

Upon completion the frigate returned to Training Flotilla 3 in Londonderry where she continued to train the cadets and midshipmen in anti submarine warfare and navigational training until 7 October when she hit No 5 wharf at Devonport. The damage done required a period in dockyard hands to correct. With the wound repaired *Loch Veyatie* sailed back to Londonderry in late October.

In December the ship received notification that her next refit planned for January would take place at Chatham Dockyard. Meanwhile, on 28 December Lieutenant Commander H P Fleming became the frigates latest commanding officer.

The start of 1954 saw the ship still under repair and refit at Chatham Dockyard. When the process neared completion the changes were tested during trials conducted in the Thames Estuary in April. The spring months saw *Loch Veyatie* operating in her role as part of the 3rd Training Squadron and during this period of her career she visited La Pallice in France in September and took part in Exercise Bright Bonfire IX towards the end of the year off Gibraltar with units of the US Navy's 6th Fleet including the submarine USS *Picuda*. December saw the frigate back with the rest of the flotilla in continuation of her training program which continued well into 1955. The early months of the New Year did, however, see the arrival onboard of the news that the ship would be reduced to reserve by the end of the year. Firstly, however, a series of summer port visits had been organised to Port Stewart, Fowey and Bayonne in May and June and the following month a further visit was made to Dunoon on 2 July before crossing the Irish Sea to Londonderry for a final spell of training until the end of the month. On 25 July *Loch Veyatie* sailed from Londonderry and headed for Plymouth exchanging identities with the aircraft carrier *Triumph*. En route the frigate arrived at Devonport two days later to pay off into reserve. Upon her arrival she secured to no 6 Buoy in Plymouth Sound on 26 July and remained there for two days. *Loch Veyatie* was moved into No 5 Basin at the end of July and remained stationary for almost a month before sailing early in the day for Sheerness on Monday 22 August. The frigate arrived off the Kent port at 0605 the following morning and

secured to No 3 buoy to take her fuel oil off into dock-yard lighters. Once complete the frigate slipped and proceeded up the River Thames bound for a refit at Green and Silley Weir Shipyard in Millwall Docks London.

January 1946 saw the ship still under refit, which had seen some over runs, finally in September harbour trials commenced. The following month saw a number of sea trials in the Thames Estuary before returning to Chatham Dockyard where workers sealed the upper deck in preparation for the ships reduction to reserve status within the dockyard.

In May 1957 she was taken to join the reserve fleet at Lissahally in Northern Ireland after dehumification plant had been fitted whilst at Londonderry in June. She remained in reserve until 19 July 1961 when she was finally placed on the disposal list. On 3 August 1965 after four years awaiting her final journey she was sold for £24,640 to W H Arnott Young for break-ing up at Dalmuir. Nine days later *Loch Veyatie* arrived for scrapping.

Chronology

25.01.1944	Ordered from Ailsa Shipbuilding
30.03.1944	Laid down
08.10.1945	Launched
13.07.1946	Completed and joined the 4th Escort Flotilla
Autumn 1946	Joint Anti Submarine Training School
01.1948	Refit at Rosyth
03.1948	Rejoined flotilla at Londonderry
01.1949	Major refit at Rosyth
08.1949	Resumed flotilla duties at Londonderry
05.1950	Rosyth
1951	Cases of malicious damage onboard
1951	Joined search for lost submarine *Affray* in English Channel
02.05.1951	Struck jetty at Lisahally
17.05.1951	Hit submarine depot ship *Montclare* on the Clyde
04.09.1951	Special equipment trials codenamed Candial
09.1951	Danish port of Horten and Kiel in Germany
19.12.1951	Struck No 2 jetty at Devonport Dockyard
08.01.1952	Salvaged Irish drift trawler *Maeve*
27.08.1952	Collided with a barge off Ymuiden in Denmark
09.1953	NATO exercise Mainbrace
15.06.1953	Coronation Review in the Solent
07.10.1953	Hit No 5 wharf at Devonport Dockyard
01.1954	Refit at Chatham Dockyard
09.1954	Exercise Bright Bonfire IX
25.07.1955	To Plymouth to pay off
23.08.1955	Sheerness
09.1955	To Green and Silley Weir Shipyard in London for refit
Late 1955	Returned to Chatham for reserve fleet
May 1957	Lisahally in the reserve fleet
12.08.1965	Arrived WH Arnott Young at Dalmuir for breaking up

HMSAS GOOD HOPE

The good layout of the Loch class is highlighted in this image of the South African HMSAS Good Hope.
(Crown Copyright/MoD)

Loch Boisdale was ordered from the shipyard of Blyth Shipbuilding on 28 December 1942. Given the yard number 297 the workers at the shipyard set to fashioning a new frigate from steel plates with the first parts laid down on the slipway on 8 November 1943. A little over a month later on 1 December the ownership of the new frigate was transferred to the South African Naval Forces and accordingly the ship was re-christened as *Good Hope* with Lieutenant Commander R P Dryden-Dymond VRD, SANF in command. As a ship of the South African force it was also decided that she should have an appropriate motto in Africkan's, 'De Hoop en beschant niet' : 'Hope does not disappoint'.

Construction continued and after the shipyard was satisfied with the ships general performance and characteristics *Good Hope* was commissioned for service on 9 November 1944. Initially she served in the Western Approaches on anti-submarine and convoy escort duties having first taken onboard supplies at Tobermory.

1945 started with the frigate operating off Iceland in the stormy seas around the island. Indeed it was these fearsome weather conditions that saw the frigate sustain severe damage to her hull plating in January requiring repair work on the River Clyde to be undertaken. Such was the extent of the damage that *Good Hope* remained out of service until March. Upon completion of her repairs the South African frigate joined the 24th Escort Group in the English Channel, Irish Sea and South West Approaches.

For a South African ship it was, in April, deemed appropriate that she should be in South African waters, so plans were made for her and the *Natal* to sail south in May. The route chosen saw a visit made to Freetown before arriving at Simonstown from

HMSAS Good Hope *arriving in Cape Town from the UK on 18 September 1945.*   *(South African Naval Museum)*

where she operated throughout the summer.

With the end of war *Good Hope* was allocated the task of escorting troopships carrying men back from the Middle East to South Africa throughout the autumn and winter months of 1945.

1946 started with the ship continuing her trooping deployment but by February with much of the work relocating men and machinery completed the frigate was placed alongside at Simonstown with a much reduced complement. The ship was destined to become part of the South African Navy but prior to the establishment of this new force the warship suffered a period in a non operational state within the dockyard. This continued until March when preparations were made to bring the frigate back to life. The occasion that had spurred this progress was the planned tour of South Africa by HM King George VI and his family in the battleship *Vanguard*.

Throughout the Royal visit *Good Hope* escorted the

battleship including the formal farewell to the King, Queen and two Princesses on 24 April when the battleship *Vanguard* sailed from Cape Town. As the ships sailed *Good Hope* took a final opportunity to exercise with the Royal Navy warships that in addition to the mighty battleship included the cruiser *Nigeria* and frigates *Actaeon* and *Nereide* during Operaton Tots Siens.

Upon completion of Operation Tots Siens she was once again placed inside the dockyard with a reduced ships company for the remainder of the year. 1948 saw a reversal in fortunes when in January she sailed for the isolated community on the island of Tristan da Cunha. Later the frigate took part in Operation Snoektown – the annexation of Marion Island and Prince Edward Island carried out together with *Natal* and *Transvaal*. These isolated islands were annexed to prevent their use as foreign military sites.

With the ship loaded with personnel and timber

Good Hope sailed from Cape Town to Marion Island where she relieved *Natal* on station. The weather conditions at Marion Island were terrible and it was some days before the conditions were suitable to attempt a landing. The men onboard the frigate eventually went ashore and quickly set about establishing a base for operations on the island.

On 16 February *Good Hope* exchanged stations with *Transvaal* and sailed back to Simonstown where in March a change of command took place with Lieutenant Commander J Johnson DSC SAN taking command of the frigate.

The spring months of 1948 saw her stationed at Salisbury Island in Durban and after only a few months in command Lieutenant Commander Johnson was succeeded by the frigates very first commanding officer who now had been promoted to Commander R P Dryden Dymond in May. The following months saw her a series of exercises in the coastal waters off Durban. In the autumn *Good Hope* along with her two sister ships *Natal* and *Transvaal* carried out an official cruise to Portuguese West Africa (now Angola) with Commodore F J Dean of the South African Navy onboard for the formal visits planned for the two month cruise. Official ports of call were made at Mossamedes, Zuhito, Quanda and Matadi.

In November 1948 the ship was reduced to Care and Maintenance at Durban and would remain there for sometime whilst her future role in the South African forces was decided. The frigate would remain in this capacity until 1954 when she was selected for conversion to a Despatch Vessel along similar lines to the Royal Navy's Surprise and *Alert*, both former Loch class frigates themselves. The refit saw her forecastle deck extended right aft to provide a deckhouse for a stateroom and extra cabins, whilst a platform for receptions and ceremonial occasions was constructed above. The bridge structure was also extended and a tall mainmast with a gaff was stepped aft. Her armament comprised a single 4-inch gun forward and two 40mm Bofors fitted on the former Squid deck. The addition of extra accommodation was primarily for senior personnel but also for cadets whilst the ship was on training cruises.

The refit was completed when *Good Hope* re-com-

missioned on 3 June 1955 as flagship of the South African Navy under the command of Lieutenant Commander R Cousens SAN. She joined the rest of the ships of the 10th Frigate Squadron. One of her first tasks in this new role was to embark the Governor General of South Africa, The Hon Dr E G Jansen and transport him to Madagascar on a formal visit as Head of State in July.

January 1956 started with exercises with visiting Royal Navy warships and other members of the 10th Frigate Flotilla whilst the rest of the year saw operations closer to home with coastal surveillance and monitoring of sea lanes of communication dominating the despatch vessels operations that year.

On 2 April 1957 *Good Hope* was present in Simonstown Naval Dockyard for the formal handing over from the Royal Navy to the South African Navy of the naval base. The officers and crew of the frigate were in best dress uniforms for the occasion which saw the last of the Royal Navy warships leave the base, which for so long had been one of the strongholds of the Royal Navy.

Later that year in December *Good Hope* became the first ship to wear the flag of a South African admiral at sea when she welcomed onboard Rear Admiral H H Biermann SA, OBE SAN for visits to Lorenco Marques and Beira in Mozambique with the frigates *Vrystaat, Kaapstad* and *Pretoria*.

The year also saw the first helicopter deck landing on a South African Navy warship, when a S55 helicopter of the South African Air Force landed onboard whilst the ship was at anchor in Saldanha Bay.

The start of 1958 saw *Good Hope* in dockyard hands for work to be undertaken on replacing the ships single 4-inch gun with a twin 4-inch Mk XVI mounting. The opportunity was also taken to upgrade some of the accommodation spaces and machinery onboard. The work continued until April when the frigate retook her place in the newly renamed 10th Frigate Squadron.

Usual operations resumed for the frigate with rare foreign visits including, in August 1959, a visit to Angola that required a journey seventy miles up the Congo River before berthing alongside at Matadi.

1964 saw the ship continue her planned deployment

An aerial view of Good Hope, *showing the large deck extension aft (covered in Burma teak) used for receptions. An honour guard can be seen on deck surrounding the ashes of the late Admiral Sir Herbert Packer KCB CBE (C-in-C South Atlantic 1950-52) which were about to be committed to the sea.*
(South African Naval Museum)

until July when a new commanding officer assumed command. He was Commander R D Kingon SAN, who would later in life be promoted to Commodore SAN. The following month after a massive effort by the ships company to clean the ship the State President of South Africa Charles Robberts Swart embarked on board the frigate for the passage to East London. The visit was to honour the South African Navy with the freedom of the city. The official visit was a huge success and men from the ship paraded through the streets of East London in front of cheering crowds.

After the pageantry and spectacle the frigates next role was positively mundane in comparison, fisheries protection between September and December. The role required the frigate to intercept trawlers and inspect their catch and fishing gear. In January 1965 *Good Hope* resumed the role of flag frigate and visited a number of ports across South Africa. She continued this deployment until withdrawn from service in October and paid off into reserve.

Good Hope would remain in reserve for a decade until her fate was decided; eventually the old frigate was declared suitable for use as an artificial reef for recreational divers in False Bay near Cape Town. Suitably cleaned of all contaminants by divers and explosives experts from the South African Navy the warship was sent to the bottom on 12 December 1978.

Chronology

28.12.1942	Ordered from Blyth Shipbuilding
08.11.1943	Laid down
01.12.1943	Transferred to South African Naval Forces and renamed HMSAS *Good Hope*
09.11.1944	Commissioned into service
01.1945	Off Iceland sustained storm damage
01.1945	After repairs joined 24th Escort Group
05.1945	Sailed for South Africa
Late 1945	Repatriation duties in Indian Ocean
24.04.1946	Royal Visit to South Africa with battleship *Vanguard*. Operation Tots Siens
01.1948	Tristan da Cunha
01.1948	Operation Snoektown
Autumn 1948	Cruise of Portuguese West Africa
11.1948	Reduced to care and maintenance at Durban
1954	Selected for conversion to Despatch Vessel
03.06.1955	Recommissioned as flagship of South African Navy
02.04.1957	Present at handover of Simonstown Dockyard from the Royal Navy
10.1964	Paid off into reserve
12.12.1978	Scuttled in Smitswinkel Bay, South Africa

HMSAS NATAL

Ordered as Loch Cree *the future* HMSAS Natal *was launched on 19 June 1944 into the River Tyne at Swan Hunters shipyard.* *(Crown Copyright/MoD)*

Loch Cree was ordered from the Newcastle shipyard of Swan Hunters on 13 February 1943. The initial components of the new frigate had been prepared off site and on 18 October 1943 the first of these were brought together on the slipway. As more component parts were added the frigate slowly took shape before being launched into the River Tyne on 19 June 1944. The name *Loch Cree* would not be assigned to this vessel for long because it had been decided that the frigate would transfer to the South African Naval Force and in January 1945 the name was changed to HMSAS *Natal*. After commissioning on 1 March 1945 the final finishing touches to the ship were completed a week later and the frigate came to life with a crew from South Africa with Lieutenant Commander David Hall DSC SANF in command.

Upon receiving his orders to sail immediately Hall has asked permission that the ship delay her departure for two days to allow his crew to better familiarise themselves with the ship and her systems as they were new to such vessels. A postponement of forty eight hours was duly allowed.

At around 0900 on the 14 March *Natal* sailed with a group of warships from the River Tyne bound for Scapa Flow and en route heard the news from the merchantman *Sheaf Crown* that the steamship SS *Magne* had been sunk off St Abbs in the Firth of Forth, by the German Type VIIC submarine *U-714* under the command of Kapitanleutnant Hans-Joachim Schwebcke. U-714 had attacked convoy FS 1753 and sunk the small Norwegian naval trawler *Nordhav II* and four days later attacked and sank the Swedish steam mer-

chant vessel *Magne* from convoy FS 1756. After the attack on the *Magne Natal* along with the elderly destroyer *Wivern* searched for survivors from the U-boat, sadly all fifty men onboard the submarine perished.

In his action log Commander Hall recounted the day's events: "I was preceding independently from Newcastle to Methil, speed 12 knots, with twin Foxers streamed. This was the ships first voyage since commissioning on the 1st of March.

"At 1325 SS *Sheaf Crown*, sound bound, reported a merchant ship just sunk astern of her; about five miles ahead of me. I immediately ordered Defence Stations to be piped. At 1335 a lifeboat with survivors and two rafts were sighted near a large oil patch about two miles ahead.

"HMS *Wivern*, steaming in the vicinity reported that she was carrying out a search and picking up survivors and requested me to give assistance by carrying out a square search of four miles using the rafts as a datum point. (lat 55deg. 52min.N. long. 1 deg. 53.5 min W)

"The ship's company was immediately brought to A/S Action Stations and speed was reduced to eight knots in order to recover Foxer gear. An initial course of 309 degrees from datum point was decided upon, and search was commenced at 1350.

"At 1411 when two miles from datum point a good echo was reported. The extent was eight degrees with echo pitch slight to moderate high, classified as submarine. This was confirmed by A/S CO, due to definite slight high pitch and recorder trace. Use was made of the STU for a short period which gave a clear sharp echo with a slight trace. Bearing movement, echo pitch, RSA and plot indicated that the submarine was approaching at slow speed. During the last stages of the attack the submarine appeared to take avoiding action by turning to starboard.

"A very faint trace was obtained on the 147B

HMSAS Natal *seen in her wartime colour scheme.* *(Crown Copyright/MoD)*

Recorder. Little reliance was placed on this as the tuning was unsatisfactory even after adjustments before leaving Newcastle and the operator was inexperienced. However it indicated that the submarine was above bottom. On opening out after the attack the range was extreme before turning and contact was lost, but was soon regained at extreme range, and reclassified as submarine. During the run in on the second attack the submarine appeared to be zig-zagging at slow speed towards, as indicated by bearing recorder.

"At about 1200 yards range in the third attack echo appeared to be woolly. When in scale 10 the first part of the recorder trace indicated a non-sub echo and A/S CO advised me to break off attack, so I broke the ATW switch. Due to a bearing movement and a longer trace it seemed that the No.1 operator was cutting across the submarine and its wake so the A/S CO suggested that the attack be carried out. Unfortunately the captain's ATW switch was not made.

"In the fourth run the echo was very woolly and after changing to scale 10 the trace disappeared and A/S CO said there was no trace to fire on. After 'lost contact' procedure had been carried out a new arc was with no result. An all round sweep was ordered but contact was not regained.

"After the first attack a large amount of oil came to the surface. Officers and E.R said that in their opinion it smelled strongly of Diesolene. In addition a heavy cylindrical tank came to the surface and was later recovered. It appeared to be made of prefabricated steel of sturdy structure. When opened a pair of leather bellows was visible inside and these were seen to start pumping. The ships doctor applied his stethoscope and as no tickle could he heard and as the cylinder was empty then it was presumed safe. The second attack brought up more oil and another such smaller metal tank which later sank." For this action *Natal* was later awarded the Royal Navy Battle Honour of North Sea 1945.

Having arrived safely at Tobermory *Natal* continued her work up from 17 March before joining the rest of the 8th Escort Group for escort duties (based out of Greenock) in the Irish Sea and South West Approaches. After a brief visit to Milford Haven, the

frigate returned to Clydeside for some repairs and whilst there the war in Europe ended. The ships company celebrated the end of the European war with the people of Glasgow in style.

Unlike her Canadian sister ships, which were returned to the Royal Navy soon after VE Day, the three frigates assigned to South Africa were retained by that nation to form the nucleus of a future fleet and in June two of the frigates, *Natal* and *Good Hope* (ex *Loch Boisdale*) sailed to South Africa with a fuelling stop at Freetown. The pair arrived at Cape Town on 30 June.

The ships war service, however, was not complete as the frigate was, in July, prepared for further service with the British East Indies Fleet. With the Kamikaze threat still prevalent *Natal* was fitted with additional AA armament (Two single 40mm Bofors replaced the two twin 20mm Oerlikons on the after gundeck, while a further two single 40mm were mounted on the quarterdeck. The two 20mm were repositioned on the quarterdeck. On 20 August she set sail for Singapore from her temporary base of Durban.

On 1 September *Natal* joined up with a convoy taking passage from Colombo to Singapore before arriving safely. Later that month she escorted a 20-ship convoy across the Bay of Bengal and on to Port Swettenham on the Malay peninsula. She also escorted a small relief convoy to Singapore, arriving not long after the Japanese surrender there. She was then attached to the East Indies Escort Force where she operated in and around the Malacca Straits and Singapore.

After taking part in the Allied occupation of Malaya and Singapore *Natal* relieved the cruiser *Nigeria* as guardship off Sabang, at the north-western tip of Sumatra.

By November with the end of the war in the Pacific *Natal*; was allocated the task of repatriating South African personnel from Egypt to South Africa. After loading these extra men onboard the relatively small frigate she sailed making a visit to Mauritius before finally arriving back home in Durban on the last day of November. The number of South African personnel distributed across the globe was a logistical nightmare to try and get them all home as quickly as possible and

Natal proved her value as she took part in these so called 'magic carpet' operations. In December she was again back in Egypt having made a passage to Suez. Christmas was spent in the desert sun as men and stores were loaded onboard *Natal* for the return passage to Durban, which started on 4 January. After a fortnight at sea, *Natal* pulled into the wide harbour at Durban and unloaded her precious cargo. She would make another two trooping runs before being released for other duties in March and a return to Cape Town.

After a few months operating in the waters off Cape Town the ship was put into "limited availability" for the remainder of 1946. The New Year brought a new commanding officer Lieutenant Commander R P D Dymond SANF who took the ship to sea on 7 January 1947 with the intention of re-affirming the declared status of Marion Island and Prince Edward Island as sovereign territory of South Africa. *Natal* relieved sister ship *Transvaal* at Marion Island as her part of Operation Snoektown on 12 January. Bad weather at the island prevented the planned unloading of equipment and stores and the frigate had to make for open waters where she could ride out the storm, which would last for four days before another attempt could be made to unload.

On her arrival on the 18 January the crew assisted the supply ship HMSAS *Gamtoos* into Transvaal Cove after cutting a path through a kelp bed that had prevented the supply ship from anchoring. *Natal* spent the next ten days at Marion Island conducting routine patrols and observations before she was relieved by sister ship *Good Hope* on 28 January. The next month was spent in waters off Cape Town whilst March saw *Natal* once again returning to Marion Island loaded with aviation fuel and a variety of livestock for the inhabitants of the island. Upon completion *Natal* returned to Cape Town with passengers onboard from the construction party that had built a number of structures on the island for the inhabitants to use.

Upon her return to Cape Town the frigate was one of the many assembled off Simon's town to welcome the British battleship *Vanguard* in April on her tour of South Africa. On board the battleship were King George VI, Queen Elizabeth and the two Princesses

Margaret and Elizabeth. The South African's gave this mission the title of Operation Tot Siens. *Natal* would be one of the warships that also escorted the battleship out of South African waters after a most successful visit by the Royal Party.

Natal continued to operate with the South African Navy throughout 1948 on local coastal patrols and in March 1949 carried out a hydrographical survey in the Marion Island area. This was a foretaste of things to come for the frigate as in years to come she would be converted to serve as a survey vessel. The hydrographical mission lasted until April. Later in the year in November the frigate was nominated for a refit, which started the following month. Natal was taken in hand for a refit at HM Dockyard Simon's town that lasted until the following February. Following sea trials and acceptance the frigate resumed her operational programme with visits paid to Durban and Cape Town by the end of the year.

By 1952 *Natal* had been used quite extensively in survey work but had been reduced to reserve status having been relieved by *Simon Van Der Stel* in service. *Natal* remained in care and maintenance until late 1955 when she was refitted at Simon's town Naval Dockyard for further service as a dedicated survey ship. The refit would involve the removal of most of the ships weapon systems and replacing them with sonar and equipment for hydrographic research. The work entailed stripping back large sections of the superstructure and the erection of new deckhouses along similar lines to the Royal Navy survey vessel conversions carried out on four Loch class ships.

The refit lasted until 25 October 1957 when, with a new pennant number of A301 and a new white overall colour scheme, the ship re-commissioned into service with the South African Navy. The survey ship's latest commanding officer was Lieutenant Commander J C Walters SAN(H), who oversaw the ships post refit and sea trials programme before deploying in November 1957 for service during the International Geophysical Year.

Natal's first surveying mission only lasted until December when the ship sailed as far south as 51.30S to make surveys near Antarctica. The following year saw surveys in Lamberts Bay, Cape Agulhas and St

Helena Bay and a cruise in southern waters.

Natal rarely got mentioned in the headlines as her work, for the most part, went unnoticed by the media, but throughout 1959 she worked hard towards finding a route for an undersea cable near Table Bay as well as ferrying supplies to Marion Island.

For the next five years the ship continued to survey large areas of ocean around South Africa and also further into the Indian Ocean as well as providing a base for climate scientists and oceanographers to study the world's oceans. In August 1964 *Natal* sustained structural damage during heavy storms around two hundred miles south east of Durban following a successful survey of Cape St Lucia and Zululand. Such was the extent of the storm that some pieces of deck equipment were ripped from their davits and lost overboard including a ships' launch. *Natal* returned to Simon's town for repairs which lasted until the end of the year.

In early 1966 the ship visited Bouvet Island for the scientific purpose of trying to establish a metrological station on the island. Unfortunately the assessment by the scientists saw no practical use for the island in this function. On her return natal visited Millers Point, False Bay, Khysna Harbour, Alphard Banks and St Helena Bay.

On the night of 13 July 1968 *Natal* went to the aid of the Greek oil tanker *World Glory*, which had sunk some distance off Durban. Two bodies and two survivors were recovered from the sea for which the ships latest commanding officer Commander de Witt received the Gold Medal of the Greek Maritime Marine for his efforts in their recovery.

1970 saw *Natal* as busy as ever with an extensive survey between Cape Agulhas and Duivenoks river completed by March followed by further work that completed a 140 mile stretch of coastline from the border with Mozambique to St Helena Bay by the end of the year.

SAS Natal *was converted to serve as a survey ship from November 1957.* (South African Naval Museum)

SAS Natal's *final moments were as a target. She was sunk by gunfire from the frigate* SAS President Steyn.
(South African Naval Museum)

1971 was to be *Natal*'s final full year in commission and started with a calibration of the South African and Namaqualand Decca Chains as well as paying her last visits to Port Elizabeth, East London and Durban. On 15 March 1972 *Natal*'s colours were lowered on the quarterdeck for the last time as the ship was finally decommissioned from service. She didn't have to wait long for the end, when in September 1972 she was towed to a position some fourteen and a half miles south west of Cape Point and sunk by gunfire from the frigate SAS *President Steyn* as a target.

Chronology

13.02.1943	Ordered from Swan Hunters Shipbuilders
18.10.1943	Laid down
19.06.1944	Launched
.01.1945	Transferred to South African Naval Force
01.03.1945	Commissioned as HMSAS *Natal*
14.03.1945	Went to aid of Sheaf Crown sunk by *U-714*
.03.1945	Joined 8th Escort Group at Greenock
VE Day	Celebrations at Glasgow
30.06.1945	Arrived Capetown for the first time
.07.1945	Joined British East Indies Fleet based at Singapore
.11.1945	Repatriation of South African forces back to South Africa
25.12.1945	Egypt before passage to Durban
1946	At limited availability status
12.01.1947	Operation Snoektown
.04.1947	Royal Visit to South Africa with battleship *Vanguard*
1955	Refitted at Simonstown as survey vessel
25.10.1957	Refit completed
13.07.1968	Went to aid of Greek tanker *World Glory*
15.03.1972	Decommissioned
19.09.1972	Sunk as target by *SAS President Steyn*

HMSAS TRANSVAAL

Ordered as Loch Ard, HMSAS Transvaal *never served in the Royal Navy, transferring to South African control in*
May 1945. *(Crown Copyright/MoD)*

The shipyard of Harland and Wolff received a number of Loch and Bay class contracts, one of which was for the construction of *Loch Ard* on 2 May 1943. Construction started on 20 January 1944 and the frigates hull was launched on 2 August by Miss D Newman. The hull was towed from Belfast to the Clyde where at the Renfrew shipyard of Lobnitz she was fitted out with weaponry and other systems. Whilst on the Clyde *Loch Ard* became one of three Loch class frigates transferred to the South African Naval Defence Force (SANF) and was renamed as HMSAS *Transvaal*. Final fitting out was completed on 21 May 1945 too late to see active wartime service under the command of Lieutenant Commander H E Fougstedt SANF. She conducted her trials programme in the Clyde areas after commissioning on 22 May.

June was spent working up the ship but with the war in Europe over she siled for South Africa, arriving at

Table Bay on 28 July 1945. After calling at Port Elizabeth and East London she arrived at Durban on 9 August. With the end of the war with Japan *Transvaal*'s planned deployment to the region was cancelled and a new role to transport personnel was initiated instead. She sailed in August to the Middle East to take South African personnel back home. This role continued into 1946 with numerous voyages between the Middle East and South Africa.

Once released from repatriation duties *Transvaal* returned to operational tasking in April but with a much reduced complement onboard. The 1 May 1946 was an auspicious date for the SANF, not only did it mark the creation of the South African Naval Force as a permanent part of the defence structure of the country but a new commanding officer was appointed to *Transvaal*. Lieutenant Commander J K Mallory took command of the frigate and her tasking was to carry

In March 1947 HMSAS Transvaal *was present in Durban for the opening of a new dry dock in Durban's port district.* (Ken Kelly Collection)

out training in local waters until the end of the year.

In 1947 the British battleship *Vanguard* visited South Africa carrying His Majesty King George VI and HM Queen Elizabeth and the two princesses Elizabeth and Margaret. The *Transvaal* was one of the ships that were detailed to act as escorts for the tour. As such, she was guardship at East London, Port Elizabeth and Durban during the visit of the great battleship and the Royal Navy throughout February. Indeed at Durban *Transvaal* was host ship for the Royals and on 3 March Princess Elizabeth embarked in the frigate for passage to open a new dry dock in Durban's port district.

At the end of the *Vanguard*'s Royal tour of South Africa in April *Transvaal* was one of the ships that bid the battleship a fond farewell as she steamed with the Royal party onboard from Cape Town. The affairs of the South African Navy then took precedence and the frigate operated in local waters until July when a new commanding officer in the shape of Lieutenant Commander J Fairbairn was appointed.

The South African Government had in 1947 decided to annex two islands, Marion Island and Prince Edward Island for the state due to their important strategic location and the mission was assigned to the Navy. They would land men on the two islands and leave brass plates on each together with deeds of sovereignty. The operation was given the name Operation Snoektown and the frigate *Transvaal* was assigned to the task. Stores and special equipment were loaded onboard in late December and on the 21st of the month the ship slipped her moorings bound for the first of the islands, Marion Island. On 29 December men were put ashore, although the landing was somewhat delayed by bad weather.

On 4 January 1948 the frigate landed a number of personnel on Prince Edward Island with the intention of officially annexing the island for the South African Nation. The men laid a brass plate and a Deed of Sovereignty before returning to Marion Island and then home.

In February *Transvaal* made a return visit to Marion Island with a cargo of stores and letters from home for the men manning the outpost on the island and upon arrival on 15 February relieved sister ship *Good Hope*

as support ship. By the beginning of March the situation on both Marion Island and Prince Edward Island was becoming much clearer and a regular supply routine had been established allowing the frigates to conduct more normal operations. In the case of *Transvaal* this meant training and anti-submarine exercises throughout the summer months.

On 4 November the frigate went to the aid of the stricken oil tanker *Esso Wheeling* which had run aground in bad weather conditions near to Quoin Point. The ship's captain and her forty one man crew had already abandoned the ship and had taken to the lifeboats. *Transvaal* rescued the men from the very choppy seas and took them safely to shore.

On 16 November the frigate was taken in hand for a refit that would last a month with the completion date being 14 December. The closing days of the year were spent on post refit trials under the command of her new commanding officer Lieutenant Commander J J Rice VRD.

On 15 January 1949 the ship visited the remote island of Tristan da Cunha. The return leg of the journey, however, was more eventful with faulty radio equipment found to be onboard. The ship was delayed by a day until suitable replacement equipment could be found and dispatched to the frigate. Its arrival was just in time as *Transvaal* was sent to assist the MV *Pequena*, the support ship for the island, which had lost her rudder.

The support ship was located after three days steaming and a tow was passed over from the frigate. The tow broke once en route back to Cape Town, however, but the pair of ships eventually arrived safely in February.

For the rest of the year the frigate operated in local waters with visits made to Durban and Saldadana Bay before a planned refit on 4 November. The work on the frigate was finished on 12 December.

The first six months of 1950 saw the frigate carrying out operational duties around South African waters but in June *Transvaal* was listed for reduction to reserve at Durban. After three months of inactivity the frigate rejoined the fleet in September and carried out exercises off the Cape of Good Hope under the command of Lieutenant Commander J Johnson.

In December 1950 *Transvaal* had the honour of sailing to Australia to represent South Africa for the RAN Jubilee celebrations. She sailed on Boxing Day from Durban for Amsterdam Island. The ship celebrated New Year en route to Fremantle where she arrived on 10 January. The crew enjoyed a great many social and official celebrations and exchanges during the visit. On 30 January the South African frigate put to sea with Australian warships and the Royal Navy submarine *Taciturn* and Pakistani and Indian units for anti-submarine training.

In February *Transvaal* took part in further manoeuvres en route to Melbourne and Adelaide where great runs ashore were had by the crew. *Transvaal* herself was open to the public during both port visits attracting large crowds.

The South African warship started her return journey and made a second visit to Fremantle on the 15 February.

Upon her return to South Africa *Transvaal* resumed her normal operational duties that included exercises in the Cape area in May and August. After a visit to Marion Island in October, the frigate had a short two month refit from November.

In January 1952 Lieutenant Commander R C Cousens took command of the frigate. *Transvaal* made operational visits to Marion Island in March and later in August ventured as far as Diego Suarez, Madagascar, Mombasa and Dar es Salaam during an Indian Ocean cruise.

Upon her return to Simon's Town in October she was dry docked for routine maintenance and an inspection that lasted the remainder of the year.

1953 saw the frigate conducting local patrols along the South African coastline with visits made to Port Elizabeth and East London and exercises in Salahana Bay. In December Lieutenant Commander B V Hegarty DSC took command of the frigate.

1954 was dominated by local training interspersed with a visit to Marion Island in April. The summer months saw more exercises in and around Salahana Bay and she also paid an official visit to Cape Town. *Transvaal* took part in a major navy exercise in June, prior to entering refit in July and August.

Once the refit was completed the frigate carried out a shakedown followed by further visits to Marion Island, Cape Town and Port Elizabeth until the end of the year.

In January 1955 *Transvaal* was detailed to take part in a special radar survey with a new Commanding Officer at the helm, Lieutenant Commander D H Farr. On 30 January she sailed to conduct a survey of the snow-covered Bouvet Island situated on the Antarctic Ridge, some 1,700 miles south-south-west of Cape Town. The work was completed nine days later after which the frigate sailed to visit Mossell Bay and areas around the Cape of Good Hope in March.

After a period of leave for the crew *Transvaal* took part in a large South African Navy exercise around Salahana Bay on 18 April. On 8 May a new Commanding Officer was appointed in the form of Commander C J F Nettleburgh DSC.

The summer months saw the frigate making a series of visits and undertaking an East Coast Cruise that started on 25 August that included ports of call to Port Elizabeth and East London. On 9 September she returned to Simon's Town and ten days later started a refit package that kept her out of service until 25 November. The remainder of the year saw *Transvaal* conducting post refit trials.

In January 1956 *Transvaal*'s latest Commanding Officer Lieutenant Commander G N Green was appointed as the frigate took part in South African Navy manoeuvres. The frigate also visited the British-possessed Gough Island some 200 miles south west of Tristan da Cunha to conduct an underwater survey of the area with other units of the South African Navy.

The early months of 1957 saw the frigate making a series of port visits as well as a period under repair at Simon's Town. On 2 April *Transvaal* was one of the South African Navy ships present for the formal handing over of Simon's Town Dockyard from the Royal Navy to the South African Navy. The following month she sailed to visit Tristan da Cunha, Marion Island and Gough Island. The South African Government announced in the summer its intention to modernise *Transvaal* to the same standard as her sister ships in the Royal Navy.

In September *Transvaal* was taken in hand at Simon's Town to be decommissioned prior to her

HMSAS Transvaal *looking very smart later in her career with the South African Navy.*
(South African Naval Museum)

modernisation within the dockyard. The work was extensive and would take until July 1960 to complete. DUring the modernisation her single 4-inch gun was replaced by a twin 4-inch Mk XVI mounting and improved radar and communications equipment was fitted. Her light AA armament was removed and replaced by six 40mm Bofors comprising a twin water-cooled Mk V mounting aft, two single Mk 9 guns on the raised after gun deck and two similar mountings, one on each bridge wing.

After post refit trials the ship was re-commissioned under the command of Commander B V Hergarty DSC on 24 August 1960. He finished the trials in September before the frigate was reduced to reserve status in December. She spent the next seven months in reserve at Simon's Town.

In August 1961 *Transvaal* was re-commissioned into service with the new designation of SAS *Transvaal* following South Africa's withdrawal from the British Commonwealth. The autumn months proved to be busy ones with the evacuation of Tristan da Cunha in October following a volcanic eruption on the island. This operation continued through until the end of the year.

In January 1962 *Transvaal* returned to Tristan da Cunha with scientists onboard who ventured ashore to assess the damage caused by the volcanic eruptions.

She continued this operation until August and her release from the operation.

The ship underwent a further refit at Cape Town in the latter part of 1962, during which her machinery and boilers were overhauled and and her forecastle deck was extended aft to provide additional accommodation for trainees. Following this refit she was primarily used as a training ship.

In September 1963 the frigate deployed to Antarctica in support of the first American overflight of the South Pole. Her role was to provide air and sea rescue if an emergency was declared. Once released from this role she carried out underwater surveys in the Indian Ocean as part of the International Geophysical Year Project in December. On her return journey to South Africa the ship suffered a mechanical breakdown when her starboard propeller shaft broke. The shaft and other damage were repaired upon *Transvaal*'s return to Simon's Town.

In July 1964, however, it was announced that the ship would be paid off into reserve the following month and on 18 August her ensign was lowered for the last time. *Transvaal* remained in reserve until 1978 when she was listed for disposal as a target ship. She was towed out to sea on 8 August to False Bay and was sunk by gunfire.

Chronology

02.05.1943	Ordered from Harland and Wolff
20.01.1944	Laid down
02.08.1944	Launched and towed to Lobnitz shipyard at Renfrew for completion
1944	Transferred to South African Naval Defence Force
1944	Renamed *Transvaal*
21.05.1945	Completed
22.05.1945	Commissioned
06.1945	Sailed for South Africa
1945	Repatriation duties in Indian Ocean
1946	Training in local waters
03.03.1947	Princess Elizabeth boarded ship at Durban
1947	Annexation of Marion Island and Prince Edward Island (Operation Snoektown)
04.01.1948	Landed personnel on Prince Edward Island
04.11.1948	Went to assistance of tanker *Esso Wheeling*
16.11.1948	Under refit
14.12.1948	Refit completed
15.01.1949	Tristan da Cunha
02.1949	Towed stricken MV *Pequena* to Capetown
06.1950	Reduced to reserve at Durban
09.1950	Recommisioned
12.1950	Attended RAN jubilee celebrations in Fremantle
02.1951	Melbourne and Adelaide
15.02.1951	Fremantle
01.1951	Special radar survey at Bouvet Island
11.1951	Diego Saurez, Madagascar, Mombasa and Dar es Salaam
1955-1957	Local operations
02.01.1957	At Simonstown for official handover of dockyard from Royal Navy
09.1957	Refit that would last until July 1960
24.08.1960	Recommissioned
12.1960	Reserve for seven months
08.1961	Recommissioned
10.1961	Evacuation of Tristan da Cunha after volcanic eruption
01.1962	Took scientists to island to study the volcano
Late 1962	Refit and assumed training role
09.1962	Visited Antarctica
07.1964	Announcement of her withdrawal from service
18.08.1964	Decommissioned and placed in reserve
1978	Listed for disposal as target ship
08.08.1978	Sunk by gunfire in False Bay.

APPENDIX ONE

Technical Specifications

Length overall:	307ft 4ins
Length between perpendiculars:	286ft 0ins
Breadth moulded:	38ft 6ins
Depth moulded to UD:	17ft 9ins
Mean draught (deep):	12ft 3.5ins
Displacement (deep):	2,260 tons
Speed (deep):	18.5 knots
Endurance at 15knots (clean bottom):	7,000 miles

Machinery

Legend of weights

Hull:	811 tons
Machinery:	390 tons
Equipment:	170 tons
Armament:	100 tons
Oil fuel:	724 tons
Diesel oil:	30 tons
Reserve feed water:	35 tons

Armament & Equipment

Main Gun:	1 x 4-inch gun,;
AA Guns:	1 x Quad 2-pdr Pom-Pom; 2 x twin 20mm Oerlikon or 2 x single 40mm Bofors. In some vessels there were up to 8 single 20mm Oerlikons.
ASW:	2 x triple-barreled Squid mortars: 1 depth charge rail; 2 throwers.
Radar:	Type 271 or 272 was fitted to the earlier ships. Type 277 became available for later vessels.
Sonar:	Sonar Type 144 and Type 147B provided search and targeting for the Squid.

APPENDIX TWO

Class Build Details

Twenty five vessels were completed for the Royal Navy with a further three for the South African Navy. A number of vessels were completed as Bay class AA frigates, Survey vessels, Despatch vessels and Depot Ships. The careers of these later ships will be included in a seperate volume, but their details are included here for completeness, as are those vessels which were cancelled. The pennant numbers listed are those assigned to the vessels on completion. Those ships which went on to serve post war had the 'K' superior replaced by the 'F' superior. For those vessels where the pennant number differed significantly, this is indicated in the tables.

1. Loch Class vessels completed for the Royal Navy

Name	Penn No	Builder	Laid Down	Launched	Completed
Loch Achanalt	K424	Henry Robb (Leith)	14.09.43	23.03.44	11.08.44
Loch Achray	K426	Smiths Dock (Middlesborough)	13.12.43	07.07.44	01.02.45
Loch Alvie	K428	Barclay Curle (Whiteinch)	31.08.43	14.04.44	21.08.44
Loch Arkaig	K603	Caledon (Dundee)	01.11.44	07.06.45	17.11.45
Loch Craggie	K609	Harland & Wolff (Belfast)	28.12.43	23.05.44	23.10.44
Loch Dunvegan	K425	Charles Hill (Bristol)	29.09.43	25.03.44	30.06.44
Loch Eck	K422	Smiths Dock (Middlesborough)	25.10.43	25.04.44	07.11.44
Loch Fada	K390	John Brown (Clydebank)	08.06.43	14.12.43	10.04.44
Loch Fyne	K429	Burntisland Shipbuilding	08.12.43	24.05.44	09.11.44
Loch Glendhu	K619	Burntisland Shipbuilding	29.05.44	18.10.44	23.02.45
Loch Gorm	K620	Harland & Wolff (Belfast)	28.12.43	08.06.44	18.12.44
Loch Insh	K433	Henry Robb (Leith)	17.11.43	10.05.44	20.10.44
Loch Katrine	K625	Henry Robb (Leith)	31.12.43	21.08.44	29.12.44
Loch Killin	K391	Burntisland Shipbuilding	22.06.43	29.11.43	12.04.44
Loch Killisport	K628	Harland & Wolff (Belfast)	28.12.43	06.07.44	09.07.45
Loch Lomond	K437	Caledon (Dundee)	07.12.43	19.06.44	16.11.44
Loch More	K639	Caledon (Dundee)	16.03.44	03.10.44	24.02.45
Loch Morlich	K517	Swan Hunter (Wallsend)	15.07.43	20.01.44	02.08.44
Loch Quoich	K434	Blyth Dry Dock	03.12.43	02.09.44	11.01.45
Loch Ruthven	K645	Charles Hill (Bristol)	04.01.44	03.06.44	08.10.44
Loch Scavaig	K648	Charles Hill (Bristol)	31.03.44	09.09.44	22.12.44
Loch Shin	K421	Swan Hunter (Wallsend)	06.09.43	23.02.44	10.10.44
Loch Tarbert	K431	Ailsa (Troon)	30.11.43	19.10.44	22.02.45
Loch Tralaig	K655	Caledon (Dundee)	26.06.44	12.02.45	04.07.45
Loch Veyatie	K658	Ailsa (Troon)	30.03.44	08.10.45	13.07.46

2. Loch Class vessels completed for the South African Navy

Name	Penn No	Builder	Laid Down	Launched	Completed
Loch Ard (renamed *SANS Transvaal*)	K602	Harland & Wolff (Belfast)	21.04.44	02.08.44	21.05.45
Loch Boisdale (renamed *SANS Good Hope*)	K432	Blyth Dry Dock	08.11.43	05.07.44	01.12.44
Loch Cree (renamed *SANS Natal*)	K430	Swan Hunter (Wallsend)	18.10.43	19.06.44	08.03.45

3. Ships completed as Bay Class AA Frigates

Name	Penn No	Builder	Laid Down	Launched	Completed
Loch Achility (renamed *St Brides Bay*)	K600	Harland & Wolff (Belfast)	30.05.44	16.01.45	15.06.45
Loch Arklet (renamed *Start Bay*)	K604	Harland & Wolff (Belfast)	31.08.44	15.02.45	06.09.45
Loch Arnish (renamed *Tremadoc Bay*)	K605	Harland & Wolff (Belfast)	31.08.44	29.03.45	11.10.45
Loch Bracadale (renamed *Enard Bay*)	K435	Smiths Dock (Middlesborough)	27.05.44	31.10.44	04.01.46
Loch Carloway (renamed *Bigbury Bay*)	K606	Hall Russell (Aberdeen)	30.05.44	16.11.44	10.07.45
Loch Coulside (ii) (renamed *Padstow Bay*)	K608	Henry Robb (Leith)	25.09.44	24.08.45	11.03.46
Loch Fannich (renamed *Hollesley Bay*)	K614	Smiths Dock (Middlesborough)	27.11.44		Cancelled
Loch Foin (renamed *Largo Bay*)	K423	W Pickersgill (Sunderland)	08.02.44	03.10.44	26.01.46
Loch Frisa (renamed *Widemouth Bay*)	K615	Harland & Wolff (Belfast)	26.04.44	19.10.44	13.04.45
Loch Garasdale (renamed *Wigtown Bay*)	K616	Harland & Wolff (Belfast)	24.10.44	26.04.45	19.01.46
Loch Harport (ii) (renamed *Burghead Bay*)	K622	Charles Hill (Bristol)	21.09.44	03.03.45	20.09.45
Loch Heilen (renamed *Morecambe Bay*)	K624	W Pickersgill (Sunderland)	30.04.44	01.11.44	11.03.46
Loch Kilbernie (renamed *Mounts Bay*)	K627	W Pickersgill (Sunderland)	23.10.44	08.06.45	11.08.49
Loch Laxford (renamed *Cardigan Bay*)	K630	Henry Robb (Leith)	14.04.44	28.12.44	25.06.45

Name	Penn No	Builder	Laid Down	Launched	Completed
Loch Lubnaig (renamed *Whitesand Bay*)	K633	Harland & Wolff (Belfast)	08.08.44	16.12.44	30.07.45
Loch Lyddoch (renamed *St Austell Bay*)	K634	Harland & Wolff (Belfast)	30.05.44	08.11.44	29.05.45
Loch Maddy (renamed *Carnarvon Bay*)	K636	Henry Robb (Leith)	08.06.44	15.03.45	20.09.45
Loch Muick (ii) (renamed *Porlock Bay, ex- Loch Seaforth* (ii))	K650	Charles Hill (Bristol)	22.11.44	14.06.45	08.03.46
Loch Roan (renamed *Cawsand Bay*)	K644	Blyth Dry Dock	24.04.44	26.02.45	13.11.45
Loch Swannay (renamed *Veryan Bay*)	K651	Charles Hill (Bristol)	08.06.44	11.11.44	13.05.45

4. Ships completed as Despatch Vessels

Name	Penn No	Builder	Laid Down	Launched	Completed
Loch Carron (renamed *Surprise*, ex-*Gerrans Bay*)	K346	Smiths Dock (Middlesborough)	21.04.44	14.03.45	09.09.46
Loch Scamadale (renamed *Alert*, ex-*Dundrum Bay*)	K647	Blyth Dry Dock	28.07.44	10.07.45	24.10.46

5. Ships completed as Survey Vessels

Name	Penn No	Builder	Laid Down	Launched	Completed
Loch Eil (renamed *Dampier*, ex-*Herne Bay*)	K611	Smiths Dock (Middlesborough)	07.08.44	15.05.45	06.06.48
Loch Glass (renamed *Dalrymple*, ex-*Luce Bay*)	K427	W Pickersgill (Sunderland)	29.04.44	12.04.45	10.02.49
Loch Mochrum (renamed *Cook*, ex-*Pegwell Bay*)	K638	W Pickersgill (Sunderland)	30.11.44	01.09.45	20.07.50
Loch Muick (i) (renamed *Owen*, ex-*Thurso Bay*)	K640	Hall Russell (Aberdeen)	30.09.44	19.10.45	23.09.49

Pendant numbers on completion were *Cook* A311; *Dalrymple* A302; *Dampier* A303 and *Owen* A311

6. Ships completed as HQ vessels

Name	Penn No	Builder	Laid Down	Launched	Completed
Loch Assynt (renamed *Derby Haven*)	K438	Swan Hunter (Wallsend)	11.02.44	14.12.44	02.08.45
Loch Torridon (renamed *Woodbridge Haven*)	K654	Swan Hunter (Wallsend)	02.05.44	13.01.45	19.10.45

During service pendant numbers changed - *Derby Haven* P59 and *Woodbridge Haven* P58.

7. Cancelled Vessels

Name	Penn No	Builder	Laid Down	Launched	Cancelled
Loch Affric	K601	Ailsa (Troon)			1945
Loch Awe		Harland & Wolff (Belfast)			1945
Loch Badcall		W Pickersgill (Sunderland)			1945
Loch Caroy		W Pickersgill (Sunderland)			1945
Loch Clunie	K607	Ailsa (Troon)			1945
Loch Coulside (i)		Barclay Curle (Whiteinch)			1945
Loch Creran		Smiths Dock (Middlesborough)			1945
Loch Doine		Smiths Dock (Middlesborough)			1945
Loch Earn		Charles Hill (Bristol)			1945
Loch Enoch		Harland & Wolff (Belfast)			1945
Loch Ericht	K612	Ailsa (Troon)			1945
Loch Erisort	K613	Barclay Curle (Whiteinch)			1945
Loch Eye		Harland & Wolff (Belfast)			1945
Loch Eynort		Harland & Wolff (Belfast)			1945
Loch Garve	K617	Hall Russell (Aberdeen)			1945
Loch Glashan	K618	Smiths Dock (Middlesborough)			1945
Loch Goil		Harland & Wolff (Belfast)			1945
Loch Griam	K621	Swan Hunter (Wallsend)			1945
Loch Harport (i)		Hall Russell (Aberdeen)			1945
Loch Harray	K623	Smiths Dock (Middlesborough)			1945
Loch Hourne		Harland & Wolff (Belfast)			1945
Loch Inchard		Harland & Wolff (Belfast)			1945
Loch Ken	K626	Smiths Dock (Middlesborough)			1945
Loch Kirbister	K629	Swan Hunter (Wallsend)			1945

Name	Penn No	Builder	Laid Down	Launched	Cancelled
Loch Kirkaig		Harland & Wolff (Belfast)			1945
Loch Kishorn		Henry Robb (Leith)			1945
Loch Knockie		W Pickersgill (Sunderland)			1945
Loch Laro		Harland & Wolff (Belfast)			1945
Loch Linfern	K631	Smiths Dock (Middlesborough)			1945
Loch Linnhe	K632	W Pickersgill (Sunderland)			1945
Loch Lurgain		Harland & Wolff (Belfast)			1945
Loch Lyon	K635	Swan Hunter (Wallsend)			1945
Loch Maberry		Hall Russell (Aberdeen)			1945
Loch Minnick	K637	Smiths Dock (Middlesborough)			1945
Loch Nell	K641	Henry Robb (Leith)			1945
Loch Odairn	K642	Henry Robb (Leith)			1945
Loch Ossian	K643	Smiths Dock (Middlesborough)			1945
Loch Ronald		Harland & Wolff (Belfast)			1945
Loch Ryan	K646	W Pickersgill (Sunderland)			1945
Loch Scridain	K649	W Pickersgill (Sunderland)			1945
Loch Seaforth (i)		Caledon (Dundee)			1945
Loch Sheallag		Harland & Wolff (Belfast)			1945
Loch Shiel		Harland & Wolff (Belfast)			1945
Loch Skaig		Smiths Dock (Middlesborough)			1945
Loch Skerrow		Charles Hill (Bristol)			1945
Loch Stemster		Harland & Wolff (Belfast)			1945
Loch Stennes		Smiths Dock (Middlesborough)			1945
Loch Striven		Harland & Wolff (Belfast)			1945
Loch Sunart		Harland & Wolff (Belfast)			1945
Loch Swin		Harland & Wolff (Belfast)			1945
Loch Tanna	K652	Blyth Dry Dock			1945
Loch Tilt	K653	W Pickersgill (Sunderland)			1945
Loch Tummell		Harland & Wolff (Belfast)			1945
Loch Urigill	K656	Blyth Dry Dock			1945
Loch Vanavie		Harland & Wolff (Belfast)			1945
Loch Vennacher	K657	Blyth Dry Dock			1945
Loch Watten	K659	Blyth Dry Dock			1945